D1136742

HIPPOCRENE HANDY DICTIONARIES

Korean

HIPPOCRENE HANDY DICTIONARIES

For the traveler of independent spirit and curious mind, this practical series will help you to communicate, not just to get by. Common phrases are conveniently listed through key words. Pronunciation follows each entry and a reference section reviews all major grammar points. *Handy Extras* are extra helpful—offering even more words and phrases for students and travelers.

ARABIC
 $8.95 • 0-87052-960-9

CHINESE
 $8.95 • 0-87052-050-4

CZECH EXTRA
 $8.95 • 0-7818-0138-9

DUTCH
 $8.95 • 0-87052-049-0

FRENCH
 $8.95 • 0-7818-0010-2

GERMAN
 $8.95 • 0-7818-0014-5

GREEK
 $8.95 • 0-87052-961-7

HUNGARIAN EXTRA
 $8.95 • 0-7818-0164-8

ITALIAN
 $8.95 • 0-7818-0011-0

JAPANESE
 $8.95 • 0-87052-962-5

KOREAN
 $8.95 • 0-7818-0082-X

PORTUGUESE
 $8.95 • 0-87052-053-9

RUSSIAN
 $8.95 • 0-7818-0013-7

SERBO-CROATIAN
 $8.95 • 0-87052-051-2

SLOVAK EXTRA
 $8.95 • 0-7818-0101-X

SPANISH
 $8.95 • 0-7818-0012-9

SWEDISH
 $8.95 • 0-87052-054-7

THAI
 $8.95 • 0-87052-963-3

TURKISH
 $8.95 • 0-87052-982-X

(All prices subject to change.)

TO PURCHASE HIPPOCRENE BOOKS contact your local bookstore, or write to: HIPPOCRENE BOOKS, 171 Madison Avenue, New York, NY 10016. Please enclose check or money order, adding $5.00 shipping (UPS) for the first book and $.50 for each additional book.

HIPPOCRENE HANDY DICTIONARIES

Korean

Compiled by
Thomas Eccardt with Oh Wonchul (오 원철)

HIPPOCRENE BOOKS
New York

Copyright© 1993 by Thomas Escardt with Oh Wonchul.

Second printing, 1995.

All rights reserved.

For information, address:
HIPPOCRENE BOOKS, INC.
171 Madison Avenue
New York, NY 10016

ISBN 0-7818-0082-X

Printed in the United States of America.

Table of Contents

Outline of Korean Grammar

The following abbreviations are used in this Grammar:

dest.	destination
i.o.	indirect object
obj.	object
poss.	possessive
sub.	subject

INTRODUCTION

The Korean language is not related to the European languages most readers are familiar with, and it differs enormously from them. Instead, it is similar to Japanese. So Korean may be a challenge for you to speak — you may even wonder how Koreans can communicate in such a strange medium. But English presents similar problems to Koreans. The way for anyone to learn a foreign language is to accept the new concepts that the language presents, and to try to do without the familiar standbys of his or her native language. This grammar presents an outline of the most useful items of Korean grammar; some new concepts (bound nouns, postpositions) must be introduced, while many of the traditional grammatical concepts (articles, plurals) will not be found here.

THE WORD IN KOREAN

Korean words may seem discouragingly long to the beginner. What makes them long are the endings, which are easy to get used to, since they don't change very much. Generally there are two kinds of endings: noun endings and verb endings. Although many linguists believe the noun endings should be written separately, Koreans generally attach them, so they will be treated as endings in this book. There are very few prefixes (attached to the beginnings of words) in Korean.

PARTS OF SPEECH

In this dictionary, you can recognize the part of speech of most of the Korean words used in the sentence examples by their endings. This is not true of English: *works* could be a noun or a verb, depending on the way it is used. The careful distinction which Korean makes between endings for verbs and endings for nouns is important enough to make nouns and verbs a major division between the two parts of this grammatical summary. In addition, this dictionary follows certain conventions when defining a word in isolation. Nouns are given without endings, since you may hear them this way in a sentence. Verbs are given with the ŏ-yo ending attached, which represents a kind of present tense: **mŏgŏ-yo** = **mŏg** + **ŏ-yo**, *(I/you/he) eats.* Adjectives are really a kind of verb in Korean, so you may see them in a Korean sentence with the verb ending: **choha-yo** = **choh** + **a-yo**, *it is good.* But in isolation, this dictionary lists adjectives in the

Pronounce: a father; e let; i machine; o note; ŏ löng; u rude; ü fürther

MODIFICATORY form: **chohün** = **choh** + **ün** *good.* This is the more ordinary form: **chohün ch-heg,** *a good book.*

SYNTAX

One of the most unfamiliar aspects of Korean is the order of words in sentences, or the SYNTAX. In English, we say the subject first, then the verb, and then the object: *The cat eats the bird.* In Korean, the subject comes first, but then the object appears, while the verb is left for the end:

> **ko-yang-i serl mögö-yo**
> [cat   bird eats]

An important characteristic of Korean grammar is that the verb usually comes at the very end of sentences and clauses. This enables the Koreans to use a verb ending (**-go**) as a kind of conjunction (to translate *and*), since it will appear at the end of one clause, just before the second one to be connected with it:

> every morning I eat breakfast and go to school
> **me-il ach-himl mög-go haggyo-e ka-yo**
> [everyday breakfast eat-and school-to go]

In this dictionary we use three dots... to indicate something you can fill in to complete a sentence. For example, *I'd like...* could be filled in to read *I'd like coffee.* Since Korean word order is often the reverse of English, the three dots often end up on the opposite side of the sentence: ...**rl chushibshi-o .**

> I need...
> ...**ül p-hiryo he-yo**
> [...object need do]

Sometimes you say something about what you are saying, for example: *I wish I could go.* In English, the gist of the sentence, *I could go,* ends up after the comment about it, *I wish.* This is because *I could go* is the OBJECT of *I wish.* In Korean, again, the OBJECT comes before the verb, so that much of the sentence is reversed:

> (I) wish that (I) could go.
> **kamyön chok-hessö-yo.**
> [go-if would-be-good]

NOUNS

In one way, Korean nouns are simpler than English ones. When an English speaker wants to use a noun, he must decide (unconsciously, of course) if there is one or more than one of the thing represented by the noun, and then use the singular or plural form of the noun. You must say *cats* if you are talking about more than one cat—you have no alternative. Koreans need make no such decisions. They do have a kind of plural, **dl,** but they use it only when they want to emphasize plurality. In fact, it would not be used in the expression *three cats.* Here it is redundant, since the word *three* already indicates plurality. In the same way, Korean has no articles like English *the* and *a.* But if emphasis is needed, there are words such as **kü** *this* and **han** *one* to express

Pronounce: a father; e let; i machine; o note; ö löng; u rude; ü fürther

these ideas. In this dictionary, many words given in the English plural will be given without **dl** in the Korean.

saram	a person, the person, people
kemi	an ant, the ant, ants
kemidl	ants

NOUN ENDINGS

In another sense, Korean nouns are more complicated than English ones because of the endings which indicate the use of the noun in the sentence. Every time a Korean uses a noun, instead of worrying about singular or plural, he has to decide whether the noun is to be the subject, object, indirect object, or the TOPIC of the sentence. In English, we show this by word order: *man bites dog* versus *dog bites man*. The Korean endings correspond roughly to CASES in other languages, or to the PARTICLES in Japanese. Fortunately there are no declensions, but unfortunately some of the endings change, depending on whether the attached word ends in a vowel or a consonant:

Type	Used After:		Exapmles	
	Vowel	Consonant		
Topic	**nün**	**n**	**ch-ha-nün**	**ch-heg-n**
Subject	**ka**	**i**	**ch-ha-ga**	**ch-heg-i**
Object	**rl**	**l**	**ch-ha-rl**	**ch-heg-l**
I.O.	**ege**	**ege**	**saram-ege**	

a man reads a book
sarami ch-heg-l ilgö-yo
[man-sub book-obj read]

that man listens to the radio
kü saram-n radi-o-rl trö yo
[that man-topic radio-obj listens]

(I'm) writing to the teacher
sönseng-nim-ege ssö-yo
[teacher-i.o.   write]

PRONOUNS

In Korean, there are words which translate English pronouns, but only approximately. Some of these should be used only in very familiar conversations, but none of them are used as often as in English. Koreans prefer to continue using a name or a title instead of a pronoun, whereas English speakers immediately switch to *he* or *she* after the person has been identified once. English pronouns represent grammatical classifications, such as *he* vs. *she*, which Koreans do not ordinarily make, and which is difficult for them to learn. The moral is to use the following list of pronouns as infrequently as possible.

Pronounce: a father; e let; i machine; o note; ö löng; u rude; ü fürther

	Ordinary	Respectful
I	**na**	**chö**
you	**nö**	**tang-shin**
we	**uri**	
you pl.	**nöhe**	**tang-shindl**

You will hardly ever have an opportunity to use **nö,** or **nöhe,** except to young children. For the third person, you can say **kü saram** *that person,* or **kü yöja** *that female,* for *he* or *she.* Still it is better to repeat the title or the name, or better yet, just leave out the subject or object entirely. This strategy is obligatory in the case of the pronoun *it,* since there is no such word in Korean.

> where do I (you, etc) get off?
> **ödisö neryö-yo?**
> [where-at get-off]

> when does it go?
> **önje ch-hulbal he-yo**
> [when depart do]

> I can't hear you.
> **chal tlliji anö-yo**
> [well hear   not]

As a matter of fact, the pronouns really aren't a separate grammatical category at all, since they use the same endings as the nouns:

> I am a student.
> **nanün   hagseng-i-e-yo**
> [I-topic student-be]

> does (he) see me?
> **narl   pwa-yo?**
> [I-obj see?]

HOW YOU SAY *YOU*

Although the word **tang-shin,** *you,* is considered a respectful form, most Koreans are uncomfortable using it. Perhaps it sounds a little like *hey you!* sounds to us. As mentioed before, Koreans prefer to use a title instead of the word *you.* If the title refers to an important person, it may be followed by **nim,** which means *esteemed*:

sönseng-nim	**kisa-nim**	**chibe-in-nim**	**abö-nim**
teacher, ma'am	driver, sir	Mr. Manager	Father, Dad

A word which means *guest,* **son-nim,** refers to customers, passengers, hotel guests, etc. Despite its convenience, **nim** cannot be used without a title, and not with all titles, either. A tour guide can simply be called *tour guide,* **an-ne-wön;** a nurse can be called *nurse,* **kan-ho-sa.** A waiter can be called **ajöshi,** *uncle;* and a waitress can be called **agashi,** *young lady.* These last two can also be used if you don't know the profession of the person serving you. In any case, remember that

Pronounce: a father; e let; i machine; o note; ö löng; u rude; ü fürther

all the words given in this section are not just titles, but should also be used in place of the English word *you*.

MORE ON THE NOUN ENDINGS

The term TOPIC was mentioned in the noun section. In the example given there, the word ending in **-nün** was the topic, but it would have been considered the SUBJECT in English:

> that man listens to the radio
> **kü saram-n radi-o-rl trö-yo**
> [that man-topic radio-obj listens]

Even linguists disagree as to the difference between a topic and a subject, so distinctive to Korean and Japanese. Suffice it to say that a Korean topic seems to be less closely related to the verb than a Korean subject, although both are often translated as a subject in English:

> my back hurts
> **nanün tng-i ap-hö-yo**
> [I-topic back-sub hurt]

> I like Korea
> **nanün han-gugi choha-yo**
> [I-topic Korea-sub be-pleasing]

In the above sentences a rendering of the meaning of TOPIC might be *as for* : *As for me, the back hurts; As for me, Korea is nice*. Another ending which can also replace the subject or object ending is **do**, meaning *also* or *even*. It is always attached directly to the *additional* item:

> I also want to see the DMZ.
> **hyujönsödo pogo ship-hünde-yo**
> [DMZ-also see want]

The possessive ending is **e**. It is used like *'s* in English, but it is applied to pronouns, too. It can even turn a noun into an adjective:

> our house
> **uri-e chib**
> [we + poss house]

> my friend
> **na-e (ne) ch-hin-gu**
> [me-poss friend]

> American
> **migug-e**
> [America + poss]

Pronounce: a father; e let; i machine; o note; ö löng; u rude; ü fürther

The ending **üro** has two other forms, **ro** and **lo**, to be used when it follows a vowel or the letter *L*. It indicates *means, method, way,* etc. But it can also indicate a destination:

by air(plane)
piheng-gi-ro
[airplane + means]

go to the hotel
hot-hel-lo ka-yo
[hotel + dest go]

Another ending, also pronounced **e**, indicates location or time. It translates English *in, at, on,* etc.

he's at the hotel
hot-her-e issö-yo
[hotel-at is]

at eight o'clock
yödölshi-e
[8-hour-at]

But if you are describing where some activity takes place, rather than merely location, you must use **esö**. This ending also means *from*.

they meet at the hotel
hot-her-esö manna-yo
[hotel-from meet]

he came from the hotel
hot-her-esö wassö-yo
[hotel-from came]

Many ideas expressed by prepositions in English are expressed by endings in Korean, as shown above. However some English prepositions are nouns in Korean. These POSTPOSITIONS generally use the ending **e**. And they follow the word which would be the object of the preposition in English.

(I) am in the room
pang an-e issö-yo
[room in-at be]

after dinner
chönyög hu-e
[dinner after-at]

Pronounce: a father; e let; i machine; o note; ö löng; u rude; ü fürther

The ending **boda** corresponds to the English word *than*. When comparing things, you can use the word **tö** to translate *more*:

> He is smaller than I.
> **k-nün   na-boda tö chaga-yo**
> [he-topic I-than more is-small]

HERE, THERE AND YONDER

Koreans distinguish the meanings *there* and *yonder*, which we no longer do in English. So Korean has three place words where English only has two. *Yonder* simply means *not near you or me* or *over there*. In Korean, *there* always means *near you*. So, too, Korean has three different adjectives which translate *this* and *that*.

TYPE	HERE	THERE	YONDER
Adjective	**i**	**kü**	**chö**
	this	that	*yonder*
Noun	**igöd**	**kgöd**	**chö-göd**
	this (thing)	that (thing)	*yonder* thing
Adverb	**yögi**	**kögi**	**chögi**
	here	there	*yonder*

QUESTION WORDS

Question words in Korean also behave like nouns, in that many of them take the appropriate noun endings. But they never take **nün**, the topic ending. So as subjects, they use **ga:**

> when (do we) arrive?
> **önje toch-hag he-yo?**
> [when arrive   do]

> where (do I) catch the bus?
> **pös-rl ödi-sö   t-ha-yo?**
> [bus-obj where-from catch]

> what do you want?
> **mu-ös-l wön hase-yo?**
> [what-obj want do]

> who did it?
> **nu-ga   hessö-yo?**
> [who-sub did]

Other question words are:

> what, which
> **musn**

Pronounce: a father; e let; i machine; o note; ö löng; u rude; ü fürther

what kind of
öd-dön

how
öd-dök-he

VERBS

The sound changes which take place in Korean when endings are added to stems are most obvious in the VERBS. You cannot use a verb without an ending, and both the stems and the endings are divided into consonant-types and vowel-types. The stems either end in a vowel or end in a consonant. The endings either begin with a vowel or begin with a consonant. There are also some subdivisions. However, the main changes simply involve the weak vowel **ü**: it is dropped when it would appear next to a vowel, or it is added to prevent two consonants from coming together. In the chart on the next page, the verbs are listed vertically, and their various forms are listed across the page. This is by no means a complete list of the verbs used in this book – not even of the verb categories. The most frequently used verbs are shown in order to give you an idea of the possible changes you are likely to encounter in speaking and hearing Korean. You will also find adjectives in the list, since they undergo the same changes as regular verbs; as mentioned previously, there is practically no difference between these two parts of speech in Korean. Have a look at the chart, not worrying about the meaning or use of the particular forms listed, but concentrating on the sound changes that each verb undergoes. When you refer to a verb in general, you use the **da** form, in the first column of the table.

TENSES

There are three tenses in Korean: present, past and future. Later we will see how adjectives can have the same tenses as well. The present and the past tenses make use of **ö** (or **a**), the so-called infinitive form of the verb (a vowel ending), while the future tense is a consonant ending. You will notice that the ending **yo** is also added to the end – this is the way form the INFORMAL POLITE mode. So that the present tense ending is **ö-yo**, the past is **össö-yo** and the future is **gessö-yo**.

PRESENT	PAST	FUTURE
go!	he went	they will go
ka-yo	**kassö-yo**	**kagessö-yo**
he eats rice	we ate rice	I will eat rice
pabl mögö-yo	**pabl mögössö-yo**	**pabl möggessö-yo**
who is coming?	who came?	(I) will come again
nuga wa-yo?	**nuga wassö-yo?**	**tashi ogessö-yo**

As stated above, pronouns are infrequently used in Korean. And there is no change in the verb for person or number. So the translations provided for some of the above examples are arbitrary. You must let the context clarify who or what the subject is. These tenses are used similarly to the corresponding English tenses, except that the present tense may be used more often in Korean than in English, such as for commands (*go!*). Also, the future tense can imply mere uncertainty, and is closely associated with the verbs **alda** *to know, to understand* and **morda** *not to know*:

Pronounce: a father; e let; i machine; o note; ö löng; u rude; ü fürther

Some Common Korean Verbs

English	Citation form	Infinitive	Modificatory	Honorific Pres.	Conditional	Formal Polite
do	hada	he	han	hase-yo	hamyŏn	hamnida
become	dweda	dwe	dwen	dwese-yo	dwemyŏn	dwemnida
does that	krŏt-ha	kre	krŏn	krŏse-yo	krŏmyŏn	krŏhsmnida
go	kada	ka	kan	kase-yo	kamyŏn	kamnida
go out	nada	na	nan	nase-yo	namyŏn	namnida
come	oda	wa	on	ose-yo	omyŏn	omnida
see	poda	pwa	pon	pose-yo	pomyŏn	pomnida
be	ida	yŏ	in	i-e-yo	imyŏn	imnida
not be	anida	anyŏ	anin	ani-e-yo	animyŏn	animnida
be big	k-hŭda	k-hŏ	k-hŭn	k-hŭse-yo	k-hŭmyŏn	kmnida
be bad	nab-bda	nab-bŏ	nab-bn	nab-bse-yo	nab-bmyŏn	nab-bmnida
write/use	ssda	ssŏ	ssn	ssŭse-yo	ssmyŏn	ssmnida
be far	mŏlda	mŏrŏ	mŏn	mŏse-yo	mŏlmyŏn	mŏmnida
not know	morda	molla	morn	morse-yo	mormyŏn	mormnida
exist/be	it-da	issŏ	issn	kyese-yo	issmyŏn	issmnida
not exist/lack	ŏbda	ŏbsŏ	ŏbsn	an-gyese-yo	ŏbsmyŏn	ŏbsmnida
not (true)	ant-ha	anŏ	anŭn	anse-yo	anmyŏn	ansmnida
be good	chot-ha	choha	chohŭn	chohŭse-yo	chot-hamyŏn	chohsmnida
want	shipt-ha	ship-hŏ	ship-hŭn	ship-hŭse-yo	ship-hŭmyŏn	shipsmnida

Pronounce: a father; e let; i machine; o note; ŏ löng; u rude; ü fürther

I don't know (wouldn't know)   Do you understand?
morgessö-yo   **algessö-yo?**

TO BE OR NOT TO BE

There are some little verbs which are frequently used in Korean, but rather differently from their English translations. Some have separate verbs to express the negative of them.The verb to be, **ida,** is used to show that one thing is equal to another thing; it is never used with adjectives, as in *the house is green.* How to translate this sentence is explained in the section on adjectives. Unlike other verbs, *to be* is attached to the end of the second noun; it appears as **e-yo** before nouns ending in a vowel, and as **i-e-yo** after those ending in a consonant.

he is a teacher
kü saramn   sönseng-nim-i-e-yo
[that person-topic teacher-is]

it's a friend!
ch-hin-gu-e-yo
[friend-is]

The opposite, *not to be, is not,* is expressed by **anida:**

it's not a friend
ch-hin-guga   ani-e-yo
[friend-topic is-not]

The verb **it-da** means *to exist, to be there.* It translates the English verb *to be* when it tells WHERE:

he is home
chibe   issö-yo
[house-at exists]

It is a way of expressing *to have*:

I have money
nanün toni   issö-yo
[I-topic money-sub there-is]

Notice that the possessor is the TOPIC, while the possessed is the SUBJECT. Literally, it means *As for me, money exists.* The opposite meaning *does not exist, is not there, is lacking* is expressed by the verb **öbda:**

he is not home
chibe   öbsö-yo
[house-at not-exist]

Pronounce: a father; e let; i machine; o note; ö löng; u rude; ü fürther

I have no money
nanün toni öbsö-yo
[I-topic money-sub is-lacking]

PARTICIPLES

Korean has several verb endings which do not correspond to tenses, but rather loosely to other verbal forms of English, such as -*ing* as in *working*. The participles are used either alone or with other verbs which might be called auxiliaries. Sometimes the participles are followed by the noun endings, besides. The infinitive is actually one of these participles, so the present tense is sort of an *absence of tense.*   The infinitive, when followed by **it-da** forms the PRESENT PROGRESSIVE tense, meaning *to be doing*:

(I) am standing
sö   issö-yo
[stand   be]

It is used to form compound verbs:

he comes back	I go in
tora ka-yo	**trö ka-yo**
[turn go]	[enter go]

And it is used (with the noun ending **do**) to ask for or give permission:

may I go?
nega kado choha-yo?
[I-sub go-even is-good]

With the ending **ya** plus the verb **he-yo**, the infitive is used to express the meaning *to have to* or *must:*

I must go
ka-ya he-yo
[go-**ya** do]

Another important participle is formed with **go**; it is a consonant ending which conjugates just like the citation form **da.** With **it-da,** it forms another present progressive tense with a slightly different meaning:

I am living in Seoul
sö-uresö salgo issö-yo
[Seoul-from living am]

In the SYNTAX section, an example has already been given of the use of this participle as a translation for *and.*   An important participial ending is **ji**, a consonant ending like **da** and **go.** Like the infinitive, it can be followed by the ending **yo** to form a kind of present tense. However, this tense implies a casual attitude toward what is being said, like the words *you know* and *isn't*

Pronounce: a father; e let; i machine; o note; ö löng; u rude; ü fürther

it and *I suppose* in English. Although spelled as two syllables, they are pronounced as one, like the word *Joe*.

It's expensive, isn't it?
kabshi pissaji-yo
[price-sub expensive]

Another important use of the **ji** participle is to form NEGATIVE sentences. After the verb in the **ji** participle, you use the verb **ant-ha,** *does not*:

I don't eat kimchee
kimch-hirl mögji anö-yo
[kimchee-obj eat-ji do-not]

As mentioned above, the COMMAND form is the same as the present tense. But the negative command (*don't!*) is formed with the **ji** participle, plus the verb *to avoid,* **malda:**

don't eat kimchee
kimch-hirl mögji mase-yo
[kimchee-obj eat-ji avoid]

You can also express the meaning of the conjunction *but* with this participle, plus the ending **man:**

he lives here but he's not in now.
yögisö saljiman chigmn yögi-e öbsö-yo
[here-from live-ji-but now-topic here-at lacks]

The consonant participle ending **gi** is used in statements relating to time or reason. Notice that *it's raining* is expressed as *rain comes:*

because it's raining I cannot go
piga   ogi ddemune   kal suga öbsö-yo
[rain-sub come-gi reason-at go   cannot]

it's starting to rain
piga   ogi   shijag he-yo
[rain-sub come-gi begin do]

let's go before it rains
piga   ogi   chöne uri ka-yo
[rain-sub come-gi before we   go]

Another consonant ending is **ge,** which makes an adjective (really a verb) into an adverb.

is early	come early
njö-yo	**ndge wa-yo**
[be-early]	[early come]

This ending is also used to express cause or permission with the verb **hada:**

Pronounce: a father; e let; i machine; o note; ö löng; u rude; ü fürther

I made him stay home
chibe idge hessö-yo
[home-at be-ge made]

The ending **ümyön**, the CONDITIONAL, is generally a vowel ending. The first vowel in it drops before a verb which ends in a vowel. But it behaves differently with verbs that have an l/r which drops (see **mölda** in the chart). The ending **ümyön** is a way to express the English word *if*:

If it rains (I) will stay home
piga   omyön chibe issl gö-e-yo
[rain-sub come-if house-at stay-will]

It can be used to translate *hope*. Instead of saying *I hope it rains,* you say *if it rains, it will be good:*

I hope it rains
piga   omyön chok-hessö-yo
[rain-sub come-if good-will-be]

This ending can also be used with the noun ending **sö** to translate *while*:

I read a book while I eat
pabl mögümyönsö, ch-hegl ilgö-yo
[rice-obj eat-if-from, book-obj read]

ADJECTIVES

As mentioned before, Korean adjectives are almost indistinguishable from verbs. In fact, the MODIFICATORY or adjective form can also be used to modify nouns, as a means of translating *which* or *who*. This form actually has three tenses, present past and future:

the person coming	the person who came	the person who will come
onün saram	**on saram**	**ol saram**
[coming person]	[came person]	[will-come person]

As you can see, the endings are **nün, (ü)n**, and **(ü)l**. This is yet another way in which Korean word order is different from English. Instead of saying *the letter which he received,* you say *the he-received letter.* And since you put the verb after the object, to translate *I wrote the letter which he received,* you must say *I the he-received letter wrote:*

I wrote the letter which he recieved
nanün kü sarami padn p-hyönjirl ssössö-yo
[I-topic that person-sub read   letter-obj wrote]

After this explanation, the ordinary adjectives should be easy. All you do is use the PAST tense of the modificatory form. Compare the ordinary present tense – which means *to be bad* – with the modificatory form, meaning simply *bad:*

the book is bad	the bad book
ch-hegi nab-bö-yo	**nab-bn ch-heg**
[book-sub bad-is]	[bad-mod book]

Pronounce: a father; e let; i machine; o note; ö löng; u rude; ü fürther

In this dictionary an English adjective is given in the Korean modificatory form, while an English verb is given in the Korean present tense. This is done so that you have to make as few changes to the verbs as possible. Although the modificatory forms are generally easy, there are some *classes* of verb/adjectives which are a little more complicated. So it is not always easy to go from one form to the other. However, if you need to say *the book is bad* or *the student is bad*,but you only know the modificatory form **nab-bn,** you can simply say:

the book is a bad thing   the sudent is a bad person
ch-hegn   nab-bn göshi-e-yo   **hakseng-n nab-bn sarami-e-yo**
[book-topic bad   thing-is]   [sudent-topic bad person-is]

This sounds a lot better in Korean than it does in English.

BOUND NOUNS

Besides the participles, Korean has another way to express certain English items which are related to verbs or conjunctions: BOUND NOUNS. These little words are nouns, sometimes taking the noun endings, but they cannot stand alone without modification. In other words, you must use a verb/adjective in the modificatory form before them. The bound noun **göd/gös,** *thing* has already been presented as a way of using the modificatory form to mean *is somehow.* When you talk about *the fact that...* in English, you say *the thing* in Korean:

I know that he came
kü sarami on   gösl ara-yo
[that person-sub having-come thing-obj know]

To say *it seems...* or *I think...,* in Korean you say *...thing is likely:*

I think that he came
kü sarami on   göd kat-ha-yo
[that person-sub having-come thing is-likely]

To express the meaning *can, is able* you use the future modificatory form, plus the bound noun **su,** *possibility,* plus the verb **it-da,** *to exist:*

I can eat
mögl su   issö-yo
[will-eat possibility exists]

To express the meaning of the English present perfect tense, *have you (ever)...?,* use the modificatory form, plus the bound noun **il,** *act* (as a subject), plus **it-da:**

Have you (ever) seen an American?
migug saraml pon   iri issö-yo?
[American person-obj having-seen act-sub exist]

Two bound nouns, **god/gos,** *place,* and **dde,** *time,* are used instead of the English conjunctions *where* and *when:*

Pronounce: a father; e let; i machine; o note; ö löng; u rude; ü fürther

when we get back
toragal dde
[return-will time]

when we got back
toragassl dde
[returned-will **dde**]

where I left it
nega nerin   kod
[I-sub having-left place]

YES/NO

English *yes* is translated by **ne**; *no* is translated by **ani-yo.** However, Koreans answer *yes* much more than English speakers; it may simply mean, *I understand.* On the other hand, a better translation for **ne** would be *correct* and for **ani-o** *incorrect,* because each refers to the literal interpretation of what was said before:

Did you do your homework? Yes, I did.
sugjerl hessö-yo?   ne hessö-yo
No, I didn't.
ani-yo, haji anössö-yo

Didn't you do your homework?   *No,* I did
sugjerl haji anössö-yo?   ani-yo, hessö-yo
Yes, I didn't
ne, haji anössö-yo

VERBS/ADJECTIVES IN HADA

Hundreds of years ago, many verbs and adjectives came into Korean from Chinese, a language which does not have endings. Fortunately, Koreans were ready for these borrowings, for they already had a way to make a noun (which may lack an ending) into a verb. *To such-and-such* in Korean is simply: *such-and-such do.* That is, a foreign verb is considered a noun — with or without the object ending — after which you use the verb **hada.** Today, Koreans use this mechanism to borrow words from European languages such as English.

I think
nanün seng-gag he-yo
[I-sub thinking do]

When will we arrive?
önje t-hoch-hag he-yo?
[when arrival do?]

Pronounce: a father; e let; i machine; o note; ö löng; u rude; ü fürther

did he clean (it)?
k-hürin hessö-yo?
[cleaning did?]

Similarly, adjectives can be formed with **hada** in its modificatory form,   **han:**

an excellent book
hullyung   han ch-heg
[excellence doing book]

RESPECTFUL LANGUAGE

Expressions like *sir, if you please, may I ask,* and *if I could,* are ways to show respect to speakers of English. Korean has many more ways to show respect than English. Some of them are endings, and their absence may indicate a lack of respect for the person you are speaking with.   Fortunately, most Koreans are aware that their respectful language is difficult to master and will forgive an ignorance of its subtleties.   But they are not likely to speak a pidgin Korean to you, leaving out the respectful parts.   So be prepared to hear the following endings, which are part of the FORMAL POLITE style:

USE	VERB ENDING	EXAMPLE	
statement	**smnida**	**omnida**	*he comes*
question	**smnig-ga?**	**mögsmnig-ga?**	*does he eat?*
command	**shibshi-o**	**chushibshi-o**	*give, please give me...*
suggestion	**shibshida**	**kashibshida**	*let's go*

We have been using the INFORMAL POLITE style in this grammatical summary   and throughout the body of the dictionary, except in "fixed expressions."   This is the simplest style to use, since it doesn't change for questions,   commands, etc., and it will not be considered out of place in most   situations.   It is formed by ending all sentences with **yo.** We gave the tenses of verbs with the **yo** already added, to guarantee that it would be used.   The FORMAL POLITE style endings given above of course are themselves verb endings, so you will not hear a **yo** after them.   But you also may hear Korean men speaking with none of the above endings.   If they use the plain infinitive form without **yo,** they are using the INFORMAL PLAIN style.   Women are less likely to use this plain or non-polite style, just as women are less likely to use rough language in English.   Man or women, you are advised to stay with the INFORMAL POLITE style.

Another way to express respect is to use the HONORIFIC ending, **shi,** which comes just after the verb stem and before the other endings. We gave examples of the honorific plus the present tense in the verb table.   There it appears as **se.** Technically, this ending does not mean *you,* but rather shows respect for the subject of the verb, whoever he or she is.   But it is so frequently used to refer to the listener, that you might consider it the Korean equivalent of French *vous,* German *Sie,* or Spanish *Vd.* The honorific plus the past tense has the form **shyöss.** Only with consonant endings like the future tense does the honorific have its full form **shi.** Incidentally, there are still other aspects of respect language which there is no room to describe here.

Pronounce: a father; e let; i machine; o note; ö löng; u rude; ü fürther

COUNTING THINGS

Koreans use two sets of numbers; one is Chinese, and one is native Korean:

Value	Chinese	Korean
1	il	han / hana
2	i	tu
3	sam	sed
4	sa	ned
5	o	tasöd
6	yug	yösöd
7	ch-hil	ilgob
8	p-hal	yödölb
9	ku	ahob
10	shib	yöl
11	shibil	yörana
12	shibi	yöldul
13	shibsam	yölsed
14, etc.	shibsa	yölned
20	ishib	smul
21, etc.	ishibil	smul hana
30	samshib	sörn
40	sashib	mahün
50	oshib	swin
60	yugshib	yesn
70	ch-hilshib	irn
80	p-halshib	yödn
90	kshib	ahün
100	peg	
200, etc.	ibeg	
1000	ch-hön	
2000, etc.	ich-hön	
10,000	man	
20,000, etc.	iman	
100,000	shimman	
200,000, etc.	ishimman	
1,000,000	pengman	
2,000,000, etc.	ibengman	

Notice that the Korean numbers do not go beyond 90. Each thing to be counted or enumerated determines the appropriate set of numbers to be used, Chinese or Korean, they are not interchangeable. So one says **han saram** *one person* (not **il saram**) and **shib wön** *ten Won* (not **yöl wön**). Koreans generally write the Arabic numerals (1,2,3...), rather than spelling out the numbers. This makes it easier for us to read, but impossible to tell which set of numbers is being used. In Korean, you use a *measure* after a number more often than in English. Both languages can measure beer in glasses:

Pronounce: a father; e let; i machine; o note; ö löng; u rude; ü fürther

have a glass of beer
megju hanjan mashibshi-o
[beer one-glass drink]

But it is hard for English speakers to see why Koreans always need to use a measure when they count books:

I bought two books
ch-hegl tugwön sassö-yo
[book-obj two-volume bought]

As with ordinary nouns, some measures require the Chinese numbers and some the Korean numbers:

Used With Korean Numbers:		Used with Chinese numbers:	
saram	people	**ch-hüng**	floors
sal	years of age	**nyön**	years
pun	honored people	**wön**	Won
mari	animals	**peg**	hundreds

DATES AND TIME

Korean dates and time are given with the largest unit first, followed by smaller and smaller units. This is sometimes different from the English:

June 21, 1992 at 8:30 PM
chön kubeg kushib inyön yuwöl ishibiril ohu   yödolshi...
[1000 900 90   2-year June   21-day afternoon 8-hour...
...**samshib-bun**
...thirty-minute]

You can leave out the year, month, or any other unit, but what remains must remain in the same order. Notice that years, days, months and minutes require the Chinese numbers, whereas hours require the Korean numbers. Instead of thirty minutes, you may say *half past:*

half past nine
ahöbshi pan
[nine-hour half]

To express minutes before the hour, say *before:*

ten minutes before five
tasösshi shib-bun   chön
[five-hour ten-minutes before]

Pronounce: a father; e let; i machine; o note; ö löng; u rude; ü fürther

English / Korean

KOREAN PRONUNCIATION

1. The most important thing to remember is to pronounce the vowels as indicated at the bottom of each page:

Pronounce: a father; e let; i machine; o note; ö löng; u rude; ü fürther

That is, pronounce the letter **a** as it is pronounced in the word **father,** pronounce the letter **e** as in the word **let,** etc. There are no silent vowels in Korean, like the silent **e** in English **rose.**

2. The consonants are pronounced as in English. There are no silent letters; every letter is pronounced fully. The pronunciation of **g** is always hard, as in **gift** (not as in **gin**). The letter **r** is never dropped, but it is flapped as in Italian or Spanish, or as in the North American pronunciation of **tt** in **butter.** The letter **s** is always pronounced like **ss** in **hiss,** never like **z** as in **rose.**

3. The double letters (**bb, dd, jj, gg**) are pronounced extra strong or extra long. In the middle of words, we place a hyphen between the letters to remind you to pronounce them that way. (see 5 below).

4. There is no stress (accent) in Korean, so try to give each syllable equal weight.

5. The hyphens have no special meaning. They are used to help you avoid certain English spelling conventions, such as pronouncing **ph** as if it were **f** as in **phone.** For example, **p-he-iji** is the Korean word for **page.** For the first syllable, pronounce a **p** plus a strong **h** followed by the vowel **e** as in **let.** Then say **eejee** (**i** is always as in **machine**). That makes three syllables altogether. Although **p-he-iji** is now a Korean word, it came originally from English. And it is pronounced very much like **page** with a Korean accent.

6. There are many sound changes that occur with the consonants. These changes are shown in the pronunciation, so you don't have to learn them to use this dictionary. But if you learn Hungul, the native Korean alphablet, you should try to become familiar with the changes, because they are not shown there. These changes also affect the way a Korean pronounces words that come from English. Typically, when two consonants come together, the first one disappears but causes the second to be pronounced long. But this does not always happen. Also, when a consonant comes at the beginning of a word, its pronunciation changes, typically becoming less voiced or nasalized: **b** becomes **p, t** becomes **t,** etc, and **m** becomes **mb,** etc. Also, before another consonant or at the end of a word, **r** becomes **l.** Sometimes **i** becomes **y,** and **u** becomes **w** before another vowel.

A

a (one) 한 han
a la carte 알라 카아트 alla k-ha-at-hü
a.m.: at 9 a.m. 오전 아홉시 ojön ahobshi
abacus 주판 chup-han
abalone 전복 chönbog
abbreviation 생략 seng-ryag
able 할 수 있는 hal su innün; I wasn't able to 할 수 없었어요 hal su öbsössö-yo; she isn't able 할 수가 없어요 hal suga öbsö-yo
about 약 yag; about 15 약 십오 yag shibo; about 40 years old 약 마흔살 yag mahünsal; how about a ...? ...는 어때요? ...nün öd-de-yo?; we heard about that 그 일에 관해서 들었어요 kü ire kwanesö trössö-yo; I'll think about it 잘 생각해 보겠어요 chal seng-gak-he pogessö-yo; I'm worried about her 그녀를 걱정 해요 knyörl kögjöng he-yo; I'm really angry about it 나는 화가 많이 났어요 nanün hwaga mani nassö-yo; I've got a complaint about the room 방에 관해 불평 할께 있어요 pang-e kwane pulp-hyöng halg-ge issö-yo; it's nothing to laugh about 웃을 것 없어요 usl göd öbsö-yo
above 위에 wi-e
abroad 외국 wegug
abscess 종기 chong-gi
absolutely 절대로 chöldero; absolutely not (that is wrong) 전혀 아네요 chönyö anye-yo; that's absolutely right 완전히 옳으세요 wanjöni orshyö-yo; I'm absolutely sure 정말 확실 해요 chöng-mal hwagshil he-yo
accelerator 악셀 agsel
accept 받아요 pada-yo; please accept

my apologies 내 잘못을 용서해 주십시오 ne chalmosl yong-söhe jushibshi-o; please accept it 제발 받으세요 chebal padse-yo; do you accept checks? 수표를 받으세요? suphyorl padse-yo?; do you accept American money? 미국 돈을 받으세요? migug tonl padse-yo?
accident 사고 sago; road accident 교통 사고 kyot-hong sago; excuse me, it was an accident 미안 합니다만, 실수였어요 mi-an hamnidaman, shilsu-yössö-yo
accommodations (room) 방 pang
according to ... ...의 하면 ...e hamyön
account: bank account 은행 구좌 üneng kujwa
accurate 정확 한 chöng-wag han
ache (be painful) 아퍼요 ap-hö-yo; I have a stomach ache 배가 아파요 pega ap-ha-yo
across ... ... 건너서 ... könnösö; the shop across the street 길 건너편에 있는 상점 kil könnöp-hyöne innün sangjöm
act (of play) 막 mag; don't act silly 어리석은 짓을 하지 마세요 örisögn chisl haji mase-yo
action 활동 hwaldong
action film 활극 hwalgüg
activity 행사 heng-sa
actor 배우 pe-u
actress 여배우 yöbe-u
actually 참으로 ch-hamro
acupressure 지압 chi-ab
acupuncture 침치료 ch-himch-hiryo
ad 광고 kwang-go
adapter 아답터 adabt-hö
additional 추가의 ch-huga-e; is that an additional expense? 그것은 추가 비용이에요? kgösn ch-huga pi-yong-i-e-yo?
address 주소 chuso; forwarding address

새로운 주소 sero-un chuso; home address 집 주소 chib chuso; what's the address? 주소를 알려 주시겠어요? chusorl allyö jushigessö-yo?; please send it to this address 이 주소로 부쳐 주세요 i jusoro puch-hyö juse-yo
address book 주소록 chusorog
adhesive tape 접착 테이프 chöbch-hag t-he-ip-hü
admission 입장료 ibjang-ryo; free admission 무료 입장 muryo ibjang; what's the admission price? 입장료는 얼마에요? ibjang-ryonün ölma-e-yo?
adult 어른 örn
advance: in advance 미리 miri; must I get tickets in advance? 표를 미리 사야 돼요? p-hyorl miri sa-ya dwe-yo?
advertisement 광고 kwang-go
advise 충고 해요 ch-hung-go he-yo; what do you advise? 어떻게 하면 좋을지 가르쳐 주십시오 öd-dök-he hamyön chohülji karch-hyö jushibshi-o
aerogram 항공 엽서 hang-gong öbsö
afraid 무서워 한 musöwö han; afraid so 미안 합니다만, 그래요 mi-an hamnidaman, kre-yo; I'm afraid we can't help you 미안 합니다만, 도울 수가 없어요 mi-an hamnidaman, to-ul suga öbsö-yo
Africa 아프리카 ap-hürik-ha
after 후에 hu-e; after 7 o'clock 일곱시 지나서 ilgobshi chinasö; after dark 해 가 진 후에 hega chin hu-e; the day after tomorrow 모레 more
afternoon 오후 ohu; this afternoon 오늘 오후에 onl ohu-e; tomorrow afternoon 내일 오후 ne-il ohu; yesterday afternoon 어제 오후 öje ohu; sometime this afternoon 오늘 오후 언젠가 onl ohu önjen-ga
aftershave 면도후에 바르는 로션 myöndohu-e parnün roshyön
afterwards 나중에 najung-e

again 다시 tashi; let's meet again 또 만나요 ddo manna-yo; please come again 또 오세요 ddo ose-yo; half as much again 한배 반 hanbe pan; till we meet again 그럼 다시 또 만날 때 까지 kröm tashi ddo mannal dde ggaji; that will not happen again 그런 일은 다신 일어나지 않을 거에요 krön irn tashin irönaji anl kö-e-yo; I'm sure we'll meet again 또 만나뵙게 되겠지요 ddo mannabwebge dwegedji-yo
against (not supporting) 반대 한 pande han; against the law 불법으로 pulböbro; I'm against that 그것에 반대 해요 kgöse pande he-yo
age 나이 na-i; you don't look your age 자기 나이로 보이지 않어요 chagi na-iro po-iji anö-yo
age limit 연령 제한 yönryöng chehan
agency 대리점 terijöm; travel agency 여 행사 yöheng-sa; car rental agency 렌 트카 회사 rent-hük-ha hwesa
agent: real estate agent 부동산 업자 pudong-san öbja
ago 전에 chöne; two months ago 이개 월 전에 igewöl chöne; three years ago 삼년 전 samnyön chön; that happened long ago 훨씬 이전에 일어난 일이에요 hwölshin ijöne irönan iri-e-yo
agree 동의 해요 tong-e he-yo; do you agree? 동의 하세요? tong-e hase-yo?; kimchee doesn't agree with me. 김치는 내 몸에 안 맞아요. kimch-hinün ne mome an maja-yo.
ahead (forward, in front) 앞에 ap-he; 5 kilometers ahead 오킬로미터 더 앞에 ok-hillomit-hö tö ap-he; go straight ahead 똑 바로 가세요 ddog paro kase-yo
aid: first aid 응급 치료 üng-gb ch-hiryo; hearing aid 보청기 poch-höng-gi
AIDS 에이즈 e-ijü

air 공기 kong-gi; sea air 바닷 공기 padad kong-gi; I need some fresh air 신선 한 공기가 필요 해요 shinsön han kong-giga p-hiryo he-yo

air conditioning 냉방 장치 neng-bang chang-ch-hi; could you turn the air conditioning off? 에어콘을 꺼 주시겠어요? e-ök-honl ggö jushigessö-yo?; can you put the air conditioning on? 에어콘을 켜 주시겠어요? e-ök-honl k-hyö jushigessö-yo?

air mattress 고무 침대 komu ch-himde

airfare 항공 료 hang-gong ryo; what is the airfare to New York? 뉴욕까지 비행기 요금이 얼마에요? nyu-yogg-gaji piheng-gi yogmi ölma-e-yo?

airline 항공 hang-gong

airmail 항공 우편 hang-gong up-hyön

airmail envelope 항공 우편 봉투 hang-gong up-hyön pong-t-hu

airplane 비행기 piheng-gi; by airplane 비행기로 piheng-giro

airport 공항 kong-ang; would you take me to the airport? 공항까지 데려다 주시겠어요? kong-ang-ggaji teryöda jushigessö-yo?

airport bus 에어 포오트 버스 e-ö p-ho-ot-hü pösü

airport tax 공항 세금 kong-ang segm

aisle 통로 t-hong-ro

alarm (warning) 경보 kyöng-bo; fire alarm 화재 경보 hwaje kyöng-bo

alarm clock 자명종 chamyöng-jong; travel alarm clock 여행용 알람 시계 yöheng-yong allam shigye

alcohol 알콜 alk-hol; does it contain alcohol? 알콜이 들어 있어요? alk-hori trö issö-yo?

alive 살아 있는 sara innün

all (adjective) 모든 modn; all hotels 모든 호텔 modn hot-hel; all of them 모두 modu; all of it 모두 modu; all my belongings 내 모든 것 ne modn göd; all right, fair enough 좋아, 됐어요

choha, dwessö-yo; it's all arranged 다 정리 했어요 ta chöng-ri hessö-yo; it's all gone 다 없어졌어요 ta öbsöjyössö-yo; that's all right 괜찮아요 kwench-hana-yo; what does all that come to? 모두 얼마에요? modu ölma-e-yo?; I dislike all of them 아무것도 싫어요 amugöddo shirö-yo; I'm sunburned all over 나는 온몸이 볕에 탔어요 nanün onmomi pyöt-he t-hassö-yo; we've spent all our money 돈을 다 썼어요 tonl ta ssössö-yo; it's gotten all wet 다 젖었어요 ta chöjössö-yo

allergy 알레르기 allergi

alley 골목 kolmog

allowance: baggage allowance 수하물 중량 제한 suhamul chung-ryang chehan

allow 허락 해요 hörag he-yo; is camping allowed here? 여기에서 캠프를 해도 되요? yögi-esö k-hemp-hürl hedo dwe-yo?

almonds 아몬드 amondü

almost 거의 kö-e; almost 10,000 won 거의 만원 kö-e manwön

alone 혼자 honja; leave us alone! 제발 혼자 있게 해 주십시오! chebal honja idge he jushibshi-o!; I came alone 혼자 왔어요 honja wassö-yo; I am travelling alone 혼자 여행 하고 있어요 honja yöheng hago issö-yo

along ... ...을 따라 ...l ddara; along the road 일을 따라 irl ddara

aloud (adverb) 소리를 내어 sorirl ne-ö; could you read it aloud? 소리 내어 읽어 주시겠어요? sori ne-ö ilgö jushigessö-yo?

already 벌써 pölssö; I've already ordered 벌써 주문 했어요 pölsö chumun hessö-yo; we have already eaten 우리는 벌써 먹었어요 urinün pölsö mögössö-yo; it has already been paid for 대금을 벌써 끝냈어요 tegml pölsö ggt-hnessö-yo

also 도 to

alter 고쳐요 koch-hyö-yo
alteration 고침 koch-him
alternative 다른 방법 tarn pang-böb
although ... ... 하지만 ... hajiman
altogether 모두 modu; what does that come to altogether? 전부 얼마나 됐어요? chönbu ölmana dwessö-yo?
aluminum foil 은박지 ünbagji
always 항상 hang-sang; Seoul's main streets are always crowded 서울의 큰 거리는 항상 붐벼요 sö-ure k-hün körinün hang-sang pumbyö-yo
amazing 놀라운 nolla-un
ambassador 대사 tesa
ambulance 구급차 kugbch-ha; call an ambulance! 구급차 좀 불러 주세요! kugbch-ha chom pullö juse-o!
America 미국 migug; a stamp for America, please 미국으로 우표를 주세요 migugro up-hyorl chuse-yo; if you should come to America 만일 미국에 가보면 manil miguge kabomyön; I want to send this to America 이것을 미국에 보내고 싶은데요 igösl miguge ponego ship-hünde-yo; I want to make a call to America 미국에 전화 하고 싶은데요 miguge chönwa hago ship-hünde-yo
American (adjective) 미국 (의) migug (e); Americans 미국 사람 migug saram; the American market 미국 시장 migug shijang; I'm an American 나는 미국 사람이에요 nanün migug sarami-e-yo; do you accept American money? 미국 돈을 받으세요? migug tonl padse-yo?; she isn't an American 그녀는 미국 사람이 아니에요 knyönün migug sarami ani-e-yo
American Embassy 미국 대사관 migug tesagwan
among ... ... 가운데 ... ka-unde
amount (money) 금액 kmeg
amp 앰프 emp-hü; a 15 amp fuse 십오 암페어 의 퓨즈 shibo-amp-he-ö e p-

hyujü
amusement park 유원지 yuwönji
ancestor 선조 sönjo
anchovies 멸치 myölch-hi
anchovy 앤초우비 ench-ho-ubi
ancient 고대 의 kode e
and (between nouns) 와 / 과 wa / gwa; Seoul and New York 서울과 뉴욕 sö-ulgwa nyu-yog
anesthetic 마취제 mach-hwich-he
angry 성난 söng-nan; I'm really angry about it 나는 화가 많이 났어요 nanün hwaga mani nassö-yo
animal 동물 tong-mul
ankle 발목 palmog; I think my ankle is broken 발목이 부러진 것 같아요 palmogi puröjin göd kat-ha-yo; I've twisted my ankle 발목을 뺐어요 palmogl bbyössö-yo
anniversary (wedding) 결혼 기념일 kyöron kinyömil
annoy (harass) 괴롭혀요 kwerop-hyö-yo; it's really annoying 몹시 귀찮게 해요 mobshi kwich-hyank-he he-yo
another 다른 tarn; another blanket, please 담요를 한 장 더 주시겠어요 tamyorl han chang tö jushigessö-yo; another serving 더 한 그릇 tö han krd; is there another mail delivery? 우체부가 오늘 또 와요? uch-hebuga onl ddo wa-yo?; please call another hotel for me 다른 호텔에 전화 좀 걸어 주세요 tarn hot-here chönwa chom körö juse-yo; please give us another bottle 한 병 더 주세요 han pyöng tö juse-yo; would you like another? 더 하나 어때요? tö hana öd-de-yo?; can we move to another table? 다른 테이블로 옮겨 주시겠어요? tarn t-he-ibllo olgyö jushigessö-yo?; I want to stay another week 일주일간 더 묵고 싶은데요 ilju-ilgan tö muggo ship-hünde-yo
answer (noun) 대답 tedab; there was no answer 대답이 없었어요 tedabi öbsössö-

yo

answering machine 자동 응답기 chadong üng-dabgi

ants 개미들 kemidl

antacid 제산제 chesanje

antibiotics 항생제 hang-seng-je

antifreeze 부동액 pudong-eg

antihistamine 안티히스타민제 ant-hihist-haminje

antique 골동품 koldong-p-hum

antique shop 골동품상 koldong-p-humsang

antiseptic 방부제 pang-buje

any: in any case 어떠한 경우에도 öd-döhan kyöng-u-edo; got any matches? 성냥 있어요? söng-nyang issö-yo?; are you any better? 좀 나으세요? chom nase-yo?; are there any other colors? 다른 색이 있어요? tarn segi issö-yo?; is there any good fishing around here? 이 근처에 좋은 낚시터가 있어요? i gnch-hö-e chohün nag-gshit-höga issö-yo?; are there any leaflets on ...? ...에 관한 리플렛 있어요? ...e kwanan rip-hülled issö-yo?; are there any letters for me? 나에게 편지가 있어요? na-ege p-hyönjiga issö-yo?; is there any news? 무슨 별다른 일이 있어요? musn pyöldarn iri issö-yo?; are there any other sizes? 다른 사이즈가 있어요? tarn sa-ijga issö-yo?; they haven't got any change 잔돈이 없어요 chandoni öbsö-yo; it doesn't make any difference 큰 차이는 없어요 k-hün ch-ha-inün öbsö-yo; there is hardly any money left 돈이 거의 남지 않았어요 toni kö-e namji anassö-yo; do you have any vacancies? (rooms) 빈방이 있어요? pinbang-i issö-yo?; I don't need any ... ...가 필요 없어요 ...ga p-hiryo öbsö-yo

anyone, anybody 누구든지 nugudnji; has anyone called me? 나한테 전화 온 데 있어요? nahant-he chönwa on te

issö-yo?; is anyone hurt? 부상자가 있어요? pusang-jaga issö-yo?; is there anyone who can help? 누구 도와줄 사람 있어요? nugu towajul saram issö-yo?

anything 아무것 amugöd; anything else? 그밖에 다른 것은 없어요? kbag-ge tarn gösn öbsö-yo?; is there anything cheaper? 더 싼 것은 없어요? tö ssan gösn öbsö-yo?; I don't need anything 아무 것도 필요 없어요 amu göddo p-hiryo öbsö-yo; I didn't buy anything 아무것도 사지 않았어요 amugöddo saji anössö-yo; do you have anything else? 다른 것이 있어요? tarn göshi issö-yo?; he did not say anything 그는 아무것도 말하지 않았어요 knün amugöddo maraji anössö-yo

apartment 아파트 ap-hat-hü; our apartment hasn't been cleaned yet 우리 아파트는 아직 청소가 안 됐어요 uri ap-hat-hünün ajig ch-höng-soga an dwessö-yo

aperitif 반주 panju

apology 사죄 sajwe

apparently 일견 해 ilgyön he

appetite 식욕 shigyog; I lost my appetite 식욕을 잃어 버렸어요 shigyogl irö pöryössö-yo

appetizer 에퍼타이저 ep-höt-ha-ijö

apple 사과 sagwa

apple pie 사과 파이 sagwa p-ha-i

appliances: electrical appliances 가전 제품 kajön chep-hum

application form 신청용지 shinch-höng-yong-ji

apply: you must apply in writing 서류 신청을 해야 돼요 söryu shinch-höng-l he-ya dwe-yo

appointment 약속 yagsog; do I need to make an appointment? 예약 해야 돼요? ye-yag he-ya dwe-yo?

approach (come near) 접근 해요 chöbgn he-yo

appropriate 적당 한 chögdang han
approve 찬성 해요 ch-hansöng he-yo;
we don't approve 찬성 하지 않아요 ch-
hansöng haji ana-yo
apricot 살구 salgu
April 사월 sawöl
aquamarine (stone) 남옥 namog
aquarium 수족관 sujoggwan
Arabic (language) 아랍어 arabö
arcade: shopping arcade 상가 sang-ga
archeology 고고학 kogohag
archery 궁도 kung-do
architect 건축가 könch-hugga
architecture 건축 könch-hug
are 이에요 i-e-yo; are you alone? 혼자
계세요? honja kyeshyö-yo?; are there
Western or Korean meals? 음식은
양식이에요, 한식이에요? ümshign yang-
shigi-e-yo, hanshigi-e-yo?; are you
sure? 확실 하세요? hwagshil hase-yo?;
are there any other colors? 다른 색이
있어요? tarn segi issö-yo?; are you
married? 결혼 했어요? kyöron hessö-
yo?; are you OK? 어떠세요? öd-döse-
yo?; are there ...? ...가 있어요?
...ga issö-yo?; are they coming? 그
사람들은 와요? kü saramdrn wa-yo?;
how are you doing? 안녕 하십니까
annyöng hashimnig-ga; where are you
from? 어디서 오셨어요? ödisö oshyössö-
yo?; there are ... ...가 있어요 ...ga
issö-yo; there you are (here it is) 여
기 있어요 yögi issö-yo
area 지역 chi-yög; what's the area code
for ...? ...의 지역번호는 뭐에요? ...e
chi-yögbönonün mwö-ye-yo?; I don't
know this area 그 근처를 몰라요 kü
gnch-hörl molla-yo
area code 시외 국번 shiwe kugbön
Argentina 아르헨티나 arhent-hina
arm 팔 p-hal
army 육군 yuggun
around (on all sides) 사방에 sabang-e;
around 8 o'clock 여덟시 경 yödölshi

kyöng; around noon 정오 경 chöng-o
kyöng; is it around here? 이 근처에
있어요? i gnch-hö-e issö-yo?; I'm
travelling around 여기저기 여행 하고
있어요 yögijögi yöheng hago issö-yo;
can I look around? 구경 해도 좋아요?
kugyöng hedo choha-yo?; let's take a
walk around the town 도시에 산책
나갈까요 toshi-e sanch-heg nagalg-ga-
yo; I like just wandering around 어슬
렁 어슬렁 돌아다니기를 좋아 해요
ösllöng ösllöng toradanigirl choha he-
yo; is there any good fishing around
here? 이 근처에 좋은 낚시터가 있어요? i
gnch-hö-e chohün nag-gshit-höga
issö-yo?; I want to go and look
around 가서 답사를 하고 싶은데요 kasö
tabsarl hago ship-hünde-yo
arrangements 준비 chunbi; please make
the arrangements 준비를 해 주십시오
chunbirl he jushibshi-o
arranging: flower arranging 꺾꽃이
ggögg-goch-hi
arrest 체포 해요 ch-hep-ho he-yo; she
was arrested 그는 체포 됐어요 knün ch-
hep-ho dwessö-yo
arrival 도착 toch-hag
arrive 도착 해요 toch-hag he-yo; when
will he arrive? 언제 도착 해요? önje
toch-hag he-yo?; please let me know
when they arrive 그들이 도착 하면 곧
알려 주십시오 kdri toch-hag hamyön
kod allyö jushibshi-o
art 미술 misul; folk art 민속 예술
minsog yesul
art gallery 화랑 hwarang; modern art
gallery 현대 미술관 hyönde misulgwan
arthritis 관절염 kwanjöröm
artificial 인공의 in-gong-e
artist 예술가 yesulga
as: as much as possible 될 수 있는 대로
많이 dwel su innün tero mani; as soon
as possible 가능한 한 빨리 kanüng-an
han bballi; as a special case 예외로서

Pronounce: a father; e let; i machine; o note; ö löng; u rude; ü further

yewerosö; as far as I'm concerned 나에
관한 한 na-e kwanan han; as ... as
possible 되도록 ... dwedorog ...; as
usual 전과 같이 chön-gwa kat-hi;
twice as much 두배의 분량 tube-e
punryang; I'm here as a tourist 관광하
러 왔어요 kwan-gwang-arö wassö-yo;
that's just as good 그것 만큼 좋아요
kgöd man-k-hüm choha-yo
ashore 해변에 hebyöne; to go ashore 상
륙 해요 sang-ryug he-yo
ashtray 재떨이 ched-döri
Asia 아시아 ashi-a
Asian (adjective) 아시아 의 ashi-a e;
(person) 아시아 사람 ashi-a saram
ask (for) 부탁 해요 put-hag he-yo;
please ask that policeman over there
저기에 있는 경찰에게 물어보세요
chögi-e innün kyöng-ch-harege
muröbose-yo; will you ask him? 그에
게 물어 봐 주시겠어요? k-ege murö
pwa jushigessö-yo?; this is not what I
asked for 이건 내가 주문한 것이
아니에요 igön nega chumunan göshi
ani-e-yo; excuse me, I'd like to ask a
question 실례지만, 말씀 좀 묻겠어요
shillyejiman, malsm chom mudgessö-
yo
asparagus 아스파라거스 asp-haragösü
aspirin 아스피린 asp-hirin
assault (violation) 폭행 p-hok-heng;
she's been assaulted 그는 피해를
당했어요 knün p-hiherl tang-essö-yo
assistant (helper) 조수 chosu; (shop) 점
원 chömwön
assume (suppose) 추측 해요 ch-huch-
hüg he-yo
asthma 천식 ch-hönshig
at ... ...에(서) ...e(sö); at 9 a.m. 오
전 아홉시 ojön ahobshi; at 10 o'clock
열시에 yölshi-e; at the beginning 처음
에 ch-hö-me; at the bottom of the
hill 언덕의 밑에 öndöge mit-he; at the
seaside 해변에 hebyöne; at sunrise 새벽

녘에 sebyög nyök-he; at the end of
the road 길 끝에 kil ggt-he; at home
집에(서) chibe(sö); at my hotel 내
호텔에(서) ne hot-here(sö); at last 마
침내 mach-himne; at the latest 늦어도
njödo; at night 밤에 pame; at once 곧
kod; at 7:00 p.m. 오후 일곱시에 ohu
ilgobshi-e; at present 현재 hyönje; at
what time do you close? 몇시에 문을
닫으세요? myöt-hshi-e munl tadse-yo?;
look at him 그를 좀 봐요 krl chom
pwa-yo; the guy at reception 접수부에
있는 사람 chöbsubu-e innün saram; I'm
still at school 나는 아직 학생이에요
nanün ajig hagseng-i-e-yo; please let
me off at ... ...에서 내려 주세요
...esö neryö juse-yo
athlete 운동 선수 undong sönsu
Atlantic Ocean 대서양 tesö-yang
atmosphere 분위기 punwigi
attache case 서류 가방 söryu kabang
attack: heart attack 심장마비 shimjang-
mabi
attend 참석 해요 ch-hamsög he-yo; I
want to attend the religious services
today 오늘 예배에 참석 하고 싶은데요
onl yebe-e ch-hamsög hago ship-
hünde-yo
attendant: flight attendant (woman) 스
튜어디스 st-hyu-ödisü
attention 주의 chu-e; pay attention 주
의 해요 chu-e he-yo
attractions 구경거리 kugyöng-göri;
main attractions 가장 볼만 한 구경 거리
kajang polman han kugyöng köri
attractive 매력 있는 meryög innün
auburn (color) 갈색 kalseg
auction 경매 kyöng-me
audience 관객 kwan-geg
August 팔월 p-harwöl; in August 팔월
에 p-harwöre
aunt 아주머니 ajumöni
Australia 호주 hoju
Australian (adjective) 호주 (의) hoju

Pronounce: a father; e let; i machine; o note; ö löng; u rude; ü fürther

(e); (person) 호주 사람 hoju saram
author 저자 chöja; the author of this
book is ... 이 책의 저자가 ...이에요 i
ch-hege chöjaga ...i-e-yo
auto mechanic 자동차 정비공 chadong-
ch-ha chöng-bigong
automatic 자동 식 chadong shig
automatic transmission 오토매틱 ot-
homet-hig
automobile 자동차 chadong-ch-ha
autumn 가을 ka-l; in the autumn 가을
에 ka-re
autumn leaves 단풍 tanp-hung
available 유효 한 yuhyo han; are
camping facilities available? 캠프
시설이 있어요? k-hemp-hü shisöri issö-
yo?; is room service available? 룸써비
스가 있어요? rumsöbisga issö-yo?
avalanche 눈사태 nunsat-he
avenue 큰길 k-hün-gil
average (ordinary) 보통 pot-hong;
below average 보통 이하 pot-hong iha
awake 깨어 있는 gge-ö innün; it keeps
me awake 그것이 나를 잠 못 들게 해요
kgöshi narl cham mod tlge he-yo
away (far) 멀리 mölli; get away! 가시
오! kashi-o!; right away 곧 kod; it's
really far away! 매우 멀어요! me-u
mörö-yo!; don't throw it away 내버리
지 말아요 neböriji mara-yo
awful 무시무시 한 mushimushi han;
what awful weather! 참 나쁜 날씨에요
ch-ham nab-bn nalshi-e-yo; it tastes
awful 맛이 아주 나빠요 mashi aju nab-
bö-yo; he has an awful hangover 숙취
가 심 해요 sugch-hwiga shim he-yo
awful-tasting 맛이 없는 mashi ömnün
axle 차축 ch-hach-hug

*

B

baby 아기 agi
baby bottle 젖병 chödbyöng
baby carrier (on back) 베이비 케리어
pe-ibi k-heri-ö
baby-sitter 애 보는 사람 e ponün saram;
please find us baby-sitter 애 보는
사람을 알아봐 주세요 e ponün saraml
arabwa juse-yo
bachelor 독신자 togshinja
back (of body) 등 tng; in back 뒤에
twi-e; come back! 돌아 와요! tora wa-
yo!; I'll be back 돌아 오겠어요 tora
ogessö-yo; we'll be back later 나중에
돌아오겠어요 najung-e tora-ogessö-yo;
I'll be back late 늦게 들어 오겠어요
ndge trö ogessö-yo; I'll come back
soon 곧 돌아오겠어요 kod tora-ogessö-
yo; on a back street 뒷골목에(서)
twidgolmoge(sö); I'll walk back 걸어
서 돌아 가겠어요 körösö tora kagessö-
yo; I'll give it back it tomorrow 내일
돌려 주겠어요 ne-il tollyö chugessö-
yo; I have a weak back 등이 약해요
tng-i yak-he-yo; when should I come
back? 언제 다시 올까요? önje tashi
olg-ga-yo?; when will they be back?
언제 돌아오시지요? önje tora-oshiji-
yo?; would you give me my money
back? 돈을 돌려 주시겠어요? tonl
tollyö jushigessö-yo?; when is the
last bus going back? 마지막 돌아오는
버스는 언제 있어요? majimag tora-onün
pösnün önje issö-yo?; I'll have to
send this food back 이 음식을 반품 해야
해요 i mshigl panp-hum he-ya he-yo;
would you tell her to call me back?
저에게 전화하라고 전해 주시겠어요?
chö-ege chönwaharago chöne

jushigessö-yo?
back door 뒷문 twinmun
back seat 뒷자리 twidjari
back street 뒷골목 twidgolmog
backache 허리 통증 höri t-hong-jng;
I've got a backache 등이 아파요 tng-i
ap-ha-yo
backgammon: Korean backgammon 윷
yuch
backpack 등짐 tng-jim
bacon 베이컨 pe-ik-hön
bad 나쁜 nab-bn; not bad! 괜찮아요
kwench-hyana-yo; that's too bad! 참
안됐군요! ch-ham andwedgunyo!; it
smells bad 나쁜 냄새가 나요 nab-bn
nemsega na-yo
badly (seriously) 심하게 shimage
badminton 배드민턴 pedmint-hön
bag 가방 kabang; (paper) 종이 봉지
chong-i pong-ji; (shopping bag) 쇼핑
백 shyop-hing peg; (luggage) 슈트케
이스 shyut-hük-he-isü; plastic bag 비
닐 봉투 pinil pong-t-hu; my bag has
been stolen 지갑을 도둑맞았어요 chigabl
todungmajassö-yo; tea bag 티백 t-
hibeg; that is her bag 그 것은 그 여자
의 가방에요 kü gösn kü yöja e
kabang-e-yo; I left my bag on the
train 차 안에 가방을 놓고 내렸어요 ch-
ha ane kabang-l nok-ho neryössö-yo;
he left his bag here 백을 여기에 놓고
갔어요 pegl yögi-e nok-ho kassö-yo;
can I use my sleeping bag? 내 침낭을
써도 돼요? ne ch-himnang-l ssödo
dwe-yo?
baggage 짐 chim; excess baggage 제한
초과 수화물 chehan ch-hogwa
suhwamul; hand baggage 수화물
suhwamul; this is my baggage 내 짐이
여기 있어요 ne chimi yögi issö-yo
baggage allowance 수하물 중량 제한
suhamul chung-ryang chehan
baggage claim 수하물 suhamul
baggage room 수하물 보관소 suhamul

pogwanso
baked 군 kun
bakery 빵집 bbang-jib
balcony (theater) 이층석 ich-hüng-sög
bald person 대머리 temöri
ball 공 kong; tennis ball 테니스 공 t-
henisü kong
ballet 발레 palle
ballpoint pen 볼펜 polp-hen
bamboo 대나무 tenamu
bamboo basket 대바구니 tebaguni
bamboo craft shop 죽세공점
chugsegong-jöm
banana 바나나 panana
band (musicians) 악단 agdan; elastic
band 고무 밴드 komu pendü; rubber
band 고무줄 komujul; watch band 손목
시계 줄 sonmog shigye chul
band-aid (tm) 일회용 반창고 irwe-yong
panch-hang-go
bandage 붕대 pung-de
bangs (hair) 단발 tanbal
bank 은행 üneng; where is there a
bank? 은행이 어디 있어요? üneng-i ödi
issö-yo?
bank account 은행 구좌 üneng kujwa
banker 은행가 üneng-ga
bar 빠 bba; cocktail bar 칵테일바 k-
hagt-he-ilba; snack bar 스낵바 snegba;
they meet in the bar 빠에서 만나요
bba-esö manna-yo; she left her bag in
the bar 백을 빠에 놓고 왔어요 pegl bba-
e nok-ho wassö-yo
barbecue (Korean style) 불고기 pulgogi
barber 이발소 ibalso
bargain (haggle) 에누리 해요 enuri he-
yo
barley 보리 pori
barley tea 보리차 porich-ha
barn 광 kwang
barrette 헤어밴드 he-öbendü
bartender 바텐더 pat-hendö
baseball 야구 yagu
baseball stadium 야구장 yagujang

Pronounce: a father; e let; i machine; o note; ö löng; u rude; ü fürther

basic 기본적인 kibonjögin

basket 바구니 paguni; bamboo basket 대 바구니 tebaguni; wastepaper basket 휴 지통 hyujit-hong

basketball 농구 nong-gu

bastard! 자식! chashig!

bath 목욕 mogyog; private bath 개인용 욕실 ke-inyong yogshil; public bath 공중목욕탕 kong-jung-mogyogt-hang; may I take a bath? 목욕을 해도 좋아요? mogyogl hedo choha-yo?; a room with a bath 욕실이 달린 방 yogshiri tallin pang

bathhouse (public) 목욕탕 mogyogt-hang

bathing 목욕 mogyog; a bathing cap 수 영모자 su-yöng-moja

bathing suit 수영복 su-yöng-bog

bathrobe 목욕가운 mogyogga-un

bathroom (for a bath) 목욕탕 mogyogt-hang; (toilet) 화장실 hwajang-shil; where's the bathroom? 화장실은 어디에 있어요? hwajang-shirn ödi-e issö-yo?; I want to go to the bathroom 화장실에 가고 싶은데요 hwajang-shire kago ship-hünde-yo

bathtub 목욕통 mogyogt-hong

battery (dry) 건전지 könjönji; (auto) 배터리 pet-höri; the battery is dead 건 전지가 다 닳았어요 könjönjiga ta tarassö-yo; do you have a battery for this? 이것에 쓰는 전지가 있어요? igöse ssnün chönjiga issö-yo?

bay 만 man; Asan Bay 아산 만 asan man

be 이에요 i-e-yo; to be satisfied 마음에 들어요 ma-me trö-yo; be careful 조심 해요 choshim he-yo; be patient 참아 주세요 ch-hama juse-yo; be quiet! 조 용 해! cho-yong he!; don't be scared 겁내지 말아요 kömneji mara-yo; I'll be back 돌아 오겠어요 tora ogessö-yo; I won't be long 빨리 하겠어요 bballi hagessö-yo; he ought to be here soon

그는 곧 도착 할 것이에요 knün kod toch-hag hal göshi-e-yo

beach 해변 hebyön; on the beach 해변에 hebyöne; is this beach safe for swimming? 이 해변에서 수영해도 안전 해요? i ebyönesö su-yöng-edo anjön he-yo?; a sandy beach 모래의 바닷가 more-e padadga

beach umbrella 비치 파라솔 pich-hi p-harasol

beads 구슬 kusl

bean curd 두부 tubu

bean sprouts 콩나물 k-hong-namul

beans 콩 k-hong

bear 곰 kom

beard 수염 su-yöm

beautiful 아름다운 armda-un; (wonderful) 훌륭한 hullyung-an; what beautiful weather! 참 좋은 날씨에요 ch-ham chohün nalshi-e-yo; it's really beautiful 참 아름다워요 ch-ham armdawö-yo

beauty parlor 미용실 mi-yong-shil

beauty salon 미용실 mi-yong-shil

because ... ... 때문에 ... ddemune; because it's getting late 늦어지기 때문에 njöjigi ddemune; because the weather is not good 날씨가 나쁘기 때문에 nalshiga nab-bgi ddemune

become 되요 dwe-yo; I want to become a member 회원이 되고 싶은데요 hwewöni dwego ship-hünde-yo

bed (Western) 침대 ch-himde; (Korean) 이부자리 ibujari; my bed has not been made 잠자리를 아직 깔지 않았어요 chamjarirl ajig ggalji anassö-yo; bunk beds 이단 침대 idan ch-himde; twin beds 트윈 베드 t-hüwin pedü; Korean bedding 이부자리 ibujari; could you get the bed ready? 잠자리를 마련 해 주시겠어요? chamjarirl maryön he jushigessö-yo?; I must go to bed early 일찍 자야 되요 ilj-jig cha-ya dwe-yo; must he stay in bed? 집에서 누워

Pronounce: a father; e let; i machine; o note; ö löng; u rude; ü fürther

있어야 돼요? chibesö nuwö issö-ya dwe-yo?

bed and breakfast 아침 식사를 포함한 숙박 ach-him shigsarl p-hohaman sugbag

bedroom 침실 ch-himshil

bee 꿀벌 ggulböl

beef 소고기 sogogi; **ground beef** 다진 쇠고기 tajin swegogi; **roast beef** 로스트 비프 rost-hü pip-hü

beef ribs 소갈비 sogalbi

beefsteak 비프 스테이크 pip-hü st-he-ik-hü

beeper (pager) 삐삐 bbib-bi

beer 맥주 megju; **draft beer** 생맥주 seng-megju; **this beer is flat** 이 맥주는 김 빠졌어요 i megjunün kim bbajyössö-yo; **a can of beer** 맥주 한깡통 megju hang-gang-t-hong; **how about a beer?** 맥주 한잔 어때요? megju hanjan öd-de-yo?

beer hall 맥주집 megjujib

before 전에 chöne; **before I go** 내가 가기 전에 nega kagi chöne; **the day before** 전 날 chön nal; **the day before yesterday** 그저께 kjög-ge; **half an hour before** 반시간 전에 panshigan chöne; **the same as before, please** 전과 같은 것을 주세요 chön-gwa kat-hün gösl chuse-yo

begin 시작 해요 shijag he-yo; **what time does the movie begin?** 영화는 몇 시에 시작 돼요 yöng-wanün myöt shi-e shijag dwe-yo

beginner 초보자 ch-hoboja; **I'm still a beginner** 나는 아직 초보자에요 nanün ajig ch-hoboja-e-yo

beginning 처음 ch-hö-m; **at the beginning** 처음에 ch-hö-me

behavior 행동 heng-dong; **her behavior** 그의 행동 k-e heng-dong; **indecent behavior** 추잡한 행동 ch-hujap-han heng-dong

behind 뒤에 twi-e

beige 베이지색 pe-ijiseg

Belgium 벨기에 pelgi-e

believe 믿어요 midö-yo; **we believe you** 당신을 믿어요 tang-shinl midö-yo; **I don't believe you** 당신을 믿지 않어요 tang-shinl midji anö-yo

bell (electric) 벨 pel; (temple) 종 chong

bellflower root 도라지 toraji

bellhop 뽀이 bbo-i

belong 속 해요 sog he-yo; **does this belong to you?** 이것은 당신의 것이에요? igösn tang-shine göshi-e-yo?

belongings 소유물 so-yumul

below (down) 아래에 are-e; (less than) 이하 iha; **below average** 보통 이하 pot-hong iha

belt (to wear) 허리띠 hörid-di; **fan belt** 팬 벨트 p-hen pelt-hü; **life belt** 구명띠 kumyöng-ddi; **seat belt** 좌석 벨트 chwasög pelt-hü; **must I wear a seat belt?** 좌석 벨트를 맬 필요가 있어요? chwasög pelt-hürl mel p-hiryoga issö-yo?

beltway 순환 도로 sunwan toro

bend (curve) 커어브 k-hö-öbü

berries 장과 chang-gwa

beside ... ... 옆에 ... yöp-he; **beside the post office** 우체국 옆에 uch-hegug yöp-he; **beside the window** 창문 옆에 ch-hang-mun yöp-he; **a seat beside the window** 창문 옆 자리 ch-hang-mun yöp chari

besides ... ... 외에 ... we-e

best 제일 좋은 che-il chohün; **which is the best route?** 어느 쪽이 제일 좋은 길이에요? önü jjogi che-il chohün kiri-e-yo?; **I consider you my best friend** 나는 당신을 제일 좋은 친구라고 생각 해요 nanün tang-shinl che-il chohün ch-hin-gurago seng-gag he-yo

bet (to wager) 걸어요 körö-yo; **I bet you 20000 won** 이만원을 걸겠어요

imanwönl kölgessö-yo

better 더 좋은 tö chohün; **a better than average hotel** 보통 이상 의 호텔 pothong isang e hot-hel; **even better** 더 좋은 tö chohün; **much better** 훨씬 좋은 hwölshin chohün; **that's better yet** 더 욱 좋아요 tö-ug choha-yo; **that is better** 그 것이 더 좋아요 kü göshi tö choha-yo; **I'm a little better** 조금 나아졌어요 chogm na-ajyössö-yo; **can you give me a better price?** 좀 싸게 해 주시겠어요? chom ssage he jushigessö-yo?

between ... ... 사이에 ... sa-i-e; **what's the difference between** ...? ...의 차이가 뭐에요? ...e ch-ha-iga mwö-e-yo?

beverage 음료수 ümryosu

beyond 저편에 chöp-hyöne

bicycle 자전거 chajön-gö; **do you rent bicycles here?** 여기에 임대 자전거 있어요? yögi-e imde chajön-gö issö-yo?

big 큰 k-hün; **it's too big** 너무 커요 nömu k-hö-yo; **it's too big a hassle** 몹시 성가신데요 mobshi sönggashinde-yo; **it's a little too big** 조금 만 작았으면 좋겠어요 chogmman chagassmyön chok-hessö-yo

bigger 더 큰 tö k-hün

bike 자전거 chajön-gö; **I fell off my bike** 자전거에서 떨어졌어요 chajön-gö-esö ddöröjyössö-yo

bikini 비키니 pik-hini; **bikini top** 비키 니 톱 pik-hini t-hob

bill 계산서 kyesansö; **the bill is wrong** 계산이 틀려요 kyesani t-hüllyö-yo; **pay the bill** 계산 해요 kyesan he-yo; **could I get the bill, please?** 계산서 주시겠어요? kyesansö jushigessö-yo?; **would you examine the bill?** 계산을 검사해 주세요? kyesanl kömsahe juse-yo?; **could we get separate bills?** 계산 서를 따로따로 주시겠어요? kyesansörl

ddarod-daro chushigessö-yo?; **would you give me change for a 5,000 won bill?** 오천원 짜리 한장을 잔돈으로 바꿔 주시겠어요? och-hönwön jjari hanjang-l chandonro pag-gwö jushigessö-yo?

billfold 접는 돈지갑 chömnün tonjigab

billiards 당구 tang-gu

bills (currency) 짜리 jjari; **I'd like the money in large bills** 큰 돈으로 주세요 k-hün tonro chuse-yo

bird 새 se

birth 출생 ch-hulseng; **birth certificate** 출생 증명서 ch-hulseng chüngmyöng-sö

birthdate 생년월일 seng-nyönwöril

birthday 생일 seng-il; **happy birthday!** 생일을 축하 해요 seng-irl ch-huk-ha he-yo

biscuit 비스켓 pisk-hed

bit 조금 chogm; **isn't that a bit too much?** 그것은 좀 지나쳤죠 kgösn chom chinach-hyödjyo; **the engine sounds a bit rough** 엔진 소리가 좀 거슬려요 enjin soriga chom gösllyö-yo

bite 물어요 murö-yo; **insect bite** 벌레 물 pölle mulm; **do you have something for insect bites?** 벌레물린데 좋은 약 있어요? pöllemullinde chohün yag issö-yo?

bitter 쓴 ssn

bitter lemon 쓴 레몬 ssn remon

black 검은 kömn; **black and white camera film** 흑백 필림 hügbeg p-hillim; **black tea** 홍차 hong-ch-ha; **a black coffee** 커피 한잔 k-höp-hi hanjan

blackout (electrical power cut) 정전 chöng-jön

blade: shoulder blade 어깨뼈 ög-gebbyö; **razor blades** 면도날 myöndonal

bland 순 한 sun han

blanket 담요 tamyo; (Korean style) 이 불 ibul; **electric blanket** 전기 담요

chön-gi tamyo
blazer 블레이저 코트 plle-ijö k-hot-hü
bleed 피가 나요 p-higa na-yo; I've got
a nose bleed 코피가 나요 k-hop-higa
na-yo
blender (food processor) 믹써 migsö
blind 눈먼 nunmön
blinds 블라인드 plla-indü; venetian
blind 차양 ch-ha-yang
blister 물집 muljib
block: sun block cream 선 블럭 크림
sön pllög k-hürim
blocked 막힌 mak-hin
blond (adjective) 금발의 kmbare
blonde (lady) 금발의 여성 kmbare
yösöng
blood 피 p-hi; her blood type is ... 그
의 혈액형은 ... 이에요 k-e hyörek-
hyöng-n ... i-e-yo
bloody mary 브러디 매리 prödi meri
blouse 브라우스 pra-usü
blow dry 드라이 tra-i
blue 파란 색 p-haran seg; dark blue 어
두운 청색 ödu-un ch-höng-seg; light
blue 연한 파란 색 yönan p-haran seg;
pale blue 여한 파란 색 yöhan p-haran
seg
Blue House (Presidential Palace) 청와대
ch-höng-wade
blusher (makeup) 볼연지 poryönji
board: full board 세끼 포함 seg-gi p-
hoham; diving board 다이빙대 ta-
ibing-de; emery board 손톱용줄 sont-
hobyong-jul
boarding house 하숙집 hasugjib
boarding pass 보딩 패스 poding p-hesü
boat (small) 보트 pot-hü; (ship) 배 pe;
fishing boat 어선 ösön; the next boat
from ... ...에서부터 다음 의 배
...esöbut-hö ta-m e pe
bobby pins 머리핀 mörip-hin
body 몸 mom; (car) 차체 ch-hach-he
body lotion 보디 로션 podi roshyön
boil: please boil the water 물을 끓여

주십시오 murl ggryö jushibshi-o
boiled egg 삶은 계란 salmn kyeran
boiled rice 밥 pab
bomb (noun) 폭탄 p-hogt-han
bone 뼈 bbyö; collar bone 쇄골 swegol;
I think the bone is broken 뼈가 부러진
것 같아요 bbyöga puröjin göd kat-ha-
yo
bonus 보너스 ponösü
book (noun) 책 ch-heg; (to reserve) 예
약 해요 ye-yag he-yo; address book
주소록 chusorog; cheque book 수표장
sup-hyojang; comic book 만화책
manwach-heg; grammar book 문법 책
munböb ch-heg; a book on Seoul 서울
에 관 한 책 sö-ure kwan han ch-heg;
phrase book 숙어집 sugöjib; that's my
favorite book 그 책은 내가 제일
좋아하는 책이에요 kü ch-hegn nega
che-il chohahanün ch-hegi-e-yo; the
author of this book is ... 이 책의
저자가 ...이에요 i ch-hege chöjaga
...i-e-yo; please find the word in this
book 이 책에서 그 말을 찾아 주세요 i
ch-hegesö kü marl ch-haja juse-yo
bookstore 서점 söjöm
boot 부츠 puch-hü; rain boots 장화
chang-wa; ski boots 스키 부츠 sk-hi
puch-hü; walking boots 등산화 tng-
sanwa
booth: telephone booth 공중 전화 박스
kong-jung chönwa pagsü
border (international) 국경 kuggyöng
boring 지루한 chiruhan
born: I was born in ... ...에
태어났어요 ...e t-he-önassö-yo
borrow 빌려 줘요 pillyö chwö-yo
boss 사장 sajang
both 양쪽 yang-jjog; please give me
both of them 두개 다 주세요 tuge ta
juse-yo
bother (annoyance) 괴로움 kwero-um
bottle 병 pyöng; baby bottle 젖병
chödbyöng; hot-water bottle 탕파 t-

hang-p-ha; thermos bottle 보온병 po-onbyöng; please bring us another bottle 한병 더 갖다 주십시오 hanbyöng tö kadda jushibshi-o
bottle opener 병따개 pyöng-ddage
bottom 밑바닥 midp-hadag
bouncer (bar) 경비원 kyöng-biwön
bourbon 버번 pöbön
bow (reverence) 인사 insa(verb) 인사 해요 insa he-yo
bowl 사발 sabal; rice bowl 밥 그릇 pab krd
bowling 볼링 polling
box 상자 sang-ja; cardboard box 상자 sang-ja; a box of chocolates 초콜릿 한 상자 ch-hok-hollid han sang-ja; fare box 요금함 yogmam; letter box 우체통 uch-het-hong
box lunch 도시락 toshirag
box office 매표소 mep-hyoso
boxing 권투 kwönt-hu
boy 남자 아이 namja a-i
boyfriend 남자친구 namjach-hin-gu
bra 브라자 praja
bracelet 팔찌 p-halj-ji
brake fluid 브레이크 오일 pre-ik-hü o-il
brakes 브레이크 pre-ik-hü; parking brake 주차 브레이크 chuch-ha pre-ik-hü; I slammed on the brakes 브레이크를 밟었어요 pre-ik-hürl palbössö-yo; something is wrong with the brakes 브레이크가 잘못 됐어요 pre-ik-hüga chalmod dwessö-yo
brandy 브랜디 prendi; double brandy 더블 브랜디 töbl prendi
brass 놋쇠 nosswe
brave 용감한 yong-gaman
Brazil 브라질 prajil
bread 빵 bbang; two slices of bread 빵 두 조각 bbang tu chogag; can I get some bread and butter? 빵과 버터를 주시겠어요? bbang-gwa pöt-hörl chushigessö-yo?
break (glass) 부숴요 puswö-yo;

somebody's broken in 강도들이 침입 했어요 kang-dodri ch-himib hessö-yo; you broke it 당신이 부쉈어요 tang-shini puswössö-yo; I think my ankle is broken 발목이 부러진 것 같아요 palmogi puröjin göd kat-ha-yo
breakdown (in car) 고장 kojang; my car has broken down 차가 고장났어요 ch-haga kojang-nassö-yo
breakfast 아침 식사 ach-him shigsa; breakfast included 아침 식사를 포함 ach-him shigsarl p-hoham; before breakfast 아침밥 전에 ach-himbab chöne; English breakfast 영국식 아침 식사 öng-gugshig ach-him shigsa; Korean breakfast 한식 아침 식사 hanshig ach-him shigsa; bed and breakfast 아침 식사를 포함한 숙박 ach-him shigsarl p-hohaman sugbag; please send breakfast to our room 아침 식사 방으로 갖다 주세요 ach-him shigsa pang-ro kadda juse-yo; when is breakfast served? 아침 식사가 몇 시에 나와요? ach-him shigsaga myöt shi-e nawa-yo?
breast 가슴 kasm; (woman's) 유방 yubang
breast-feed 젖을 줘요 chöjl chwö-yo
breath 숨 sum
breathe 숨 쉬워요 sum swiwö-yo
breathtaking 놀랄만한 nollalmanan
breeze 산들바람 sandlbaram
breezy: it's so breezy 바람이 많이 불어요 parami mani purö-yo
bride 신부 shinbu
bridegroom 신랑 shinrang
bridge (span) 다리 tari
brief (not long) 짧은 jjalbn
briefcase 서류 가방 söryu kabang
bright (hue) 밝은 palgn
bring 갖다 줘요 kadda chwö-yo; please bring us another bottle 한병 더 갖다 주십시오 hanbyöng tö kadda jushibshi-o; please bring some more bread 빵을

더 갖다 주세요 bbang-1 tö kadda juse-yo; please bring it to my hotel 호텔로 가져 오시겠어요 hot-hello kajyö oshigessö-yo; we will bring it back 가져 오겠어요 kajyö ogessö-yo; may I bring a friend? 친구를 데려와도 좋아요? ch-hin-gurl teryöwado choha-yo?

Britain 영국 yöng-gug; Great Britain 연합 왕국 yönab wang-gug

British 영국 의 yöng-gug e; British people 영국 사람 yöng-gug saram

British Embassy 영국 대사관 yöng-gug tesagwan

broccoli 브라컬리 prak-hölli

brochure 팜플렛 p-hamp-hülled

broil 구워요 kuwö-yo

broiled 불에 구운 pure ku-un

broken 부서진 pusöjin; somebody's broken in 강도들이 침입 했어요 kang-dodri ch-himib hessö-yo; my car has broken down 차가 고장났어요 ch-haga kojang-nassö-yo; the air conditioner is broken 에어콘이 고장났어요 e-ökhoni kojang-nassö-yo; I think the bone is broken 뼈가 부러진 것 같아요 bbyöga puröjin göd kat-ha-yo

brother (a man's elder) 형 hyöng; (man's younger) 동생 tong-seng; (woman's older) 오빠 ob-ba; (woman's younger) 남동생 namdong-seng; I have one brother 형제 한 명 있어요 hyöng-je han myöng issö-yo

brother-in-law (wife's brother) 처남 ch-hönam

brown 갈색 kalseg

browse: may I browse? 보기만 해도 돼요 pogiman hedo dwe-yo

bruise (injury) 타박상 t-habagsang

brunette (person) 브루네트 prunet-hü

brush (noun) 빗 pid; lip brush 립 부러쉬 rib puröswi; scrub brush 세탁솔 set-hagsol; shaving brush 면도솔 myöndosol

bucket 바께쓰 pag-gessü

Buddha 불타 pult-ha

Buddhism 불교 pulgyo

Buddhist (adjective) 불교의 pulgyo-e; (person) 불교도 pulgyodo

Buddhist temple 절 chöl

buffet 부페 pup-he

bug (insect) 벌레 pölle

build 지어요 chi-ö-yo

building 빌딩 pilding

bulb (light) 전구 chön-gu; light bulb 전구 chön-gu; I need a new light bulb 새 전구 하나 주세요 se chön-gu hana juse-yo

bulgogi 불고기 pulgogi

bull 황소 hwang-so

bump (swelling) 혹 hog

bumper 범퍼 pömp-hö

bumpy 울퉁불퉁한 ult-hung-bult-hung-an

bunk beds 이단 침대 idan ch-himde

burglar 도둑 todug

burgundy (color) 자주색 chajuseg

burn (incinerate) 태워요 t-hewö-yo;

burn (on body) 화상 hwasang; do you have an ointment for burns? 화상에 듣는 약 있어요? hwasang-e tnnün yag issö-yo?

bus 버스 pösü; airport bus 에어 포오트 버스 e-ö p-ho-ot-hü pösü; a bus to … …에 가는 버스 …e kanün pösü; hotel bus 호텔 버스 hot-hel pösü; the bus was delayed 버스가 지연 됐어요 pösga chi-yön dwessö-yo; which bus? 어느 버스 önü pösü; when does the bus leave? 버스는 몇 시에 떠나요? pösnün myöt shi-e ddöna-yo?; I missed the bus 버스를 놓쳤어요 pösrl noch-hyössö-yo; when is the last bus going back? 마지막 돌아오는 버스는 언제 있어요? majimag tora-onün pösnün önje issö-yo?; when is the next bus? 다음 버스는 언제 있어요 ta-m pösnün önje issö-yo

bus driver 버스 운전수 pösü unjönsu

Pronounce: a father; e let; i machine; o note; ö löng; u rude; ü further

bus station 정류장 chöng-ryujang
bus stop 버스 정거장 pösü chöng-göjang
bus tour 버스 관광 pösü kwan-gwang
business 사업 sa-öb; I've come on business 일 때문에 왔어요 il ddemune wassö-yo
business card: have you got a business card? 명함을 가지고 있어요? myöng-aml kajigo issö-yo?
business district 비즈니스거리 pijnisgöri
business hours 영업 시간 yöng-öb shigan
business trip 출장 ch-huljang
business woman 여류 사업가 yöryu sa-öbga
businessman 사업가 sa-öbga; (office worker) 샐러리맨 sellörimen
busy (crowded) 번잡한 pönjap-han; he's busy this evening 오늘 밤에는 바빠요 onl pamenün pab-bö-yo; in the busy season 최성기에 ch-hwesöng-gi-e
but 그러나 kröna; not these, but those 이것이 아니고, 그곳이에요 igöshi anigo, kgoshi-e-yo
butcher 정육점 chöng-yugjöm
butter 버터 pöt-hö; can I get some bread and butter? 빵과 버터를 주시겠어요? bbang-gwa pöt-hörl chushigessö-yo?
butterfly 나비 nabi
button 단추 tanch-hu
buy 사요 sa-yo; I'll buy the whole lot 모두 사겠어요 modu sagessö-yo; I didn't buy anything 아무것도 사지 않았어요 amugöddo saji anössö-yo; where can you buy ...? 어디서 ...를 살 수 있어요? ödisö ...rl sal su issö-yo?; I want to buy a small gift 작은 선물을 사고 싶어요 chagn sönmurl sago ship-hö-yo
by ... ...으로 ...ro; by airplane 비행기로 piheng-giro; by airmail 항공우편 hang-gong up-hyön; by ship 배

로 pero; by rail 기차로 kich-haro; by the river 강변에 kang-byöne; by the roadside 길가에 kilga-e; by the sea 해변에 hebyöne; quite by chance 정말로 우연히 chöng-mallo u-yöni; close by 바로 곁에 paro kyöt-he; drop by once in a while 가끔 들러 주세요 kag-gm tllö juse-yo; we're going by air 비행기로 가요 piheng-giro ka-yo; I'm going by myself 나는 혼자 가요 nanün honja ka-yo; may I pay by the day? 하루씩 지불 해도 좋아요? harusshig chibul hedo choha-yo?
bye! (see GOODBYE)

C

cab (taxi) 택시 t-hegshi
cabbage 배추 pech-hu
cabin (ship) 선실 sönshil; (hut) 오두막 집 odumagjib
cabinet (kitchen) 찬장 ch-hanjang
cable 케이블 k-he-ibl; cable (TV) 케이블 텔레비전 k-he-ibl t-hellebijön
cable car 케이블 카 k-he-ibl k-ha
caddy 캐디 k-hedi
cafe 까페 ggap-he; at the cafe 까페에(서) ggap-he-e(sö)
caffeine 카페인 k-hap-he-in
cake 케익 k-he-ig; rice cake 떡 ddög; some of that cake, please 그 케익을 조금 주세요 kü k-he-igl chogm chuse-yo
calculator 전자 계산기 chönja kyesan-gi; electronic calculator 전자 계산기 chönja kyesan-gi
calendar 달력 tallyög; lunar calendar 음력 ümryög
call 불러요 pllö-yo; call an ambulance! 구급차 좀 불러 주세오! kugbch-ha chom pullö juse-o!; call the police!

경관을 불러! kyöng-gwanl pullö!; please call me at 6:30 여섯시 반에 전화 해주세요 yösösshi pane chönwa hejuse-yo; they've called it off 중지 됐어요 chung-ji dwessö-yo; collect call 수화 인 지불 통화 suhwa-in chibul t-hong-wa; local call 시내 전화 shine chönwa; please call another hotel for me 다른 호텔에 전화 좀 걸어 주세요 tarn hot-here chönwa chom köro juse-yo; I'll call again (telephone) 다시 전화 하겠어요 tashi chönwa hagessö-yo; could you call a doctor? 의사를 불러 주시겠어요? esarl pullö jushigessö-yo?; long distance call 시외 전화 shiwe chönwa; could you call the manager? 지배인을 불러 주시겠어요? chibe-inl pullö jushigessö-yo?; international telephone call 국제 전화 kugje chönwa; what do you call this? 이것을 뭐라고 불러요 igösl mwörago pullö-yo; person to person call 특정인 호출 전화 t-hügjöng-in hoch-hul chönwa; would you tell her to call me back? 저에게 전화하라고 전해 주시겠어요? chö-ege chönwaharago chöne jushigessö-yo?; I want to make a call to America 미국에 전화 하고 싶은데요 miguge chönwa hago ship-hünde-yo; may I make a telephone call? 전화를 걸어도 좋아요? chönwarl körödo choha-yo?; I want to make a collect call to New York 수화자 지급으로 뉴욕에 전화 하고 싶은데요 suhwaja chigbro nyu-yoge chönwa hago ship-hünde-yo
calligraphy 서예 sö-ye
calm 조용한 cho-yong-an
calories 칼로리 k-hallori
camcorder (VCR camera) 캠코더 k-hemk-hodö
camera 카메라 k-hamera; movie camera 영화 카메라 yöng-wa k-hamera; your camera 당신의 카메라 tang-shine k-

hamera
camera shop 카메라점 k-hamerajöm
camp (verb) 야영 해요 ya-yöng he-yo
camping 캠핑 k-hemp-hing; are camping facilities available? 캠프 시설이 있어요? k-hemp-hü shisöri issö-yo?; is camping allowed here? 여기에 서 캠프를 해도 되요? yögi-esö k-hemp-hürl hedo dwe-yo?
camping site 캠핑장 k-hemp-hing-jang
can (tin) 깡통 ggang-t-hong;
can ....을 수 있어요 ...l su issö-yo; can she ...? (able) ...을 수가 있어요? ...l suga issö-yo?; can I have it? 가져도 좋아요? kajyödo choha-yo?; can I cook for myself? 직접 해 먹어도 되요? chigjöb he mögödo dwe-yo?; can we look around? 구경 해도 괜찮아요? kugyöng hedo kwench-hana-yo?; can you give me a better price? 좀 싸게 해 주시겠어요? chom ssage he jushigessö-yo?; can you repair it temporarily? 임시로 고칠 수 있어요? imshiro koch-hil su issö-yo?; if we can 만일 할수 있으면 manil halsu issmyön
can opener 깡통 따개 k-hang-t-hong ddage
Canada 캐나다 k-henada
Canadian (adjective) 캐나다 의 k-henada e; (person) 캐나다 사람 k-henada saram
cancel 취소 해요 ch-hwiso he-yo; he cancelled it 취소 했어요 ch-hwiso hessö-yo; I'd like to cancel my reservation 예약을 취소하고 싶은데요 ye-yagl ch-hwisohago ship-hünde-yo
cancellation 취소 ch-hwiso
candle 양초 yang-ch-ho
candy 캔디 k-hendi; a piece of candy 캔디 한개 k-hendi han-ge
candy store 과자점 kwajajöm
cap (hat) 모자 moja; lens cap 렌즈 뚜껑 renjü ddug-gyöng; shower cap 샤워

Pronounce: a father; e let; i machine; o note; ö löng; u rude; ü fürther

모자 shyawö moja; a bathing cap 수영
모자 su-yöng-moja
capital (of country) 수도 sudo;
provincial capital 도청 소재지 toch-
höng sojeji
capital city 수도 sudo
captain (ship) 선장 sönjang
car 차 ch-ha; my car has broken down
차가 고장났어요 ch-haga kojang-
nassö-yo; by car 차로 ch-haro; dining
car 식당칸 shigdang-k-han; rental car
렌트카 rent-k-ha; this car needs
servicing 이 차는 수리 해야 해요 i ch-
hanün suri he-ya he-yo; sleeping car
침대간 ch-himdegan; the car doesn't
start 시동이 걸리지 않아요 shidong-i
kölliji anö-yo; can I rent a car? 차를
빌릴 수가 있어요? ch-harl pillil suga
issö-yo?; would you move your car,
please? 차를 옮겨 주시겠어요? ch-harl
ulgyö jushigessö-yo?; would you
wash my car? 세차 해 주시겠어요?
sech-ha he jushigessö-yo?
car ferry 카페리 k-hap-heri
car keys 차 열쇠 ch-ha yölswe
car park 주차장 chuch-hajang
car phone 카 폰 k-ha p-hon
car rental 렌트카 rent-hük-ha
car rental agency 렌트카 회사 rent-hük-
ha hwesa
carafe 유리 물병 yuri mulbyöng
carat 캐럿 k-heröd; is it (14 carat)
gold? 그거 십사 금이에요? kgö shibsa
kmi-e-yo?
carbonated 탄산을 넣은 t-hansanl nöhün
carburetor 카뷰레터 k-habyuret-hö
card (business) 명함 myöng-am; (for
New Year's) 연하장 yönajang; credit
card 크레딧 카드 k-hüredid k-hadü;
identity card 신분 증명서 shinbun
chüng-myöng-sö; here is my card 제
명함이에요 che myöng-ami-e-yo; have
you got a business card? 명함을 가지고
있어요? myöng-aml kajigo issö-yo?

card game (Korean) 화투 hwat-hu
cardboard box 상자 sang-ja
cards 카드 k-hadü; what credit cards do
you take? 어떤 크레딧 카드를 받아요?
öd-dön k-hüredid k-hadrl pada-yo?; do
you take credit cards? 크레디트 카드를
받으세요? k-hüredit-hü k-hadrl padse-
yo?
care 걱정 kögjöng; day care center 탁아
소 t-hagaso; would you take care of
it? 그것을 하시겠어요? kgösl
hashigessö-yo?
careful! 주의! chu-e!
careless 조심성 없는 choshimsöng
ömnün
carnation 카네이션 k-hane-ishyön
carnival 카니발 k-hanibal
carp 잉어 ing-ö
carpet 융단 yung-dan
carrier: baby carrier (on back) 베이비
케리어 pe-ibi k-heri-ö
carrot 당근 tang-gn
carry 들어요 trö-yo; please carry this 이
것을 운반해 주세요 igösl unbane juse-
yo; do you carry English newspapers?
영어 신문 있어요? yöng-ö shinmun
issö-yo?
carry-on 기내 소지품 kine sojip-hum
carryall 큰 가방 k-hün kabang
carsick (adjective) 차멀미 한 ch-
hamölmi han;
carsick 차멀미난 ch-hamölminan
cart: push cart 손수레 sonsure
carte: a la carte 알라 카아트 alla k-ha-
at-hü
carton 용기 yong-gi
cartoon film 만화 영화 manwa yöng-wa
cartridges 카트리지 k-hat-hüriji
carved objects 조각품 chogagp-hum
carving 조각 chogag
carwash 세차 sech-ha
case (bags) 가방 kabang; attache case 서
류 가방 söryu kabang; in case she
returns 그가 돌아올 경우에는 kga tora-

ol kyöng-u-enün; pillow case 베갯잇 pegashid; in any case 어떠한 경우에도 öd-döhan kyöng-u-edo; as a special case 예외로서 yewerosö

cash 현금 hyön-gm; would you cash a check? 수표를 현금으로 바꿔 주시겠어요? sup-hyorl hyön-gmro paggwö jushigessö-yo?; we'll pay in cash 현금으로 지불하겠어요 hyön-gmro chiburagessö-yo; we're out of cash 돈 이 떨어 졌어요 toni ddörö chyössö-yo

cash machine 현금 자동 지급기 hyön-gm chadong chigbgi

cash register 금전 등록기 kmjön tngroggi

cashier 계산대 kyesande

casserole 전골 chön-gol

cassette 카세트 k-haset-hü; cassette player, cassette recorder 카세트 녹음기 k-haset-hü nogmgi

cast: plaster cast 기브스 kibsü

castle 성 söng

casual (informal) 평상의 p-hyöngsang-e

casual clothes 평상복 p-hyöng-sang-bog

cat 고양이 ko-yang-i

catalog 카탈로그 k-hat-hallogü

catastrophe 큰 재해 k-hün chehe

catch (take) 잡아요 chaba-yo; to catch the flu 몸살 나요 momsal na-yo; is it catching? 전염이 돼요? chönyömi dweyo?

catholic: Roman Catholic 천주교의 ch-hönjugyo-e; where is there a Catholic church? 성당은 어디 있어요? söng-dang-n ödi issö-yo?

cauliflower 꽃양배추 ggoch-hyang-bech-hu

cause (noun) 원인 wönin

caution 주의 chu-e

cave 동굴 tong-gul

caviar 캐비어 k-hebi-ö

cavity 충치 ch-hung-ch-hi

CD (compact disc) 콤팩트 디스크 k-

hombegt-hü tisk-hü

CD player 씨디 플레이어 sshidi p-hüllei-ö

ceiling 천장 ch-hönjang

celebration 축하 ch-huk-ha

celery 셀러리 sellöri

cellular phone 셀 방식 전화 sel pangshig chönwa

Celsius 섭씨 söbshi; 20 degrees Celsius 섭씨 이십도 söbshi ishibdo

cemetery 묘지 myoji

center 중심 chung-shim; city center 시 의 중앙 shi-e chung-ang; straight through the city center 곧장, 시의 중심을 지나서 kodjang, shi-e chung-shiml chinasö

centigrade 섭씨의 söbshi-e

centimeter 센티미터 sent-himit-hö

central 중심의 chung-shime; where is the central post office? 중앙우체국 어디 있어요? chung-ang-uch-hegug ödi issö-yo?

central heating 집중 난방 chibjung nanbang

central station 중앙역 chung-ang-yög

century 세기 segi; in the 15th century 십오 세기에 shibo segi-e

ceramics 도자기 tojagi

ceramics store 도자기점 tojagijöm

cereal (breakfast) 시리얼 shiri-öl

ceremony (opening) 개회식 kehweshig; closing ceremony 폐막식 p-hyemagshig; Confucian Ceremony 석 전제 sögjönje

certain (sure) 확실한 hwagshiran; are you certain? 확실 하세요? hwagshil hase-yo?; is that for certain? 확실 해요? hwagshil he-yo?

certainly (of course) 물론 mullon; certainly (surely) 확실히 hwagshiri; ceratainly not (unacceptable) 안 돼요 an dwe-yo; I certainly must go (there) 꼭 가야겠어요 ggog kayagessö-yo

Pronounce: a father; e let; i machine; o note; ö löng; u rude; ü further

certificate 증명서 chüng-myöng-sö;
birth certificate 출생 증명서 ch-hulseng
chüng-myöng-sö
chain 체인 ch-he-in
chair 의자 eja; deck chair 갑판 의자
kabp-han eja; folding chair 접는 의자
chömnün eja; can we get an extra
chair? 의자를 하나 더 주시겠어요? ejarl
hana tö jushigessö-yo?
champagne 샴페인 shyamp-he-in
champion 우승자 usng-ja
chance (opportunity) 기회 kihwe
change (coins) 잔돈 chandon; change
the subject 화제를 바꿔요 hwajerl pag-
gwö-yo; would you change my
bandage? 붕대를 갈아 주시겠어요?
pung-derl kara jushigessö-yo?; for a
change 기분 전환을 위하여 kibun
chönwanl wiha-yö; will you change
places with me? 나와 자리를
바꾸겠어요? nawa charirl pag-gugessö-
yo?; keep the change 거스름돈은 그만
두세요 gösrmdonün kman tuse-yo;
could you change the oil? 오일을 바꿔
주시겠어요? o-irl pag-gwö jushigessö-
yo?; will you change traveller's
checks? 여행자 수표를 바꿔 주시겠어요?
yöheng-ja sup-hyorl pag-gwi
chushigessö-yo?; they haven't got any
change 잔돈이 없어요 chandoni öbsö-
yo; would you give me change for a
5,000 won bill? 오천원 짜리 한장을
잔돈으로 바꿔 주시겠어요? och-hönwön
jjari hanjang-l chandonro pag-gwö
jushigessö-yo?; do I have to change
(trains) ? (기차를) 갈아타야 돼요?
(gich-harl) karat-ha-ya dwe-yo?
changeable 변덕스러운 pyöndögsrö-un
channel (TV) 채널 ch-henöl
chapel 교회 kyohwe
character (letter) 글자 klja; Chinese
character 한자 hanja; in Korean
characters 한글로 han-gllo; the writing
of a Chinese character 한짜 붓 글씨

쓰기 hanj-ja pud klshi ssgi
charge (expense) 비용 pi-yong; cover
charge 입장료 ibjang-ryo; reverse
charge call 수화인 지불 통화 suhwa-in
chibul t-hong-wa; service charge
(restaurant) 봉사료 pong-saryo; what
are these charges for? 이 요금은
뭐지요? i yogmn mwöji-yo?; how
much do you charge? 얼마를
청구하세요? ölmarl ch-höng-guhase-
yo?; what is the commission charge?
코미션은 얼마에요? k-homishyönün
ölma-e-yo?
charm: lucky charm 부적 pujög
charming 매력적인 meryögjögin
charter flight 전세 비행기 chönse
piheng-gi
chassis (car body) 보디 podi
chateaubriand 샤토브리앙 shyat-hobri-
ang
chauffeur 운전 기사 unjön kisa
chauvinist: male chauvinist 남성
우월주의자 namsöng uwölju-eja
cheap 싼 ssan; is there anything
cheaper? 더 싼 것은 없어요? tö ssan
gösn öbsö-yo?
cheat (deceive) 속여요 sogyö-yo; I've
been cheated 속았어요 sogassö-yo
check (bill) 계산서 kyesansö;
check (financial) 수표 sup-hyo;
check (pattern) 체크 무늬 ch-hek-hü
mune; please check the brakes 브레이
크 좀 봐 주세요 pre-ik-hü chom pwa
juse-yo; personal check 개인 수표 ke-
in sup-hyo; security check 보안 검사
po-an kömsa; traveller's check 여행자
수표 yöheng-ja sup-hyo; may I check
this coat? 이 코트를 맡길 수 있어요? i
k-hot-hürl madk-hil su issö-yo?; do
you accept checks? 수표를 받으세요?
sup-hyorl padse-yo?; could you please
check the steering? 핸들 좀 점검해
주세요? hendl chom chömgöme juse-
yo?; I have already checked 벌써 검사

했어요 pölsö kömsa hessö-yo; I'd like
to check this suitcase in 이 가방을 좀
부쳐 주세요 i gabang-l chom puch-hyö
juse-yo; would you cash a check? 수
표를 현금으로 바꿔 주시겠어요? sup-
hyorl hyön-gmro pag-gwö jushigessö-
yo?; could we get the check please?
계산서 주시겠어요? kyesansö
jushigessö-yo?

check in (verb) 체크인 해요 ch-hek-hü-
in he-yo

check out (verb) 체크 아웃 해요 ch-
hek-hü a-ud he-yo; I'm checking out
this morning 오늘 아침에 계산 하겠어요
onl ach-hime kyesan hagessö-yo

checkbook 수표장 sup-hyojang

checkered (pattern) 바둑 무늬의 padug
mune-e

checkers 체커 ch-hek-hö; Korean
checkers 바둑 padug

checkout (supermarket) 계산 kyesan

checkroom 휴대품 보관소 hyudep-hum
pogwanso

cheek (face) 뺨 bbyam

cheers (toast) 건배 könbe

cheese 치즈 ch-hijü

cheesecake 치즈 케익 ch-hijü k-he-ig

chef 주방장 chubang-jang

cherry 버찌 pöj-ji

cherry tree 벚나무 pönnamu

chess (Western) 체스 ch-hesü; (Korean)
장기 chang-gi

chest (breast) 가슴 kasm

chest cold 기침 감기 kich-him kamgi

chestnut 밤 pam

chewing gum 껌 ggöm

chicken 닭 talg; (meat) 닭고기 talgogi;
ginseng chicken 삼계탕 samgyet-hang;
a chicken sandwich 닭고기 샌드위치
talgogi sendwich-hi

chicken pox 수두 sudu

child 어린이 örini

children 어린이들 örinidl; do you have
any children? 아이들이 있으세요? a-idri

issüse-yo?

chilled 차거운 ch-hagö-un

chilly 쌀쌀 한 ssalsal han

chima chogori (traditional dress) 치마
저고리 ch-hima chögori

chimes: wind chimes 범 종 pöm chong

chimney 굴뚝 kuld-dug

chin 턱 t-hög

china 도자기 tojagi;

China 중국 chung-gug

Chinese (adjective) 중국 의 chung-gug
e; (person) 중국 사람 chung-gug
saram; (language) 중국말 chung-
gungmal

Chinese character 한자 hanja

chips: potato chips 감자 튀김 kamja t-
hwigim

chocolate 초콜렛 ch-hok-holled; a
chocolate bar 바초콜릿 pach-hok-
hollid; hot chocolate 코코아 k-hok-
ho-a

choice 선택 sönt-heg; I had no other
choice 다른 방법이 없었어요 tarn pang-
böbi öbsössö-yo

choose 선택 해요 sönt-heg he-yo;
please choose for us 우리를 위해서 선택
해 주세요 urirl wihesö sönt-heg he
juse-yo

chopsticks 젓가락 chödgarag

Christmas 크리스마스 k-hürismasü;
Merry Christmas! 메리 크리스마스!
meri k-hürismas!

church 교회 kyohwe; church service 예
배 yebe; next to the church 교회의
옆에 kyohwe-e yöp-he; where is there
a Catholic church? 성당은 어디 있어요?
söng-dang-n ödi issö-yo?

cigar 잎 담배 ip tambe

cigarette 담배 tambe; filter cigarettes 필
터가 달린 담배 p-hilt-höga tallin
tambe; would you like a cigarette? 담
배 피우겠어요? tambe p-hi-ugessö-yo?

cigarette lighter 라이터 ra-it-hö

circle: traffic circle 로터리 rot-höri

Pronounce: a father; e let; i machine; o note; ö löng; u rude; ü further

citizen 시민 shimin; senior citizen 노인
·no-in
citizenship 시민권 shimin-gwön
city 도시 toshi; capital city 수도 sudo
city center 시의 중앙 shi-e chung-ang
city hall 시청 shich-höng
city map 시내 지도 shine chido
civilian 민간인 min-ganin
civilization 문명 munmyöng
claim (application) 청구 ch-höng-gu;
baggage claim 수하물 suhamul
clam 대합 tehab
clarify 분명 하게 해요 punmyöng hage
he-yo
class (lesson) 수업 su-öb; first class 일
등석 ildngsög; second class 이등석
idng-sög
classical 고전의 kojöne
classical literature 고전 문학 kojön
munag
classical music 고전 음악 kojön ümag
clay 찰흙 ch-harlg
clean (adjective) 깨끗 한 ggeg-gd han;
clean (an object) 청소 해요 ch-höng-so
he-yo; would you clean this, please?
이것을 깨끗이 해 주시겠어요? igösl
ggeg-gshi he jushigessö-yo?
cleaner: dry cleaner 세탁소 set-hagso;
pipe cleaner 파이프 청소기 p-ha-ip-hü
ch-höng-sogi; vacuum cleaner 진공
청소기 chin-gong ch-höng-sogi
cleansing cream (for makeup) 클린싱
크림 k-hüllinshing k-hürim
clear (clean) 맑은 malgn; I hope it
will clear up 날씨가 맑으면 좋겠어요
nalshiga malgmyön chok-hessö-yo
clergyman 목사 mogsa
clerk: hotel clerk 호텔 안내원 hot-hel
annewön; sales clerk 점원 chömwön
clever 영리한 yöng-rihan
cliff 벼랑 pyörang
climate 기후 kihu
climb (go up) 올라가요 ollaga-yo;
we're going to climb up 우리는 올라

가겠어요 urinün olla kagessö-yo
climber 등산자 tng-sanja
clinic 진료서 chinryosö
clippers: nail clippers 손톱 깎이 sont-
hob ggag-gi
cloakroom 휴대품 보관소 hyudep-hum
pogwanso
clock 시계 shigye; alarm clock 자명종
chamyöng-jong; travel alarm clock 여
행용 알람 시계 yöheng-yong allam
shigye
clogs 나막신 namagshin
close (nearby) 가까운 kag-ga-un; is it
close? 가까워요? kag-gawö-yo?;
close (shut) 닫아요 tada-yo; at what
time do you close? 몇시에 문을
닫으세요? myöt-hshi-e munl tadse-yo?
closed (door) 닫힌 tat-hin; (store) 휴업
hyu-öb; it was closed 닫혀 있었어요
tat-hyö issössö-yo
closet 옷장 odjang
closing ceremony 폐막식 p-hyemagshig
cloth (fabric) 옷감 odgam; (rag) 걸레
kölle
clothes 옷 od; (made to order) 마춤복
mach-humbog; bed clothes 침구 ch-
himgu; casual clothes 평상복 p-
hyöng-sang-bog; could you wash
these clothes? 이것을 세탁 해
주시겠어요? igösl set-hag he
jushigessö-yo?
clothes dryer (machine) 드라이어 tra-
i-ö
clothes line 빨래줄 bballejul
clothespin 빨래 집게 bballe chibge
clothing: Korean clothing 한복
hanbog; women's clothing 부인복 pu-
inbog
clouds 구름 kurm
cloudy 흐린 hürin; it's cloudy 날씨가
흐려요 nalshiga hüryö-yo; it's getting
cloudy 하늘이 흐려져요 hanri
hüryöjyö-yo
clown 익살꾼 igsalg-gun

Pronounce: a father; e let; i machine; o note; ö löng; u rude; ü fürther

club 클럽 k-hüllöb; jazz club 재즈 클럽 cheju k-hüllöb; golf clubs 골프 채 kolp-hü ch-he

clumsy 솜씨 없는 somshi ömnün

clutch (auto) 클러치 k-hüllöch-hi; the clutch slips 클러치가 작동을 안해요 k-hüllöch-higa chagdong-l ane-yo

coach (bus) 장거리 버스 chang-göri pösü

coast 해안 he-an; on the coast 해안에 he-ane

coast guard 해안 경비대 he-an kyöng-bide

coat (overcoat) 코트 k-hot-hü; (jacket) 자켓 chak-hed; I left my coat under the seat 좌석 밑에 코트를 놓고 내렸어요 chwasög mit-he k-hot-hürl nok-ho neryössö-yo; may I check this coat? 이 코트를 맡길 수 있어요? i k-hot-hürl madk-hil su issö-yo?

coat hanger 양복걸이 yang-boggöri

cockroach 바퀴 벌레 pak-hwi pölle

cocktail 칵테일 k-hagt-he-il; fruit cocktail 프루트 칵테일 p-hürut-hü k-hagt-he-il

cocktail bar 칵테일바 k-hagt-he-ilba

cocoa 코코아 k-hok-ho-a

coconut 야자 열매 yaja yölme

cod (haddock) 대구 tegu

code: area code 시외 국번 shiwe kugbön; what's the area code for ...? ...의 지역번호는 뭐예요? ...e chi-yögbönonün mwö-ye-yo?

coeducation 남녀 공학 namnyö kong-ag

coffee 커피 k-höp-hi; coffee with milk 프림을 탄 커피 p-hüriml t-han k-höp-hi; coffee with sugar 설탕을 넣은 커피 sölt-hang-l nöhün k-höp-hi; coffee without sugar 설탕을 넣지 않은 커피 sölt-hang-l nöch-hi anün k-höp-hi; espresso coffee 에스프레소 커피 esp-hüreso k-höp-hi; iced coffee 아이스 커피 a-isü k-höp-hi; instant coffee 인스턴트 커피 inst-hönt-hü k-höp-hi; a

cup of coffee 커피 한잔 k-höp-hi hanjan

coffee shop 커피 숍 k-höp-hi shyob

coin 동전 tong-jön; 100 won coin 백원 짜리 동전 pegwön jjari tong-jön

Coke (tm) 코카콜라 k-hok-hak-holla; rum and coke 럼 앤 콕 röm en k-hog

cola 콜라 k-holla

cold (chilly) 차가운 ch-haga-un; chest cold 기침 감기 kich-him kamgi; head cold 두통 감기 tut-hong kamgi; I feel cold 추워 요 ch-huwö yo; a nice cold drink 아주 시원 한 음료수 aju shiwön han ümryosu; it's a little cold today 오늘은 조금 추워요 onrn chogm ch-huwö-yo; she's caught a cold 감기에 걸렸어요 kamgi-e köllyössö-yo

cold cream (makeup) 콜드크림 k-holdk-hürim

cold soup 냉면 neng-myön

collapse (faint) 기절 해요 kijöl he-yo

collar 칼라 k-halla; white collar worker 샐러리맨 sellörimen

collar bone 쇄골 swegol

colleague 동료 tong-ryo; my colleague 내 동료 ne tong-ryo

collect: I collect ... ...를 수집 해요 ...rl sujib he-yo

collect call 수화인 지불 통화 suhwa-in chibul t-hong-wa; I want to make a collect call to New York 수화자 지급으로 뉴욕에 전화 하고 싶은데요 suhwaja chigbro nyu-yoge chönwa hago ship-hünde-yo

collection 수집 sujib

college 대학 tehag

collision 충돌 ch-hung-dol

cologne 콜론 k-hollon

color 색깔 segg-gal; hair color 머리 염색약 möri yömsegyag; fall colors 단 풍 tanp-hung; are there any other colors? 다른 색이 있어요? tarn segi issö-yo?

color film 칼라 필림 k-halla p-hillim

comb (noun) 머리빗 möribid;
comb (verb) 빗어요 pisö-yo
come 와요 wa-yo; come back! 돌아
오세요! tora ose-yo!; come in! 들어
오세요! trö ose-yo!; come with me 나
와 함께 와요 nawa hamg-ge wa-yo;
come and visit us 우리 한테 놀러
오세요 uri hant-he nollö ose-yo; I've
come on business 일 때문에 왔어요 il
ddemune wassö-yo; I've come to get
my ... ...을 받으러 왔어요 ...l padrö
wassö-yo; please come into the room
방에 들어와 주세요 pang-e tröwa juse-
yo; we'll come back later 나중에 돌아
오겠어요 najung-e tora ogessö-yo;
please come again 또 오세요 ddo ose-
yo; I'll come back soon 곧
돌아오겠어요 kod tora-ogessö-yo; we
will come back next year 우리는
내년에 돌아 오겠어요 urinün nenyöne
tora ogessö-yo; she hasn't come down
yet 아직 내리지 않았어요 ajig neriji
anössö-yo; will you come and get
me? 데리러 오시겠어요? terirö
oshigessö-yo?; will you come too? 당
신도 함께 오시겠어요? tang-shindo
hamg-ge oshigessö-yo?; when will
they come? 그들은 언제 와요? kdrn
önje wa-yo?; if you should come to
America 만일 미국에 가보면 manil
miguge kabomyön; what does all that
come to? 모두 얼마에요? modu ölma-e-
yo?; both of us will come 두 사람 다
오겠어요 tu saram ta ogessö-yo
come in 들어 와요 trö wa-yo
come out 나와요 nawa-yo; these three
pictures didn't come out too well 이
사진 세장은 잘 나오지 않았어요 i sajin
sejang-n chal na-oji anassö-yo
comedian 희극 배우 hegüg pe-u
comedy 코미디 k-homidi
comfortable (cozy) 안락한 anrak-han;
it's not so comfortable 그리 안락하지
않아요 kri anrak-haji ana-yo

comic book 만화책 manwach-heg
commission: what is the commission
charge? 코미션은 얼마에요? k-
homishyönün ölma-e-yo?
common (usual) 보통의 pot-hong-e; in
common 공통으로 kong-t-hong-ro
common sense 상식 sang-shig
communist 공산주의 kong-sanju-e
compact disc 콤팩트 디스크 k-homp-
hegt-hü tisk-hü
companion 친구 ch-hin-gu
company (business) 회사 hwesa
compartment (train) 칸 k-han
compass 나침판 nach-himp-han
competition 경쟁 kyöng-jeng
complain 불평을 해요 pulp-hyöng-1 he-
yo; I'd like to complain 불만이 있어요
pulmani issö-yo
complaint 불평 pulp-hyöng; I've got a
complaint about the room 방에 관해
불평 할께 있어요 pang-e kwane pulp-
hyöng halg-ge issö-yo
complete (finish) 완성 해요 wansöng
he-yo; it's a complete fiasco 완전한
실패에요 wanjönan shilp-he-e-yo
completely 완전히 wanjöni
complicated 복잡 한 pogjab han
comprehend 이해 해요 ihe he-yo
compromise 타협 t-hahyöb
computer 컴퓨터 k-hömp-hyut-hö
concentrate 집중 해요 chibjung he-yo
concern (interest) 관심 kwanshim
concert 음악회 ümak-hwe
concert hall 연주홀 yönjuhol
concerto 협주곡 hyöbjugog
concierge (at hotel) 도어 맨 to-ö men
concussion 뇌진탕 nwejint-hang
condition (state) 상태 sang-t-he; (in a
contract) 계약 조건 kye-yag chogön;
I'm not in good condition 별로
튼튼하지 않아요 pyöllo t-hünt-hünaji
anö-yo
conditioner (hair) 헤어 컨디셔너 he-ö
k-höndishyönö

Pronounce: a father; e let; i machine; o note; ö löng; u rude; ü fürther

condom 콘돔 k-hondom
conductor (train) 차장 ch-hajang
cone: ice-cream cone 콘 아이스크림 k-hon a-isk-hürim
conference 회의 hwe-e
confirm 확인 해요 hwagin he-yo
confirmation 확인서 hwaginsö
Confucian Ceremony 석전제 sögjönje
Confucius 공자 kong-ja
confusing 복잡 한 pogjab han; it's very confusing 대단히 복잡 해요 tedani pogjab he-yo
congratulations! 축하 해요! ch-huk-ha he-yo!
connection (transportation) 갈아타는 곳 karat-hanün kod
connoisseur 감식가 kamshigga
consider 생각 해요 seng-gag he-yo; I consider you my best friend 나는 당신을 제일 좋은 친구라고 생각 해요 nanün tang-shinl che-il chohün ch-hin-gurago seng-gag he-yo
considerate 친절 한 ch-hinjöl han; that's very considerate of you 친절히 해주셔서 감사합니다 ch-hinjöri hejushyösö kamsahamnida
consomme 콩소메 k-hong-some
constipated 변비에 걸린 pyönbi-e köllin
constipation 변비 pyönbi
construction 건설 könsöl
consulate 영사관 yöng-sagwan
contact (get in touch with) 연락 해요 yönrag he-yo
contact lenses 콘택트 렌스 k-hont-hegt-hü rensü; soft contact lens 소프트 콘택트 렌즈 sop-hüt-hü k-hont-hegt-hü renjü
contagious 전염성의 chönyömsöng-e; is it contagious? 전염이 돼요? chönyömi dwe-yo?
contain: does it contain alcohol? 알콜이 들어 있어요? alk-hori trö issö-yo?
continental breakfast 양식 아침 식사 yang-shig ach-him shigsa

continue 계속 해요 kyesog he-yo
contraceptive (oral) 피임약 p-hi-imyag; (device) 피임 용구 p-hi-im yong-gu
contract (legal) 계약 kye-yag
control (management) 관리 kwanri; (to direct) 지배 해요 chibe he-yo
convenient 편리한 p-hyönrihan; it isn't convenient 편리 하지 않어요 p-hyönri haji anö-yo
cook (prepare food) 요리 해요 yori he-yo; can I cook for myself? 직접 해 먹어도 돼요? chigjöb he mögödo dwe-yo?
cooker 요리 기구 yori kigu
cookie 과자 kwaja
cool (not warm) 쌀쌀 한 ssalsal han
cop: traffic cop 교통 순경 kyot-hong sun-gyöng
corduroy 고르뎅 kordeng
cork (stopper) 코르크 마개 k-hork-hü mage
corkscrew 와인 오프너 wa-in op-hünö
corn (callous) 못 mod;
corn (veg) 옥수수 ogsusu
corner (inside) 구석 kusög; (outside) 모퉁이 mot-hung-i; it's on the next corner 다음 번 모퉁이에 있어요 ta-m pön mot-hung-i-e issö-yo
cornflakes 콘플레이크 k-honp-hülle-ik-hü
correct (adjective) 틀림없는 t-hüllimömnün
corridor 복도 pogdo
cosmetics 메이크업 me-ik-hü-öb
cost (price) 값 kab; meal cost 식비 shigbi; let's share the cost 비용을 공동으로 부담 할까요 pi-yong-l kong-dong-ro pudam halg-ga-yo
cottage 별장 pyöljang
cotton (material) 면 myön
cotton swabs 약솜 yagsom
cotton wool 탈지면 t-haljimyön
couch 소파 sop-ha
cough (noun) 기침 kich-him; (verb) 기

침 해요 kich-him he-yo; whooping cough 백일해 pegire

cough medicine 기침약 kich-himyag

cough tablets 정제로 된 기침약 chöng-jero dwen kich-himyag

counter 카운터 k-ha-unt-hö

country (land) 나라 nara; a country lane 좁은 길 chobn kil; mother country 모국 mogug; in the country 시골에(서) shigore(sö)

country music 칸츄리 뮤직 k-hanch-hyuri myujig

countryside 시골 shigol

couple (man and wife) 부부 pubu

courier 급사 kbsa

course (in school) 과정 kwajöng; of course! 그렇고 말고요! krök-ho malgo-yo!; crash course (speed learning) 집중 훈련 chibjung hunryön; golf course 골프장 kolp-hüjang; language course 어학 과정 öhag kwajöng

court (of law) 법정 pöbjöng; tennis court 테니스 코트 t-henisü k-hot-hü

courtyard 뜰 ddl

cousin 사촌 sach-hon

cover charge 입장료 ibjang-ryo

cow 암소 amso

cozy 안락 한 anrag han

crab 게 ke

crab meat 게살 kesal

cracker (biscuit) 크랙커 k-hüregk-hö

craftshop 공예품점 kong-yep-humjöm; bamboo craft shop 죽세공점 chugsegong-jöm

craftsman 공예가 kong-yega

cramp (in body) 쥐가 남 chwiga nam

crane (bird) 두루미 turumi

crane dance 학춤 hagch-hum

crash (collision) 충돌 ch-hung-dol

crash course (speed learning) 집중 훈련 chibjung hunryön

crash helmet 안전 헬멧 anjön helmed

crayfish 가재 kaje

crazy 미친 mich-hin

cream 크림 k-hürim; cleansing cream (for makeup) 클린싱 크림 k-hüllinshing k-hürim; cold cream (makeup) 콜드크림 k-holdk-hürim; ice cream 아이스 크림 a-isü k-hürim; shaving cream 면도 크림 myöndo k-hürim; whipped cream 휩 크림 wib k-hürim; a little cream 크림 조금만 주세요 k-hürim chogmman chuse-yo; sun block cream 선 블럭 크림 sön pllög k-hürim; not so much cream! 크림을 그렇게 많이 넣으면 안 돼요! k-hüriml krök-he mani nöhümyön an dwe-yo!

cream rinse 린스 rinsü

credit (financial) 외상 wesang

credit card 크레딧 카드 k-hüredid k-hadü; what credit cards do you take? 어떤 크레딧 카드를 받아요? öd-dön k-hüredid k-hadrl pada-yo?

crib (baby bed) 아기 침대 agi ch-himde

crisis 위기 wigi

Croatia 크로아티아 k-hüro-at-hi-a

crook 도둑 todug

cross (verb) 건너요 könnö-yo; cross the street 길을 건너요 kirl könnö-yo

crossing (at sea) 횡단 hweng-dan; pedestrian crossing 횡단 보도 hweng-dan podo; railroad crossing 철도 건널목 ch-höldo könnölmog

crossroads 사거리 sagöri

crosswalk 횡단 보도 hweng-dan podo

crow (bird) 까마귀 ggamagwi

crowded 붐비는 pumbinün; is it crowded? 사람이 많아요? sarami mana-yo?; Seoul's main streets are always crowded 서울의 큰 거리는 항상 붐벼요 sö-ure k-hün körinün hang-sang pumbyö-yo

crown (dental) 치관 ch-higwan

crucial 결정적인 kyöljöng-jögin

cruise (on ship) 항해 hang-e

crutches 목다리 mogdari

cry 울어요 urö-yo

cucumber 오이 o-i
cucumber kimchee 오이소박이 o-isobagi
cufflinks 커프스 단추 k-höp-hüsü tanch-hu
cuisine 요리 yori
cultural 문화의 munwa-e
culture 문화 munwa
cup 컵 k-höb; soju cup 소주잔 sojujan; could I get a cup of tea? 차 한 잔 주시겠어요? ch-ha han chan chushigessö-yo?
cupboard (closet) 벽장 pyögjang; (pantry) 찬장 ch-hanjang
curb 연석 yönsög
cure (treatment) 치료 ch-hiryo
curfew (night) 야간 통행 금지 yagan t-hong-eng kmji; is there a curfew? 통행금지가 있어요? t-hong-eng-gmjiga issö-yo?
curious (inquisitive) 호기심이 많은 hogishimi manün
curlers 파마 롤러 p-hama rollö
curly 곱슬 한 kobsl han
current (electricity) 전류 chönryu; (water) 흐름 hürm
curry 카레 k-hare
curtains 커텐 k-höt-hen
curve 커어브 k-hö-öbü
cushion 쿠션 k-hushyön; (to sit on) 방석 pang-sög
custard 카스데라 k-hasdera
custom 습관 sbgwan
Customs 관세 kwanse
customs declaration 세관 신고 segwan shin-go;
customs declaration form 세관 신고서 segwan shin-gosö
customs inspection 통관 t-hong-gwan
cut (wound) 상처 sang-ch-hö; cut the price 값을 깎아 줘요 kabsl ggag-ga chwö-yo; don't cut it too short please 너무 짧게 깎지 마세요 nömu jjalge ggag-gji mase-yo; power cut (electricity) 정전 chöng-jön; I got cut

off 전화가 그냥 끊어졌어요 chönwaga knyang ggnöjyössö-yo; could you cut a little (hair) off the top? 위만 좀 잘라 주시겠어요? wiman chom challa jushigessö-yo?
cutlets 거틀렛 köt-hülled
cycling 사이클 sa-ik-hül
cylinder (auto) 실린더 shillindö
Czechoslovakia 체코 ch-hek-ho

D

daily (every day) 매일 me-il
damage (loss) 손해 sone; it got damaged 부서졌어요 pusöjyössö-yo
damn! 제기랄 chegiral
damp (adjective) 축축한 ch-hugch-huk-han
dance (step) 춤 ch-hum; crane dance 학춤 hagch-hum; folk dance 민속 무용 minsog mu-yong; drum dance (Korean) 장고춤 chang-goch-hum; mask dance-drama 탈춤 t-halch-hum; fancy dress dance 가장 무도회 kajang mudohwe; he's a good dancer 그는 춤을 잘 춰요 knün ch-huml chal ch-hwö-yo; we'd like to go dancing 춤 추러 가고 싶은데요 ch-hum ch-hurö kago ship-hünde-yo; would you like to dance? 춤을 추시겠어요? ch-huml ch-hushigessö-yo?
dandruff 비듬 pidm
danger 위험 wihöm
dangerous 위험한 wihöman; it's too dangerous 그것은 너무 위험 해요 kgösn nömu wihöm he-yo
dark (adjective) 어두운 ödu-un
dashboard 계기판 kyegip-han
date (appointment) 약속 yagsog; what's today's date? 오늘이 며칠이에요? onri myöt-hiri-e-yo?; can we make a date?

시간 좀 내 주겠어요? shigan chom ne chugessŏ-yo?

dates (fruit) 대추 tech-hu

daughter 딸 ddal; our daughter 우리 딸 uri ddal

daughter-in-law 며느리 myönri

dawn (noun) 새벽 sebyög

day 일 / 날 il / nal; for one day 하루 에 haru-e; one day earlier 그 전날 kü jönnal; every day 매일 me-il; the day after tomorrow 모레 more; the day before yesterday 그저께 kjög-ge; the next day 다음 날 ta-m nal; have a nice day! 잘 지내 세요 chal chine se-yo

day care center 탁아소 t-hagaso

day trip 당일 여행 tang-il yöheng

dead 죽은 chugn; the battery is dead 건 전지가 다 닳았어요 könjönjiga ta tarassŏ-yo

deaf person 귀머거리 kwimögöri

deal (transaction) 거래 köre

dealer (merchant) 장사꾼 chang-sag-gun

death 죽음 chugm

December 십이월 shibiwöl

decent 점잖은 chömjanün

decide 결정 해요 kyöljöng he-yo; please decide for me 당신이 택해 주세요 tang-shini t-hek-he juse-yo; it's all been decided 다 결정 됐어요 ta kyöljöng dwessŏ-yo

decision 결정 kyöljöng

deck (ship) 갑판 kabp-han

declaration: customs declaration 세관 신고 segwan shin-go

declare (customs) 신고 해요 shin-go he-yo; I have nothing to declare 신고할 것이 없어요 shin-gohal göshi öbsö-yo

decoration (ornament) 장식 chang-shig

dedicate 바쳐요 pach-hyö-yo

deduct 공제 해요 kong-je he-yo

deep 깊은 kip-hün

deep freeze (freezer) 냉동기 neng-dong-gi

deer 사슴 sasm

definitely! 그렇고 말고 요! krök-ho malgo yo!

degree (diploma) 학위 hagwi; (temperature) 도 to; 30 degrees Fahrenheit 화씨 삼십도 hwasshi samshibdo; 20 degrees Celsius 섭씨 이십도 söbshi ishibdo

delay (postponement) 연기 yön-gi

delegate 대표 tep-hyo

deliberately 고의적으로 ko-ejögro

delicious 맛있는 mashinnün; it really was delicious 맛있게 먹었어요 mashidge mögössö-yo

deliver 배달 해요 pedal he-yo; will you deliver it? 배달 해 주시겠어요? pedal he jushigessŏ-yo?

delivery 배달 pedal; general delivery 유 치 우편 yuch-hi up-hyön

deluxe 호화스러운 hohwasrö-un

demonstration 시범 shiböm

denim (material) 무명천 mumyöng-ch-hön

denims 진 바지 chin paji

Denmark 덴마크 tenmak-hü

dent 옴폭 팬 곳 ump-hug p-hen kod

dental floss 덴탈 프로스 tent-hal p-hürosü

dentist 치과 의사 ch-higwa esa

dentures 틀니 t-hülni

deny 부정 해요 pujöng he-yo

deodorant 방취제 pang-ch-hwije

depart 출발 해요 ch-hulbal he-yo

department 부 pu; toy department 완구 부 wan-gubu; fire department 소방서 sobang-sö

department store 백화점 pek-hwajöm

departure 출발 ch-hulbal

depend 의존 해요 ejon he-yo; that depends on ... ...에 달려 있어요 ...e tallyö issö-yo

deposit (security) 보증금 pojng-gm; must I leave a deposit? 선금을 내야 돼요? sön-gml ne-ya dwe-yo?

depressed 우울 u-ul

depth 깊이 kip-hi

description 묘사 myosa

deserted 사람이 없는 sarami ömnün

design (sketch) 도안 to-an

dessert 후식 hushig

destination 목적지 mogjögji

detergent 세제 seje

detour 우회로 uhwero

develop (film) 현상 해요 hyönsang he-yo; do you develop film here? 여기서 사진 현상 하세요? yögisö sajin hyönsang hase-yo?

diabetic (person) 당뇨병 환자 tang-nyobyöng hwanja; I'm a diabetic 나는 당뇨병 걸렸어요 nanün tang-nyobyöng köllyössö-yo

diagnosis 진단 chindan

diagram 그림 krim

dialect 사투리 sat-huri

dialogue 대화 tehwa

diamond (stone) 다이아몬드 ta-i-amondü

diaper (disposable) 일회용 기저귀 irwe-yong kijögwi

diarrhea 설사 sölsa; do you have something for diarrhea? 설사에 좋은 약 있어요? sölsa-e chohün yag issö-yo?

diary (schedule) 일기장 ilgijang; (journal) 일기 ilgi

dictionary 사전 sajön; English-Korean dictionary 영한 사전 yöng-an sajön

die 죽어요 chugö-yo

diesel fuel 경유 kyöng-yu

diet 다이어트 ta-i-öt-hü; I'm dieting 다이어트 중이에요 ta-i-öt-hü chung-i-e-yo

difference 차이 ch-ha-i; what's the difference between ...? ...의 차이가 뭐에요? ...e ch-ha-iga mwö-e-yo?

different 다른 tarn; a different kind of ... 다른 종류의 ... tarn chong-ryu-e ...; that's a different story 그 렇다면 말은 달라져요 kü röt-hamyön marn tallajyö-yo; it's quite different 꽤

달라요 ggwe talla-yo; they are quite different from each other 서로 매우 달라요 söro me-u talla-yo

difficult 어려운 öryö-un; it's difficult to get there 거기에 가기는 어려워요 kögi-e kaginün öryöwö-yo

difficulty 곤란 konran

digestion 소화 sohwa

dignified: he's so dignified 그는 매우 점잖아요 knün me-u chömjana-yo

dining car 식당칸 shigdang-k-han

dining room 식당 shigdang

dinner 저녁 (식사) chönyög (shigsa); after dinner 저녁 후에 chönyög hu-e; could we cancel dinner tonight? 오늘 저녁을 취소 해주시겠어요? onl chönyögl ch-hwiso hejushigessö-yo?; I'd like to invite you to dinner 저녁 식사에 초대 하겠어요 chönyög shigsa-e ch-hode hagessö-yo

dinner jacket 턱시도 t-högshido

dinner party 만찬회 manch-hanwe

diplomat 외교관 wegyogwan

direct (adjective) 직행한 chik-heng-an

direction 방향 pang-yang; what direction is it? 어느 쪽에 있어요? önü jjoge issö-yo?

directly 똑바로 ddogbaro; it's directly opposite 바로 맞은 쪽에 있어요 paro majn jjoge issö-yo

director (movies) 감독 kamdog

directory (telephone) 전화 번호부 chönwa pönobu

dirt 먼지 mönji

dirty 더러운 törö-un

disabled person 불구자 pulguja

disappear 사라져요 sarajyö-yo; he has disappeared 사라져 버렸어요 sarajyö pöryössö-yo

disappointing 하잘것 없는 hajalgöd ömnün;

disappointment 실망 shilmang

disapprove 불찬성 해요 pulch-hansöng he-yo

disaster 재난 chenan

disc: compact disc 콤팩트 디스크 k-homp-hegt-hü tisk-hü

disc jockey 디스크 자키 tisk-hü chak-hi

disco 디스코 tisk-ho; the disco is disturbing us 디스코 음악이 너무 시끄러워요 tisk-ho ümagi nömu shiggröwö-yo

disco dancing 디스코 댄스 tisk-ho tensü

discount 할인 harin; is there a discount for seniors? 노인들에게 할인 해 줘요? no-indrege harin he chwö-yo?; is there a discount for students? 학생들에게 할인 해 줘요? hagseng-drege harin he chwö-yo?

discouraged 낙심 한 nagshim han

disease 병 pyöng; he's gotten some strange disease 그는 괴상한 병에 걸렸어요 knün kwesang-an pyöng-e köllyössö-yo

disgusting (revolting) 메스꺼운 mesggö-un

dish (food) 요리 yori; (plate) 접시 chöbshi; side dishes 반찬 panch-han

dishcloth 행주 heng-ju

dishonest 부정직 한 pujöng-jig han

dishwashing liquid 퐁퐁 p-hong-p-hong

disinfectant (noun) 소독약 sodogyag

diskette (computer) 디스켓 tisk-hed

dislike 싫어 해요 shirö he-yo; I dislike all of them 아무것도 싫어요 amugöddo shirö-yo

dislocated 탈구된 t-halgudwen

disorder 무질서 mujilsö

disposable diapers 일회용 기저귀 irwe-yong kijögwi

distance 거리 köri; long distance call 시외 전화 shiwe chönwa; it's a short distance 가까운 고리에요 kag-ga-un kori-e-yo

distilled water 증류수 chüng-ryusu

distributor (auto) 배전기 pejön-gi

disturb 방해 해요 pang-e he-yo

diving 다이빙 ta-ibing; scuba diving 스

쿠버 다이빙 sk-hubö ta-ibing; skin diving 스킨다이빙 sk-hinda-ibing

diving board 다이빙대 ta-ibing-de

divorced 이혼한 ihonan

dizzy 현기증이 나는 hyön-gijng-i nanün; she gets dizzy spells 때때로 현기증기 나요 dded-dero hyön-gijng-gi na-yo

DMZ 휴전선 hyujönsön; I also want to see the DMZ 휴전선도 보고 싶은데요 hyujönsöndo pogo ship-hünde-yo

do 해요 he-yo; do I have to wait long? 오래 기다려야 돼요? ore kidaryö-ya dwe-yo?; what do you do? 지금 뭘 하세요? chigm mwöl hase-yo?; that won't do! 안 돼요! an dwe-yo!; are you doing anything special tonight? 오늘 저녁에 특별한 일 있어요? onl chönyöge t-hügbyöran il issö-yo?; would you do that for me? 그것 좀 해 주시겠어요? kgöd chom he jushigessö-yo?; what should we do? 어떻게 해야 할까요? öd-dök-he he-ya halg-ga-yo?

docks 선착장 sönch-hagjang

doctor 의사 esa; I need a doctor 의사가 필요 해요 esaga p-hiryo he-yo; is it serious, doctor? 심각 해요, 의사님 shimgag he-yo, esanim; do you know an English-speaking doctor? 영어 할 줄 아는 의사를 아세요? yöng-ö hal chul anün esarl ase-yo?

document 서류 söryu

dog 개 ke; hot dog 핫도그 haddogü

doll 인형 inyöng

dollar 달러 tallö; what's the exchange rate for the dollar? 달러 환율이 얼마에요? tallö hwanyuri ölma-e-yo?

donkey 당나귀 tang-nagwi

door 문 mun; back door 뒷문 twinmun; next door (at neighbor's) 이웃에 i-use; the door was unlocked 문이 열려 있었어요 muni yöllyö issössö-yo

doorman 도어맨 to-ömen

doorway 문간 mun-gan

dosage 복용 pogyong
double (adjective) 두 배의 tu pe-e
double bed 이인용 침대 i-inyong ch-himde
double room 이인용 방 i-inyong pang
doubt (verb) 믿지 않어요 midji anö-yo; I doubt it 그럴까요? krölg-ga-yo?
douche 관주법 kwanjuböb
doughnut 도나스 tonasü
down 아래 are; down the road further 길을 따라 훨씬 내려간 곳에 kirl ddara hwölshin neryögan kose; calm down! 진정 하게! chinjöng hage!; slow down! 천천히 가! ch-hönch-höni ka!; upside down 거꾸로 kög-guro; he paid 15% down 십오 퍼센트를 계약 금으로 지불했어요 shibo p-hösent-hürl kyeyag kmro chiburessö-yo; I can't keep down anything I eat 나는 먹은 것을 토해 버려요 nanün mögn gösl t-hohe pöryö-yo; please put it down here 그 것을 여기에 내려놔 주세요 kgösl yögie neryönwa juse-yo; would you write it down? 이것을 써 주시겠어요? igösl ssö jushigessö-yo?; I want to go lie down 누우러 가고 싶어요 nu-urö kago ship-hö-yo
downstairs 아래층에 arech-hüng-e
downtown 시내 shine
downtown Seoul 서울의 중심가 sö-ure chung-shimga
doze (verb) 졸아요 chora-yo
dozen 다스 tasü
draft (wind) 외풍 wep-hung; it's very drafty 바람이 틈으로 새어 들어와요 parami t-hümro se-ö tröwa-yo
draft beer 생맥주 seng-megju
drain (noun) 배수 pesu
draw (picture) 그려요 kryö-yo; please draw a map for me 약도 좀 그려 주세요 yagdo chom kryö juse-yo
dream (noun) 꿈 ggum
dress (woman's) 드레스 tresü; dress pattern 무늬 mune; evening dress

(men's) 야회복 yahwebog; fancy dress dance 가장 무도회 kajang mudohwe; is evening dress necessary? 파티복을 입을 필요가 있어요? p-hat-hibogl ibl p-hiryoga issö-yo?; just let me get dressed 옷을 좀 입겠어요 osl chom ibgessö-yo
dressing (wound) 붕대 pung-de; salad dressing 새러드 소스 serödü sosü
dressmaker 양장점 yang-jang-jöm
drink (verb) 마셔요 mashyö-yo; I drank too much 너무 마셨어요 nömu mashyössö-yo; ginseng drink 인삼 음료 insam ümryo; soft drink 청량 음료 ch-höng-ryang ümryo; finish your drink 다 마셔요 ta mashyö-yo; it's his drink 그 사람의 마실 것이에요 kü sarame mashil göshi-e-yo; one last drink 마지 막 한잔 majimag hanjan; that's some drink! 훌륭한 술이에요! hullyung-an suri-e-yo!; something to drink 무엇 좀 마실 것 mu-öd chom mashil göd; is the water drinkable? 이물 마셔도 되는 거에요? imul mashyödo dwenün köye-yo?; how about a drink? 술 한잔 어때요? sul hanjan öd-de-yo?; I hardly ever drink 거의 마시지 않어요 kö-e mashiji anö-yo; a nice cold drink 아주 시원 한 음료수 aju shiwön han ümryosu; could I get a drink of water? 물을 좀 주시겠어요 murl chom chushigessö-yo; he's had a lot to drink 많이 마셨어요 mani mashyössö-yo
drive (a car) 운전 해요 unjön he-yo; could you drive slower? 좀 더 천천히 운전 해 주시겠어요? chom tö ch-hönch-höni unjön he jushigessö-yo?; how about going for a drive? 드라이브 하는게 어때요? tra-ibü hanün-ge öd-de-yo?; is it a long way to drive? 운전 하는 길이 멀어요? unjön hanün kiri mörö-yo?
driver 운전수 unjönsu; the driver behind

me 내 뒷차의 운전수 ne twidch-ha-e
unjönsu; bus driver 버스 운전수 pösü
unjönsu; taxi driver 택시 운전수 t-
hegshi unjönsu; truck driver 트럭
운전수 t-hürög unjönsu
drop (fall) 떨어져요 ddöröjyö-yo; drop
by once in a while 가끔 들러 주세요
kag-gm tllö juse-yo; would you drop
me a line? 연결 해 주시겠어요? yön-
gyöl he jushigessö-yo?
drops: ear drops 귀에 넣는 약 kwi-e
nöhnün yag; eye drops 안약 anyag
drown 빠져요 bbajyö-yo
drugs (medical) 약 yag; (narcotics) 마
약 ma-yag
drugstore 약국 yaggug; prescription
drugstore 약제사 yagjesa
drum dance (Korean) 장고춤 chang-
goch-hum
drunk (adjective) 술 취한 sul ch-
hwihan
drunken driving 음주 운전 ümju unjön
dry (adjective) 건조한 könjohan; blow
dry 드라이 tra-i
dry cleaner 세탁소 set-hagso
dry-clean 드라이 해요 tra-i he-yo
dryer: clothes dryer (machine) 드라이어
tra-i-ö; hair dryer 헤어 드라이어 he-ö
tra-i-ö
duck 오리 ori
dumb person (mute) 벙어리 pöng-öri
(stupid) 우둔한 udunan
dumplings 만두 mandu
during ... ... 중에 ... chung-e
dust 먼지 mönji
duty: are lifeguards on duty? 인명구조원
이 있어요? inmyöng-gujowöni issö-
yo?; do we have to pay duty? 관세를
내야 돼요? kwanserl ne-ya dwe-yo?
duty-free 면세의 myönse-e
dynasty 왕조 wang-jo

E

each 각각의 kaggage; each time ... 그
때마다 kd-demada; please make one
print of each 한 장씩 빼 주세요 han
chang-sshig bbe chuse-yo
ear 귀 kwi
ear drops 귀에 넣는 약 kwi-e nöhnün
yag
earache 귀앓이 kwi-ari
early 일찍 ilj-jig; one day earlier 그
전날 kü jönnal; I must leave early 일
찌기 떠나야 해요 ilj-jigi ddöna-ya he-
yo; I must go to bed early 일찍 자야
되요 ilj-jig cha-ya dwe-yo
earn 벌어요 pörö-yo
earnings 수입 su-ib
earphones 헤드 폰 hedü p-hon
earring 귀걸이 kwigöri
earth (soil) 땅 ddang
earthquake 지진 chijin
east 동쪽 tong-jjog
Easter 부활절 puhwaljöl
easy 쉬운 swi-un; within easy reach 쉽
게 갈 수 있는 거리에 swibge kal su
innün köri-e
eat (I eat) 먹어요 mögö-yo; (you eat)
잡수셔요 chabsushyö-yo; I can't eat
salt 나는 소금을 먹으면 안 되요 nanün
sogml mögmyön an dwe-yo; I seldom
eat fish 생선은 별로 먹지 않아요 seng-
sönün pyöllo mögji anö-yo; we have
already eaten 우리는 벌써 먹었어요
urinün pölsö mögössö-yo; something
hot to eat 뜨거운 음식 목을 것 ddgö-un
ümshig mogl göd; are there places to
eat here? 여기 음식점이 있어요? yögi
ümshigjömi issö-yo?; what would you
like to eat? 무엇을 드릴까요? mu-ösl
trilg-ga-yo?

Pronounce: a father; e let; i machine; o note; ö löng; u rude; ü fürther

ebb tide 썰물 ssölmul
eccentric 괴짜 kwej-ja
economic 경제(의) kyöng-je(e)
Ecuador 에쿠아도르 ek-hu-adorü
edible 식용의 shigyong-e
editor 편집자 p-hyönjibja
education 교육 kyo-yug
eel 뱀장어 pemjang-ö
egg 계란 kyeran; boiled egg 삶은 계란
salmn kyeran; fried egg 계란 후라이
kyeran hura-i; hard-boiled egg 푹 삶은
계란 p-hug salmn kyeran; poached
egg 수란 suran; scrambled eggs 풀어서
한 계란 후라이 p-hurösö han kyeran
hura-i; bacon and eggs 베이컨과 계란
pe-ik-hön-gwa kyeran
eggplant 가지 kaji
Egypt 이집트 ijibt-hü
either ... or ... ...든가 또는 ...
...dn-ga ddonün ...
elastic (noun) 고무끈 komug-gn
elbow 팔꿈치 p-halg-gumch-hi
electric 전기(의) chön-gi(e); he got an
electric shock from the ... ...에서
감전 됐어요 ...esö kamjön dwessö-yo
electric blanket 전기 담요 chön-gi
tamyo
electric fan 선풍기 sönp-hung-gi
electric heater 전기 난로 chön-gi nanro
electric light 전기 불 chön-gi pul
electric outlet 콘센트 k-honsent-hü
electric power 전력 chönryög
electric razor 전기 면도기 chön-gi
myöndogi
electrical appliance store 전자 제품점
chönja chep-humjöm;
electrical appliances 가전 제품 kajön
chep-hum
electrician 전기 기술자 chön-gi kisulja
electricity 전기 chön-gi; save
electricity 전기를 절약 해요 chön-girl
chöryag he-yo
electronic 전자(의) chönja(e)
electronic calculator 전자 계산기 chönja

kyesan-gi
electronics 전자제품 chönjajep-hum
elegant 우아한 u-ahan
elementary school 국민 학교 kungmin
haggyo
elevator 엘리베이터 ellibe-it-hö
else 그밖에 kbag-ge; anything else? 그
밖에 다른 것은 없어요? kbag-ge tarn
gösn öbsö-yo?; let's try somewhere
else 우리 다른 곳에 가 봐요 uri tarn
kose ka pwa-yo; do you have
anything else? 다른 것이 있어요? tarn
göshi issö-yo?
embarrassing 부끄러운 pug-grö-un; he's
embarrassed 그는 부끄러워 해요 knün
pug-gröwö he-yo
embassy 대사관 tesagwan; American
Embassy 미국 대사관 migug tesagwan;
British Embassy 영국 대사관 yöng-gug
tesagwan
embroidery 자수 chasu
emergency 위급 wigb; it's an
emergency 위급 해요 wigb he-yo
emery board 손톱용줄 sont-hobyong-jul
emigrate 이민 가요 imin ka-yo
emotional 감정적인 kamjöng-jögin
emperor 황제 hwang-je
employee 종업원 chong-öbwön
empty 빈 pin; is this place empty? 이
자리는 비어 있어요? i jarinün pi-ö
issö-yo?
encyclopedia 백과 사전 peggwa sajön
end (noun) 끝 ggt
endive 꽃상치 ggoch-hsang-ch-hi
endless 끝없는 ggt-hömnün
endurance 참을성 ch-hamlsöng
enemy 적 chög
energy 힘 him
engaged (to marry) 약혼한 yak-honan;
(toilet) 예약된 ye-yagdwen
engagement (wedding) 약혼 yak-hon
engagement ring 약혼 반지 yak-hon
panji
engine 엔진 enjin; the engine keeps

Pronounce: a father; e let; i machine; o note; ö löng; u rude; ü fürther

stalling 엔진이 계속 꺼져요 enjini kyesog ggöjyö-yo; the engine sounds a bit rough 엔진 소리가 좀 거슬려요 enjin soriga chom gösllyö-yo; there's a knocking noise from the engine 엔진이 노킹 해요 enjini nok-hing he-yo
engine trouble 엔진 의 고장 enjin e kojang
engineer 기술자 kisulja
England 영국 yöng-gug
English (adjective) 영국 의 yöng-gug e; (language) 영어 yöng-ö; English breakfast 영국식 아침 식사 öng-gugshig ach-him shigsa; English people 영국 사람 yöng-gug saram; in English 영어 로 yöng-öro; the English language 영어 yöng-ö; you speak English very well 영어를 잘 해요 yöng-örl chal he-yo; is there an English translation of ...? ...을 영어로 번역 한 것이 있어요? ...l yöng-öro pönyög han göshi issö-yo?; do you carry English newspapers? 영어 신문 있어요? yöng-ö shinmun issö-yo?; can you speak English? 영어를 하세요? yöng-örl hase-yo?; does it have English subtitles? 영어 자막이 있어요? yöng-ö chamagi issö-yo?; would you translate that into English? 영어로 번역 하시겠어요? yöng-öro pönyög hashigessö-yo?; is there a program in English? 영어로 된 프로그램 있어요? yöng-öro dwen p-hürogrem issö-yo?
English-Korean dictionary 영한 사전 yöng-an sajön
english-speaking: do you know an English-speaking doctor? 영어 할 줄 아는 의사를 아세요? yöng-ö hal chul anün esarl ase-yo?
Englishman 영국 사람 yöng-gug saram
engraving 조각 chogag
enjoy 즐겨요 chülgyö-yo; I enjoyed my stay 잘 지냈어요 chal chinessö-yo; I hope you enjoy it 마음에 드셨으면

좋겠어요 ma-me tshyössmyön chokhessö-yo
enjoyable 즐거운 chülgö-un
enlarge 확대 해요 hwagde he-yo
enlargement (photo) 확대 hwagde
enormous 커다란 k-hödaran
enough 충분한 ch-hung-bunan; that's enough, thanks 충분 해요, 고맙습니다 ch-hung-bun he-yo, komabsmnida; it's not enough 충분 하지 않아요 ch-hung-bun haji anö-yo; it's not chilled enough 아직 덜 차가워 졌어요 ajig töl ch-hagawö chyössö-yo; all right, fair enough 좋아, 됐어요 choha, dwessö-yo
enroll 등록 해요 tng-rog he-yo
enterprise 기업 ki-öb
entertainment 오락 orag; where can you get an entertainment guide? 공연 안내서를 어디서 구 할 수 있어요? kong-yön annesörl ödisö ku hal su issö-yo?
enthusiastic 열광적인 yölgwang-jögin
entrance 입구 ibgu; (to house) 현관 hyön-gwan
envelope 봉투 pong-t-hu; airmail envelope 항공 우편 봉투 hang-gong up-hyön pong-t-hu
environment (natural) 자연 환경 chayön hwan-gyöng
epidemic 유행병 yuheng-byöng
epileptic 간질병(의) kanjilbyöng(e)
equestrian 승마 sng-ma
equipment (facilities) 설비 sölbi; (instruments) 용구 yong-gu
era 시대 shide
eraser 지우개 chi-uge
erotic 애정 ejöng
error 실수 shilsu
escalator 에스컬레이터 esk-hölle-it-hö
escape: fire escape 비상구 pisang-gu
especially 특히 t-hük-hi
espresso coffee 에스프레소 커피 esp-hüreso k-höp-hi
essential (vital) 긴요 한 kinyo han
ethnic 이국적의 igugjöge

Pronounce: a father; e let; i machine; o note; ö löng; u rude; ü fürther

Europe 유럽 yuröb
European 유럽 사람 yuröb saram
European Community (EC) 유럽 공동체
yuröb kong-dong-ch-he
even ... ...도 ...do; even if ... 만일
... 더라도 manil ... törado; even
better 더 좋은 tö chohün
evening 저녁 chönyög; tomorrow
evening 내일 저녁 ne-il chönyög; in
the evening 저녁에 chönyöge; he's
busy this evening 오늘 밤에는 바빠요
onl pamenün pab-bö-yo; would you
like to go out this evening? 오늘밤
외출하시지 않겠어요? onlbam wech-
hurashiji ank-hessö-yo?
evening dress (men's) 야회복 yahwebog;
(woman's) 이브닝 드레스 ibning tresü;
is evening dress necessary? 파티복을
입을 필요가 있어요? p-hat-hibogl ibl
p-hiryoga issö-yo?
eventually 결국에 kyölguge
ever: we hardly ever go 좀처럼 가지
않어요 chomch-höröm kaji anö-yo; I
hardly ever eat it 거의 먹지 않어요 kö-
e mögji anö-yo; I hardly ever drink
거의 마시지 않어요 kö-e mashiji anö-
yo; it's the best meal I've ever eaten
내가 먹은 식사 중에 최고에요 nega
mögn shigsa chung-e ch-hwego-e-yo
every ... ...마다 ...mada; every day
매일 me-il; every month 매월
mewöl; every year 매년 menyön
everyone 누구든지 nugudnji
everything 무엇이든지 mu-öshidnji;
that's everything 전부 에요 chönbu e-
yo; thanks for everything 친절히 대해
주셔서 감사 합니다 ch-hinjöri tehe
jushyösö kamsa hamnida
everywhere 어디든지 ödidnji;
everywhere in the world 온 세계에서
on segye-esö; I've searched everywhere
구석 구석 찾아봤어요 kusög kusög ch-
hajabwassö-yo
exactly! 맞아요 maja-yo

exam 시험 shihöm
examine: would you examine the bill?
계산을 검사해 주세요? kyesanl
kömsahe juse-yo?
example 예 ye; for example 예를 들면
yerl tlmyön
excellent (adjective) 훌륭 한 hullyung
han; the food is excellent 음식이 훌륭
해요 ümshigi hullyung he-yo; the
service was excellent 서비스가 훌륭
했어요 söbisga hullyung hessö-yo
except 외에는 we-enün
exception 예외 yewe
excess baggage 제한 초과 수화물 chehan
ch-hogwa suhwamul
excessive 과도한 kwadohan
exchange (verb) 바꿔요 pag-gwö-yo;
foreign exchange 외국환 weguk-hwan;
can I exchange this? 이것 좀 바꿔
주시겠어요? igöd chom pag-gwö
jushigessö-yo?; would you exchange
this for ...? ...으로 이것을 바꿔
주시겠어요? ...ro igösl pag-gwö
jushigessö-yo?; what's the exchange
rate for the dollar? 달러 환율이
얼마에요? tallö hwanyuri ölma-e-yo?;
where can I exchange money? 돈을
어디에서 바꿔요? tonl ödi-esö pag-
gwi-yo?
exchange rate 환율 hwanyul
exchange student 교환 학생 kyohwan
hagseng
excitement 흥분 hüng-bun
exciting 재미 있는 chemi innün
exclusive (high class) 고급의 kogbe
excursion 관광 kwan-gwang
excuse me (to get attention) 여보세요
yöbose-yo; (didn't hear) 무엇이라고
말씀 했어요? mu-öshirago malsm
hessö-yo?; excuse me, it was an
accident 미안 합니다만, 실수였어요 mi-
an hamnidaman, shilsu-yössö-yo;
excuse me, I'd like to ask a question
실례지만, 말씀 좀 묻겠어요

Pronounce: a father; e let; i machine; o note; ö löng; u rude; ü fürther

shillyejiman, malsm chom mudgessö-yo
executive 회사 간부 hwesa kanbu
exhaust (auto) 배기 pegi
exhausted (tired) 매우 피로한 me-u p-hirohan
exhibit (verb) 전시 해요 chönshi he-yo
exhibition 전람회 chönramwe
exist 존재 해요 chonje he-yo
exit 출구 ch-hulgu; **where is the exit?** 출구가 어디 있어요? ch-hulguga ödi issö-yo?
expedition 탐험 t-hamöm
expense 비용 pi-yong; **is that an additional expense?** 그것은 추가 비용이에요? kgösn ch-huga pi-yong-i-e-yo?
expensive 비싼 pissan; **more expensive** 더 비싼 tö pissan; **they're pretty expensive** 꽤 비싸요 ggwe pissa-yo; **is it so expensive?** 그렇게나 빗싸요? krök-hena pissa-yo?
experience 경험 kyöng-öm
experienced 경험 있는 kyöng-öm innün
expert (an old hand) 노련한 사람 noryönan saram; (specialist) 전문가 chönmun-ga
expire 만료 되요 manryo dwe-yo
explain 설명 해요 sölmyöng he-yo; **could you explain it to me?** 나에게 설명 해 주시겠어요? na-ege sölmyöng he jushigessö-yo?
explore 답사 해요 tabsa he-yo
export (sell) 수출 해요 such-hul he-yo
exports (products) 수출 such-hul
express mail 속달 sogdal
express train 급행 kp-heng; **super express train** 새마을호 sema-ro
extension (phone) 교환 번호 kyohwan pöno
exterior 외부 webu
extinguisher: fire extinguisher 소화기 sohwagi
extra (additional) 여분의 yöbune; **is there an extra charge?** 할증료가 있어요? haljng-ryoga issö-yo?
extra large 엑스라지 egsraji
extremely 대단히 tedani
eye 눈 nun
eye drops 안약 anyag
eye shadow 아이 섀도우 a-i shyedo-u
eye witness 목격자 moggyögja
eyebrow 눈썹 nunsöb
eyebrow pencil 눈썹 연필 nunsöb yönp-hil
eyeliner 아이 라이너 a-i ra-inö
eyesight 시력 shiryög

F

fable 동화 tong-wa
fabric 천 ch-hyön
face 얼굴 ölgul
face mask (diving) 수중 마스크 sujung mask-hü
face powder 분 pun
facilities 시설물 shisölmul; **are camping facilities available?** 캠프 시설이 있어요? k-hemp-hü shisöri issö-yo?
facing ... ...를 향 해 ...rl hyang he
fact 사실 sashil
factory 공장 kong-jang
Fahrenheit 화씨 hwasshi; **30 degrees Fahrenheit** 화씨 삼십도 hwasshi samshibdo
fail 실패 해요 shilp-he he-yo
failure 실패 shilp-he
faint (verb) 기절 해요 kijöl he-yo; **he's fainted** 그는 기절 했어요 knün kijöl hessö-yo
fair (entertainment) 유원지 yuwönji; (commercial) 박람회 pagramwe; **trade fair** 무역 전시장 mu-yög chönshijang
fake 위조(한) wijo(an)
fall (autumn) 가을 ka-l; **in the fall**

(season) 가을에 ka-re
fall colors 단풍 tanp-hung
false (a lie) 거짓의 köjise; (fake) 위조
한 wijohan; (artificial) 인공의 in-
gong-e
false teeth 의치 ech-hi
family 가족 kajog
family name 성 söng
famous 유명한 yumyöng-an
fan (electrical) 선풍기 sönp-hüng-gi;
(folding) 부채 puch-he; (sports etc)
팬 p-hen
fan belt 팬 벨트 p-hen pelt-hü
fancy (adjective) 장식적의 chang-
shigjöge
fantastic 멋진 mödjin
far 먼 mön; how far is it from ... to
...? ...부터 ...까지 얼마나 멀라요?
...but-hö ...ggaji ölmana mölla-yo?;
is it far away? 여기서 멀어요? yögisö
mörö-yo?; it's really far away! 매우
멀어요! me-u mörö-yo!
fare 요금 yogm; half fare 반액 paneg
fare box 요금함 yogmam
farewell party 송별회 song-byörwe
farm 농가 nong-ga
farmhouse 농가 nong-ga
farther 더 멀리 tö mölli
fashion 유행 yuheng
fashionable 유행한 yuheng-an
fast 빨리 bballi; as fast as possible 가능
한한 kanüng hanan; not too fast 너무
빠르지 않게 nömu bbarji ank-he
fastener (on dress) 호크 hok-hü
fat (overweight) 살이찐 sarij-jin; (on
meat) 지방 chibang
father 아버지 aböji
father-in-law (husband's father) 시아버
지 shi-aböji; (wife's father) 장인
chang-in
fatigue 피곤 p-higon
faucet 꼭지 ggogji
fault (flaw) 결점 kyöljöm; it isn't my
fault 내 잘못이 아녀요 ne chalmoshi

anyö-yo
faulty 결점이 많는 kyöljömi mannün
favorite 제일 좋아 하는 che-il choha
hanün; this is my favorite cafe' 이곳이
내가 제일 좋아하는 까페에요 igoshi
nega che-il chohahanün ggap-he-e-yo
favorite place (regular customer) 단골
tan-gol
fax (facsimile) 팩스 p-hegsü
fear (noun) 공포 kong-p-ho; I have a
fear of heights 나는 고공 공포증이
있어요 nanün kogong kong-p-hojng-i
issö-yo
February 이월 iwöl
fee 요금 yogm
feel 느껴요 ng-gyö-yo; I feel dizzy 나
는 현기증이 나요 nanün hyön-gijng-i
na-yo; I feel cold 추워 요 ch-huwö
yo; I feel a lot better 많이 좋아졌어요
mani chohajyössö-yo; I feel ill 몸이
불편 해요 momi pulp-hyön he-yo; I
feel very warm 나는 매우 따뜻 해요
nanün me-u ddad-düd he-yo; I don't
feel like doing it 하고 싶지 않어요
hago shibch-hi anö-yo; I don't feel
well 몸이 별로 좋지 않어요 momi
pyöllo choch-hi anö-yo; how do you
feel today? 오늘은 기분이 어때요 onrn
kibuni öd-de-yo
fellow 남자 namja
felt pen 펠트펜 p-helt-hüp-hen
female 여 yö
fence 담 tam
fencing 펜싱 p-henshing; Korean
fencing 검도 kömdo
fender (auto) 밤바 pamba
ferry 페리 p-heri; car ferry 카페리 k-
hap-heri; when is the last ferry? 마지
막 페리 언제 있어요 majimag p-heri
önje issö-yo
fertilizer 비료 piryo
festival 축제 ch-hugje; Farmer's Festival
(music & dance) 농악제 nong-agje
fever 열 yöl; hay fever 건초열 könch-

ho-yöl

few (a few) 조금 chogm; a few days 며칠 myöt-hil; a few kilometers outside of town 시내에서 몇 길로미터 떨어져(서) shine-esö myöt killomit-hö ddöröjyö(sö)

fiancee 약혼녀 yak-honnyö

fiasco 실패 shilp-he; it's a complete fiasco 완전한 실패에요 wanjönan shilp-he-e-yo

fiction 소설 sosöl

field 들판 tlp-han; rice field 논 non; track and field 육상 yugsang

fifty-fifty 반반으로 panbanro

fight (noun) 싸움 ssa-um

figs 무화과 muhwagwa

figure (appearance) 모양 mo-yang; (number) 숫자 sudja

file: nail file 손톱 다듬는 줄 sont-hob tadmnün chul

filipino (adjective) 필리핀 의 p-hilliphin e; (person) 필리핀 사람 p-hilliphin saram

fill 가득 채워요 kadg ch-hewö-yo; please fill my glass 잔에 따라주세요 chane ddarajuse-yo; please help me fill out this form 이 사항에 써 넣을 것을 도와 주세요 i sahang-e ssö nöhül gösl towa juse-yo

fillet (meat) 살고기 salgogi; (of fish) 생선의 저민 고기 seng-söne chömin kogi

filling (dental) 봉 pong

film (at movies) 영화 yöng-wa; (camera) 필림 p-hillim; action film 활극 hwalgüg; cartoon film 만화 영화 manwa yöng-wa; color film 칼라 필림 k-halla p-hillim; 35mm film 삼십오 밀리 필름 samshibo milli p-hillm; disk of film 필름 한 디스크 p-hillm han tisk-hü; do you have film like this one? 이와 같은 필름 있어요? iwa kat-hün p-hillm issö-yo?; black and white camera film 흑백 필림 hügbeg p-hillim

filter 필터 p-hilt-hö; filter cigarettes 필터가 달린 담배 p-hilt-höga tallin tambe

filter-tipped 필터가 달린 p-hilt-höga tallin

filthy 더러운 törö-un

finally 마침내 mach-himne

find 찾어요 ch-hajö-yo; please find us baby-sitter 애 보는 사람을 알아봐 주세요 e ponün saraml arabwa juse-yo; please find the word in this book 이 책에서 그 말을 찾아 주세요 i ch-hegesö kü marl ch-haja juse-yo; we can't find it 찾을 수가 없어요 ch-hajl suga öbsö-yo; if you find them 만일 찾으면 manil ch-hajmyön

fine 훌륭 한 hullyung han; it's fine that way 그래로 좋아요 krero choha-yo; 50,000 won fine 벌금 오만원 pölgm omanwön

finger 손가락 son-garag; I've cut my finger 손가락을 베었어요 son-garagl pe-össö-yo

fingernail 손톱 sont-hob

finish 끝내요 ggt-hne-yo; finish your drink 다 마셔요 ta mashyö-yo; when I am finished 내가 글내면 nega kt-hnemyön; when do you finish work? 언제 일을 마치세요? önje irl mach-hise-yo?

fire 불 pul;

fire! 불이야! puri-ya!

fire alarm 화재 경보 hwaje kyöng-bo

fire department 소방서 sobang-sö

fire escape 비상구 pisang-gu

fire extinguisher 소화기 sohwagi

firefly 개똥벌레 ked-dong-bölle

fireworks 불꽃 pulg-goch

firm (company) 회사 hwesa

first (firstly) 먼저 mönjö; first class 일등석 ildngsög; first thing in the morning 아침이 되면 우선 ach-himi dwemyön usön; is this the first time? 이번이 처음이세요? iböni ch-hö-miseyo?; is this your first visit? 여기는 처음 오세요? yöginün ch-hö-m ose-yo?

first aid 응급 치료 üng-gb ch-hiryo

first aid kit 응급 처치함 üng-gb ch-höch-hiham

first class (ticket, etc) 일등석 ildng-sög

first class ticket 일등표 ildng-p-hyo

fish (broiled) 생선구이 seng-sön-gu-i; fish (food) 생선 seng-sön; (raw fish, sushi) 생선회 seng-sönwe; tuna fish 튜너 t-hyunö; I seldom eat fish 생선은 별로 먹지 않아요 seng-sönün pyöllo mögji anö-yo

fish market 수산물 시장 susanmul shijang

fisherman 어부 öbu

fishing 고기잡이 kogijabi; is there any good fishing around here? 이 근처에 좋은 낚시터가 있어요? i gnch-hö-e chohün nag-gshit-höga issö-yo?

fishing boat 어선 ösön

fishing net 어망 ömang

fishing rod 낚싯대 nag-gshidde

fishing tackle 낚시 도구 nag-gshi togu

fishing village 어촌 öch-hon

fit (healthy) 튼튼한 t-hünt-hünan;

fit (verb) 맞아요 maja-yo; this doesn't fit 이건 맞지 않는데요 igön majji annünde-yo; he's really into fitness 그는 보건 체조에 열심이에요 knün pogön ch-hejo-e yölshimi-e-yo; where is the fitting room? 옷을 입어볼 수 있는 곳이 어디에요? osl iböbol su innün koshi ödi-e-yo?

fix 수리 해요 suri he-yo; can you fix it? 수리해 주실 수 있어요? surihe jushil su issö-yo?

fixed menu 정식 chöng-shig

fixed price 정가 chöng-ga

flag (national) 국기 kuggi

flash (camera) 플래시 p-hülleshi

flashlight 플래시 p-hülleshi

flat (level) 편평 한 p-hyönp-hyöng

han; I've got a flat tire 타이어에 바람이 빠졌어요 t-ha-i-ö-e parami bbajyössö-yo

flattery 아첨 ach-höm

flavor 맛 mad

flexible (easily bent) 휘기 쉬운 hwigi swi-un; (easily changed) 융통성 있는 yung-t-hong-söng innün

flight (number) 비행기 번호 piheng-gi pöno; charter flight 전세 비행기 chönse piheng-gi; the flight was delayed 비행기 시간이 됐어요 piheng-gi shigani dwessö-yo; night flight 야간 비행 yagan piheng; scheduled flight 정기편 chöng-gip-hyön; is there a later flight than that? 그 보다 더 늦은 비행기가 있어요? kü boda tö njn piheng-giga issö-yo?; when is the next flight to Pusan? 다음의 부산행 비행기는 몇시에 있어요? ta-me pusaneng piheng-ginün myöt-hshi-e issö-yo?

flight attendant (woman) 스튜어디스 st-hyu-ödisü

flock 떼 dde

flood 홍수 hong-su

floor 마루 maru; what floor is the room on? 방이 몇 층에 있어요? pang-i myöt ch-hüng-e issö-yo?; on the second floor 이층에 ich-hüng-e; on the main floor 일층에 ilch-hüng-e; on the top floor 제일 높은 층에 che-il nop-hün ch-hüng-e

floor show 플로어쇼 p-hüllo-öshyo

flop (fiasco) 실패 shilp-he

florist 꽃집 ggojch-hib

floss: dental floss 덴탈 프로스 tent-hal p-hürosü

flour 밀가루 milgaru

flower 꽃 ggoch; bunch of flowers 꽃다발 ggodt-habal

flower arranging 꺽꽃이 ggögg-goch-hi

flower shop 꽃집 ggojch-hib

flu 몸살 momsal; to catch the flu 몸살

나요 momsal na-yo

fluently 유창 하게 yuch-hang hage; he speaks Korean fluently 그는 한국말을 유창하게 해요 knün han-gungmarl yuch-hang-age he-yo

flush: the toilet won't flush 변기가 고장났어요 pyön-giga kojang-nassö-yo

fly (housefly) 파리 p-hari; (on trousers) 바지 의 지퍼 paji e chip-hö; (verb) 날아요 nara-yo

fly killer 파리약 / 스프레이 p-hari-yag / sp-hüre-i

fog 안개 an-ge; it's foggy 안개가 짙어요 an-gega chit-hö-yo

foil: aluminum foil 은박지 ünbagji; silver foil 은박 ünbag

folding chair 접는 의자 chömnün eja

folk art 민속 예술 minsog yesul

folk dance 민속 무용 minsog mu-yong

folk songs 대중가요 tejung-ga-yo

folk village 민속촌 minsogch-hon

follow 따라 가요 ddara ka-yo

food 음식 ümshig; (western style) 양식 yang-shig; the food was nothing special 음식은 그저 그랬어요 ümshign kjö kressö-yo; frozen food 냉동 식품 neng-dong shigp-hum; gourmet food 고급 음식 kogb ümshig; no fried food 튀긴것은 안돼요 t-hwigin-gösn andwe-yo; Korean style food 한식 hanshig; I'd like some Western food 양식을 먹고 싶은데요 yang-shigl möggo ship-hünde-yo; I'll have to send this food back 이 음식을 반품 해야 해요 i mshigl panp-hum he-ya he-yo

food poisoning 식중독 shigjung-dog

food store 식료품점 shigryop-humjöm

fool 바보 pabo

foolish 어리석은 örisögn

foot 발 pal; my feet are killing me 발이 아파 죽겠어요 pari ap-ha chuggessö-yo

foot warmer 발 보온기 pal po-on-gi

football (American game) 미식축구 mishigch-huggu; (ball itself) 축구공 ch-huggugong

for ... ...위 해 ...wi he; what is this for? 뭣을 위한 것이에요? mwösl wihan göshi-e-yo?; we have been here for a week 여기에 일주일 동안 있었어요 yögi-e ilju-il tong-an issössö-yo

forbidden 금지된 kmjidwen

forecast: weather forecast 일기 예보 ilgi yebo

forehead 이마 ima

foreign 외국에 weguge; a foreign language 외국어 wegugö

foreign exchange 외국환 weguk-hwan

foreigner 외국 사람 wegug saram

forest 숲 sup

forever: it takes forever 시간이 많이 걸려요 shigani mani köllyö-yo

forget 잊어 버려요 ijö pöryö-yo; I forget 잊어 버렸어요 ijö pöryössö-yo; I forget which one it was 어느 쪽인지 잊어 버렸어요 önü jjoginji ijö pöryössö-yo; you mustn't forget 잊으면 안 돼요 ijmyön an dwe-yo

fork (for food) 포크 p-hok-hü; (crossroad) 분기점 pun-gijöm

form (hotel) 숙박계 sugbaggye; application form 신청용지 shinch-höng-yong-ji; claim form 청구 서 ch-höng-gu sö; customs declaration form 세관 신고서 segwan shin-gosö; please help me fill out this form 이 사항에 써 넣을 것을 도와 주세요 i sahang-e ssö nöhül gösl towa juse-yo

formal 형식적인 hyöng-shigjögin

former 이전의 ijöne

fortunately 다행히 taheng-i

fortuneteller 점장이 chömjang-i

forward (onward) 앞으로 ap-hüro; I'm looking forward to working with you 함께 일 하게 되어서 기쁩니다 hamg-ge il hage dwe-ösö kib-bmnida

forwarding address 새로운 주소 sero-un chuso

founder 창립자 ch-hang-ribja

fountain (structure) 분수 punsu; (drinking) 물마시는 곳 mulmashinün kod

fox (a fearsome animal in Korea) 여우 yö-u

fracture (of bone) 골절 koljöl

fragile (easily broken) 깨지기 쉬운 ggejigi swi-un

fragrance 향기 hyang-gi

frame (for photo) 사진틀 sajint-hül

France 프랑스 p-hürang-sü

fraud (crime) 사기 sagi; (person) 사기꾼 sagig-gun

free (empty) 빈 pin;

free (of charge) 무료 muryo; (not busy) 한가한 han-gahan; free admission 무료 입장 muryo ibjang; is this seat free? 이 자리는 비었어요? i jarinün pi-össö-yo?

freedom 자유 cha-yu

freezer 냉동칸 neng-dong-k-han

French (adjective) 프랑스 의 p-hürang-sü e; (language) 프랑스 말 p-hürang-sü mal

French fries 감자 튀김 kamja t-hwigim

frequent 자주 chaju

frequent customer 단골 손님 tan-gol sonnim

fresh (air, etc) 상쾌한 sang-k-hwehan; (fruit etc) 싱싱 한 shing-shing han; (bold) 건방진 könbang-jin; don't talk fresh 건방지구나 könbang-jiguna; this isn't fresh 이것은 싱싱 하지 않아요 igösn shing-shing haji ana-yo; I need some fresh air 신선 한 공기가 필요 해요 shinsön han kong-giga p-hiryo he-yo

friction tape (insulating) 절연용 테이프 chöryönyong t-he-ip-hü

Friday 금요일 kmyo-il; on Friday 금요일에 kmyo-ire; Monday through Friday 월요일부터 금요일까지 wöryo-ilbut-hö kmyo-ilg-gaji

fridge 냉장고 neng-jang-go

fried egg 계란 후라이 kyeran hura-i

fried rice 볶음밥 pok-hümbab

friend 친구 ch-hin-gu; is she your friend? 그녀는 당신의 친구에요? knyönün tang-shine ch-hin-gu-e-yo?; may I bring a friend? 친구를 데려와도 좋아요? ch-hin-gurl teryöwado choha-yo?; I consider you my best friend 나는 당신을 제일 좋은 친구라고 생각 해요 nanün tang-shinl che-il chohün ch-hin-gurago seng-gag he-yo

friendly 친한 ch-hinan

friendship 우정 ujöng

fries 감자 튀김 kamja t-hwigim

frog 개구리 keguri

from ... ...부터 ...but-hö; from time to time 때때로 dded-dero; I come from Los Angeles 나는 로스앤젤레스에서 왔어요 nanün ros-enjelles-esö wassö-yo; it's different from this one 이것과 달라요 igödgwa talla-yo; a week from today 다음 주의 오늘 ta-m chu-e onl; where are you from? 어디서 오셨어요? ödisö oshyössö-yo?; I'm expecting a call from Washington 워싱톤으로부터 전화 기다리고 있어요 wöshing-t-honrobut-hö chönwa kidarigo issö-yo; they are quite different from each other 서로 매우 달라요 söro me-u talla-yo; how far is it from ... to ...? ...부터 ...까지 얼마나 멀라요? ...but-hö ...ggaji ölmana mölla-yo?; where do you get it from? 어디서 얻어요? ödisö ödö-yo?; he got an electric shock from the ... ...에서 감전 됐어요 ...esö kamjön dwessö-yo

front 앞 ap

frozen 냉동 된 neng-dong dwen

frozen food 냉동 식품 neng-dong shigp-hum

fruit 과일 kwa-il

fruit cocktail 프루트 칵테일 p-hürut-hü k-hagt-he-il

fruit juice 과일 쥬스 kwa-il chyusü

fruit salad 과일 사라다 kwa-il sarada

frustration 좌절 chwajöl; it's very frustrating 안달이 나요 andari na-yo

fry 튀겨요 t-hwigyö-yo; no fried food 튀긴것은 안돼요 t-hwigin-gösn andwe-yo

frying pan 프라이팬 p-hüra-ip-hen

full 가득찬 kadgch-han; full board 세끼 포함 seg-gi p-hoham; I'm full 배 불러요 pe pullö-yo

full moon 보름달 pormdal

fun (enjoyment) 재미 chemi; it was really fun 정말 재미 있었어요 chöng-mal chemi issössö-yo

funeral 장례식 chang-ryeshig

funny (odd) 괴상한 kwesang-an; (amusing) 재미있는 chemi-innün

furious 격분 한 kyögbun han

furniture 가구 kagu

furrier 모피상 mop-hisang

further 그 위에 kü wi-e; further up the road 길을 따라 훨씬 내려간 곳에 kirl ddara hwölshin neryögan kose; you must go further up the hill 언덕 더 앞으로 올라가야 해요 öndög tö ap-hüro ollaga-ya he-yo; is it much further? 더 멀어요? tö mörö-yo?

fuse (electrical) 퓨즈 p-hyujü; a 15 amp fuse 십오암페어 의 퓨즈 shibo-amp-he-ö e p-hyujü

future 미래 mire; in the future 미래에 mire-e

G

gallery: art gallery 화랑 hwarang; modern art gallery 현대 미술관 hyönde misulgwan

gallon 갤런 kellön

gamble 도박 해요 tobag he-yo

game 게임 ke-im; card game (Korean)

화투 hwat-hu; mahjong game 마작 majag; Korean card game 화투 hwat-hu

game room 오락실 oragshil

garage (gas) 주유소 chu-yuso; (car repair) 자동차 수리소 chadong-ch-ha suriso; (parking) 주차장 chuch-hajang

garbage 쓰레기 ssregi

garbage can 쓰레기통 ssregit-hong

garden 정원 chöng-wön

garlic 마늘 manl

garment 옷 od

gas 가스 kasü; (gasoline) 휘발유 hwibaryu; we're out of gas 자동차에 휘발유가 없어요 chadong-ch-ha-e hwibaryuga öbsö-yo

gas pedal 악셀 agsel

gas station 주유소 chu-yuso

gas tank 가스 탱크 kasü t-heng-k-hü

gasoline 휘발유 hwibaryu; regular gasoline 보통 휘발유 pot-hong hwibaryu

gate 문 mun; (airport) 게이트 ke-it-hü

gaudy 야한 yahan

gauge 계기 kyegi

gauze 가제 kaje

gay (homosexual) 게이 ke-i

gear (car) (see also EQUIPMENT) 기어 ki-ö; low gear 저속 기어 chösog ki-ö; reverse gear 후진 기어 hujin ki-ö

gear shift 기어 레버 ki-ö rebö

gearbox 변속기 pyönsoggi

geisha (Korean) 기생 kiseng

gender 성별 söng-byöl

genealogy 족보 chogbo

general (usual) 일반저인 ilbanjö-in; in general 일반적으로 ilbanjögro

general delivery 유치 우편 yuch-hi up-hyön

generation 세대 sede

generator 발전기 paljön-gi

generous 관대 한 kwande han

gentleman / gentlewoman 신사 shinsa

genuine 진짜(의) chinj-ja(e)

Pronounce: a father; e let; i machine; o note; ö löng; u rude; ü fürther

geography 지리 chiri

German (adjective) 독일 의 togil e;
(person) 독일 사람 togil saram;
(language) 독일어 togirö

German measles 풍진 p-hung-jin

Germany 독일 togil

get 얻어요 ödö-yo; get away! 가시오!
kashi-o!; get down! 내려 요! neryö
yo!; get out! 썩 나가 ssög naga; I get
carsick 차멀미 해요 ch-hamölmi he-yo;
I get it! 알았어요! arassö-yo!; could I
get the bill, please? 계산서 주시겠어요?
kyesansö jushigessö-yo?; I don't get a
tan 볕에 그을을 수가 없어요 pyöt-he k-
rl suga öbsö-yo; can you get this
stain out? 이 얼룩을 뺄 수 있어요? i
öllugl bbel su issö-yo?; could we get
breakfast in our room? 방에서 아침
식사를 할 수 있어요? pang-esö ach-him
shigsarl hal su issö-yo?; I usually get
up late 나는 보통 늦게 일어나요 nanün
pot-hong ndge iröna-yo; may I get
past? 지나가도 돼요? chinagado dwe-
yo?; I'll go get ready 준비 하러
가겠어요 chunbi harö kagessö-yo;
would you get a taxi for me? 택시를
불러 주시겠어요? t-hegshirl pullö
jushigessö-yo?; when I get used to
the heat 더위에 익숙 해질 때에 töwi-e
igsug hejil dde-e; when I get back 돌
아갈 때 toragal dde; did my package
get here? 내 소포가 도착 했어요? ne
sop-hoga toch-hag hessö-yo?; when
does it get dark? 언제 날이 어두워져요
önje nari öduwöjyö-yo; just let me
get dressed 옷을 좀 입겠어요 osl chom
ibgessö-yo; how can I get to ...?
...에는 어떻게 가면 돼요? ...enün öd-
dök-he kamyön dwe-yo?; where do
you get it from? 어디서 얻어요? ödisö
ödö-yo?; would you go get it for
me? 가져 오시겠어요? kajyö oshigessö-
yo?; it's difficult to get there 거기에
가기는 어려워요 kögi-e kaginün

öryöwö-yo; will you come and get
me? 데리러 오시겠어요? terirö
oshigessö-yo?; I don't want to get
involved in it 말려들고 싶지 않아요
mallyödlgo shibch-hi anö-yo; please
let me know where to get off 어디서
내리는지 알려 주세요 ödisö nerinünji
allyö juse-yo; can you tell me how
to get to ...? ...으로 가는 길을 가르쳐
주시겠어요? ...ro kanün kirl karch-
hyö jushigessö-yo?

gherkins 작은 오이 chagn o-i

ghost 유령 yuryöng

gift 선물 sönmul; here is a gift for you
선물이에요 sönmuri-e-yo; I want to
buy a small gift 작은 선물을 사고
싶어요 chagn sönmurl sago ship-hö-yo

gift shop 선물 가제 sönmul kaje

gigantic 거대 한 köde han

gin 진 chin; gin and tonic 진 토닉
chin t-honig

ginger 생강 seng-gang

ginger tea 생강차 seng-gang-ch-ha

ginkgo 은행 üneng

ginseng 인삼 insam; ginseng tea 인삼차
insamch-ha; ginseng drink 인삼 음료
insam ümryo

ginseng chicken 삼계탕 samgyet-hang

ginseng shop 인삼 가게 insam kage

girdle: panty girdle 팬티거들 p-hent-
higödl

girl 여자 아이 yöja a-i

girlfriend 여자 친구 yöja ch-hin-gu

give 줘요 chwö-yo; give regards 안부
전해 줘요 anbu chöne chwö-yo; please
give us two beers 맥주 두병을 주십시오
megju tubyöng-1 chushibshi-o; please
give me just a little 조금만 주십시오
chogmman chushibshi-o; please give
me both of them 두개 다 주세요 tuge
ta juse-yo; I'll give you a lift home
차로 집까지 데려 다 드리겠어요 ch-
haro chibg-gaji teryö ta trigessö-yo;
I'll give you 10000 won 만원을

드리겠어요 manwön1 trigessö-yo; please give me a hamburger to go 햄버거를 한개 싸 주세요 hembögörl hange ssa juse-yo; please give me that one instead 그 대신에 저것을 주세요 kü deshine chögösl chuse-yo; please give us more water 물을 더 주세요 murl tö juse-yo; let's give a party 파티를 해요 p-hat-hirl he-yo; please give me a receipt 영수증을 주세요 yöng-sujng-1 chuse-yo; I'll give it back it tomorrow 내일 돌려 주겠어요 ne-il tollyö chugessö-yo; can you give me a better price? 좀 싸게 해 주시겠어요? chom ssage he jushigessö-yo?; could you give me ...? ... 좀 주시겠어요? ... chom chushigessö-yo?; do you give lessons? 가르치세요? karch-hise-yo?; could you give me some more? 더 주시겠어요? tö jushigessö-yo?; would you give me a shave? 면도 좀 해 주시겠어요? myöndo chom he jushigessö-yo?; could you give me some? 좀 주시겠어요? chom chushigessö-yo?; will you give me these? 이것들을 주시겠어요? igöddrl chushigessö-yo?; would you give this to Mr ...? 이것을 미스터 ...에게 주시겠어요? igösl mist-hö ...ege chushigessö-yo?

glad 기쁜 kib-bn
gland 선 sön
glass (substance) 유리 yuri; (cup) 잔 chan; **magnifying glass** 돋보기 todbogi; **wine glass** 포도주 잔 p-hodoju chan; **please fill my glass** 잔에 따라주세요 chane ddarajuse-yo
glasses (eyeglasses) 안경 an-gyöng
gloomy 어두운 ödu-un
gloss: lip gloss 립글로스 ribgllosü
gloves 장갑 chang-gab
glue (substance) 아교 agyo
go 가요 ka-yo; **go straight, please** 똑바로 가세요 ddogbaro kase-yo; **go**

straight? 똑바로 가요? ddogbaro ka-yo?; go that way 저쪽으로 가세요 chöj-jogro kase-yo; to go ashore 상륙해요 sang-ryug he-yo; I go home tomorrow 나는 내일 집에 돌아가요 nanün ne-il chibe toraga-yo; I'll go and get it 가져 오겠어요 kajyö ogessö-yo; he's gone 그는 없어졌어요 knün öbsöjyössö-yo; let's go now 자 지금 가요 cha chigm ka-yo; let's go see a movie 우리 영화 보러 가요 uri yöngwa porö ka-yo; I'll go pack 가서 짐을 꾸리겠어요 kasö chiml ggurigessö-yo; I'll go get ready 준비 하러 가겠어요 chunbi harö kagessö-yo; let's go for a stroll 산보 하러 갈까요 sanbo harö kalg-ga-yo; before I go 내가 가기 전에 nega kagi chöne; I must go to bed early 일찍 자야 되요 ilj-jig cha-ya dwe-yo; would you go get it for me? 가져 오시겠어요? kajyö oshigessö-yo?; it's all gone 다 없어졌어요 ta öbsöjyössö-yo; shall we go into the lobby? 로비에 들어 갈까요? robi-e trö kalg-ga-yo?; may I go with you? 함께 가도 좋아요? hamg-ge kado choha-yo?; let me go! 놓아 줘! noha chwö!; I must go 가야 해요 ka-ya he-yo; do you go near ...? ... 근처로 가세요? ... knch-höro kase-yo?; where did you go? 어디에 갔다 오셨어요? ödi-e kadda oshyössö-yo?; I want to go and look around 가서 답사를 하고 싶은데요 kasö tabsarl hago ship-hünde-yo; we hardly ever go 좀처럼 가지 않어요 chomch-höröm kaji anö-yo; I certainly must go (there) 꼭 가야겠어요 ggog ka-yagessö-yo; I have to go to the toilet 화장실에 가야 해요 hwajang-shire ka-ya he-yo; I want to go home 집에 돌아가고 싶어요 chibe toragago ship-hö-yo; I'd like to go with you 당신과 함께 가고 싶은데요 tang-shinwa hamg-ge kago ship-

hünde-yo; would you like to go out
this evening? 오늘밤 외출하시지
않겠어요? onlbam wech-hurashiji ank-
hessö-yo?; I was just going to go 나
는 막 가려고 했어요 nanün mag
karyögo hessö-yo
goal (sports) 득점 tgjöm
goat 염소 yömso
god 신 shin
goddess 여신 yöshin
gold 금 km
gold plated 금도금 kmdogm
goldfish 금붕어 kmbung-ö
golf 골프 kolp-hü; do you play golf?
골프 치세요? kolp-hü ch-hise-yo?
golf clubs 골프 채 kolp-hü ch-he
golf course 골프장 kolp-hüjang
good 좋은 chohün; good evening 안녕
하세요 annyöng hase-yo; good! 좋아요
! choha-yo!; good idea! 좋은 생각
chohün seng-gag; good luck! 행운을
빕니다! heng-unl pimnida!; good
morning 안녕 하세요 annyöng hase-
yo; good quality 양질 의 yang-jil e;
good night (sleep well) 안녕히
주무세요 annyöng-i chumuse-yo; he's
a good dancer 그는 춤을 잘 춰요 knün
ch-huml chal ch-hwö-yo; it's no
good 안돼요 andwe-yo; it looks good
on you 잘 어울려요 chal ö-ullyö-yo;
that looks good (to eat) 그것은 맛있게
보여요 kgösn mashidge po-yö-yo;
that's just as good 그것 만큼 좋아요
kgöd man-k-hüm choha-yo; do you
know a good restaurant? 좋은 음식점을
아세요? chohün ümshigjöml ase-yo?
good-looking 매력 있는 meryög innün
goodbye (to someone leaving) 안녕히
가세요 annyöng-i kase-yo; (to
someone staying) 안녕히 계세요
annyöng-i kese-yo; goodbye, take
care! 안녕, 몸조심 하십시오! annyöng,
momjoshim hashibshi-o!
goose 거위 köwi

gorgeous (woman) 아름다운 armda-un
gosh: oh my gosh! 어마! öma!
gospel 복음 pogm
gourmet 미식가 mishigga
gourmet food 고급 음식 kogb ümshig
government 정부 chöng-bu
governor (of a province) 도지사 tojisa
graceful 인자 한 inja han
grade crossing 건널목 könnölmog
gradually 점차적으로 chömch-hajögro
graduate (finish study) 졸업 해요 choröb
he-yo; (person) 졸업생 churöbseng
graduation 졸업 choröb
gram 그램 krem
grammar 문법 munböb
grammar book 문법 책 munböb ch-heg
granddaughter 손녀 sonnyö; our
granddaughter 우리 손녀 uri sonnyö
grandfather 할아버지 haraböji; my
grandfather 우리 할아버지 uri haraböji
grandmother 할머니 halmöni; my
grandmother 우리 할머니 uri halmöni
grandson 손자 sonja; our grandson 우리
손자 uri sonja
grapefruit 그레이프프루트 kre-ip-hüp-
hürut-hü
grapefruit juice 그레이프프루트 쥬스
kre-ip-hüp-hürut-hü chyusü
grapes 포도 p-hodo
grass 풀 p-hul
grateful 감사 한 kamsa han
gratitude 감사 kamsa
gravy 고기 국물 kogi kungmul
gray 회색 hweseg
grease (auto) 그리스 krisü; (food) 지방
chibang
greasy (food) 기름기 많은 kirmgi
manün
great 위대한 widehan; what a great
view! 잠, 아름다운 경치에요! cham,
armda-un kyöng-ch-hi-e-yo!; thank
you, that's great 고맙습니다, 매우 훌륭
했어요 komabsmnida, me-u hullyung
hessö-yo; how are you -- great,

thanks 어떠세요? -- 아주 건강 해요 öd-döse-yo? - aju kön-gang he-yo

Great Britain 연합 왕국 yönab wang-gug

Greece 그리스 krisü

greedy (overeating) 많이 먹는 mani möngnün; (jealous) 욕심 많은 yogshim manün

Greek (language) 그리스어 kris-ö; It's all Greek to me 모두지 무슨 말인지 모르겠어요 moduji musn marinji morgessö-yo

green 녹색 nogseg; the green one 녹색 의 것 nogsege göd

green pepper 피망 p-himang

green tea 녹차 nogch-ha

grilled 석쇠에 구운 sögswe-e ku-un

grocery store 식품점 shigp-humjöm

ground (land) 땅 ddang

ground beef 다진 쇠고기 tajin swegogi

grounds (sports) 운동장 undong-jang

group 단체 tanch-he; the rest of the group 나머지 그룹 namöji krub

grumble 불편 해요 pulp-hyön he-yo

guarantee (document) 보증 pojng; does it have a guarantee? 보증 해요? pojng he-yo?

guardian 보호자 pohoja

guest 손님 sonnim

guest room 객실 kegshil

guesthouse 여관 yögwan

guide (person) 안내원 annewön; tour guide 관광 안내원 kwan-gwang annewön; where can you get an entertainment guide? 공연 안내서를 어디서 구 할 수 있어요? kong-yön annesörl ödisö ku hal su issö-yo?

guidebook 안내서 annesö

guilty 유죄의 yujwe-e

guitar 기타 kit-ha; guitar music 기타 음악 kit-ha ümag

gull: sea gull 갈매기 kalmegi

gum (of teeth) 잇몸 inmom; (chewing gum) 껌 ggöm

gun (rifle) 총 ch-hong; (pistol) 피스톨 p-hist-hol

guy 남자 namja; the guy at reception 접수부에 있는 사람 chöbsubu-e innün saram; that guy hit me 그 사람은 나를 때렸어요 kü saramn narl dderyössö-yo

gymnasium 체육관 ch-he-yuggwan

gymnastics 체조 ch-hejo

gynecologist 부인과 의사 pu-in-gwa esa

H

hair 머리카락 mörik-harag; please part my hair on the left 가름마를 왼쪽으로 해 주세요 karmmarl wenj-jogro he juse-yo

hair color 머리 염색약 möri yömsegyag

hair dryer 헤어 드라이어 he-ö tra-i-ö

hair spray 헤어 스프레이 he-ö sp-hüre-i

hairbrush 빗 pid

haircut (for men or women) 헤어 커트 he-ö k-höt-hü; an ordinary haircut 보통의 이발 해주세요 pot-hong-e ibal hejuse-yo

hairdresser 미용사 mi-yong-sa

half 반 pan; half a dozen 반 다스 pan tasü; half an hour before 반시간 전에 panshigan chöne; half as much 반 만큼 pan man-k-hüm; a half serving 반 정도 pan chöng-do

half fare 반액 paneg

halibut 넙치 nöbch-hi

hall (corridor) 복도 pogdo; (for meetings) 홀 hol; beer hall 맥주집 megjujib; city hall 시청 shich-höng; concert hall 연주홀 yönjuhol; town hall (government) 시청 shich-höng

ham 햄 hem

hamburger 햄버거 hembögö; please give me a hamburger to go 햄버거를 한개 싸 주세요 hembögörl han-ge ssa juse-

yo
hammer (tool) 망치 mang-ch-hi
hand 손 son; can you lend a hand? 나를 도와 주시겠어요? narl towa jushigessö-yo?
hand baggage 수화물 suhwamul
hand lotion 핸드 로션 hendü roshyön
handbag 손 가방 son kabang
handicapped (see DISABLED)
handicrafts 수공예품 sugong-yep-hum
handkerchief 손수건 sonsugön
handle (of cup, etc) 손잡이 sonjabi
handmade 수제품 sujep-hum
handsome 잘 생긴 chal seng-gin
hang 걸어요 körö-yo; where can I hang my laundry? 세탁물을 어디서 널면 돼요? set-hangmurl ödisö nölmyön dwe-yo?
hang up (telephone) 끊어요 ggnö-yo
hanger (coat hanger) 옷 걸이 od köri
hangover 숙취 sugch-hwi; he has an awful hangover 숙취가 심 해요 sugch-hwiga shim he-yo
happen 일어나요 iröna-yo; how did that happen? 어떻게 일어났어요? öddök-he irönassö-yo?; that will not happen again 그런 일은 다신 일어나지 않을 거에요 krön irn tashin irönaji anl kö-e-yo; such things often happen 그런 일은 자주 일어나요 krön irn chaju iröna-yo
happiness 행복 heng-bog
happy 행복 한 heng-bog han; happy birthday! 생일을 축하 해요 seng-irl ch-huk-ha he-yo; happy new year! 새해에 복 많이 받으세요 sehe-e pog mani padse-yo
harbor 항구 hang-gu
hard 단단한 tandanan; (difficult) 어려운 öryö-un; hard luck! 불은 purn; it's hard to choose 선택 하기가 어려워요 sönt-heg hagiga öryöwö-yo; work hard 수고 해요 sugo he-yo
hard lenses 하드 렌즈 hadü renjü

hard-boiled egg 푹 삶은 계란 p-hug salmn kyeran
hardly 좀처럼 ...지 않어요 chomch-höröm ...ji anö-yo; we hardly ever go 좀처럼 가지 않어요 chomch-höröm kaji anö-yo; there is hardly any money left 돈이 거의 남지 않았어요 toni kö-e namji anassö-yo
hardware store 철물점 ch-hölmuljöm
harm (injury) 손해 sone
harmony 조화 chohwa
harsh 거친 köch-hin
harvest 추수 ch-husu
hassle 말다툼 maldat-hum; it's too big a hassle 몹시 성가신데요 mobshi söng-gashinde-yo
hat 모자 moja
hate (detest) 싫어 해요 shirö he-yo; I hate ... ...를 싫어 해요 ...rl shirö he-yo
have 있어요 issö-yo; have you got a business card? 명함을 가지고 있어요? myöng-aml kajigo issö-yo?; have a nice day! 잘 지내 세요 chal chine se-yo; have you got ...? ... 있어요 ... issö-yo; have you ever been to ...? ...에 가본 적이 있어요? ...e kabon chögi issö-yo?; have fun 재미 있게 놀아요 chemi idge nora-yo; have one of mine 나의 것을 부탁 해요 na-e gösl put-hag he-yo; have you got a pen? 펜이 있어요? p-heni issö-yo?; have you got something for an upset stomach? 위통에 좋은 약 있어요? wit-hong-e chohün yag issö-yo?; I have an ache here 여기가 아퍼요 yögiga ap-hö-yo; I have none 없어요 öbsö-yo; I have high blood pressure 나는 고혈압이 있어요 nanün kohyörabi issö-yo; I have no cash 현금이 없어요 hyön-gmi öbsö-yo; we have already eaten 우리는 벌써 먹었어요 urinün pölsö mögössö-yo; we have been here for a week 여기에 일주일 동안 있었어요 yögi-e ilju-

il tong-an issössö-yo; I have to go 나
는 가지 않으면 안돼요 nanün kaji
anmyön andwe-yo; I have ... 가
있어요 ka issö-yo; I'll have this 이거
주세요 igö juse-yo; we have
reservations 예약 했어요 ye-yag hessö-
yo; I have to go to the toilet 화장실
에 가야 해요 hwajang-shire ka-ya he-
yo; do you have any milk? 우유
있어요? u-yu issö-yo?; can I have it?
가져도 좋아요? kajyödo choha-yo?;
do we have to pay duty? 관세를 내야
돼요? kwanserl ne-ya dwe-yo?; do
you have any children? 아이들이
있으세요? a-idri issüse-yo?; do you
have our reservation? 예약을
받으셨어요? ye-yagl padshyössö-yo?;
could we have some water? 물을 좀
주시겠어요? murl chom chushigessö-
yo?; we don't have ... ...이 없어요
...i öbsö-yo; I don't have much time
시간이 별로 없어요 shigani pyöllo
öbsö-yo; I don't have the time 시간이
없어요 shigani öbsö-yo; I don't have
it with me 지금은 가지고 있지 않아요
chigmn kajigo idji anö-yo; do you
have anything else? 다른 것이 있어요?
tarn göshi issö-yo?; you could have
told me 나에게 알렸어야 했어요 na-ege
allyössö-ya hessö-yo; can I have a
try? 시험 해 봐도 좋아요? shihöm he
pwado choha-yo?

hay fever 건초열 könch-ho-yöl
hazelnuts 개암 ke-am
he 그는 knün; he was very helpful 그
는 많이 도움이 됐어요 knün mani to-
umi dwessö-yo
head 머리 möri; I bumped my head 머리
가 부딪쳤어요 möriga pudijch-hössö-
yo
head cold 두통 감기 tut-hong kamgi
head waiter 헤드 웨이터 hedü we-it-hö
headache 두통 tut-hong; a severe
headache 악성의 두통 agsöng-e tut-

hong; I've got a splitting headache 나
는 두통이 매우 심 해요 nanün tut-
hong-i me-u shim he-yo
headlights 헤드라이트 hedra-it-hü
headline 제목 chemog
headphones 헤드폰 hedp-hon
headquarters 본부 ponbu
health 건강 kön-gang; to your health!
건배! könbe!
healthy (person) 건강 한 kön-gang
han; (healthful) 건강에 좋은 kön-
gang-e chohün
hear 들어요 trö-yo; we heard about that
그 일에 관해서 들었어요 kü ire
kwanesö trössö-yo; I can't hear you
들리지 않아요 tlliji anö-yo
hearing aid 보청기 poch-höng-gi
heart (in body) 심장 shimjang; (mind)
마음 ma-m
heart attack 심장마비 shimjang-mabi
heat 열 yöl; when I get used to the
heat 더위에 익숙 해질 때에 töwi-e
igsug hejil dde-e
heat wave 열파 yölp-ha
heater (auto) 히터 hit-hö; electric
heater 전기 난로 chön-gi nanro; space
heater 실내 남방기 shilne nambang-gi
heating 난방 nanbang; central heating
집중 난방 chibjung nanbang
heavy 무거운 mugö-un
hedge 울타리 ult-hari
heel 뒤축 twich-hug
height 키 k-hi; (uplands) 고지 koji;
what is its height? 높이는 얼마나 돼요?
nop-hinün ölmana dwe-yo?
helicopter 헬리콥터 hellik-hobt-hö
hell! 빌어먹을! pirömögl!; it's hell! 지
옥 같아요! chi-og kat-ha-yo!; like
hell it is! 그럴리가 없어요! krölliga
öbsö-yo!
hello! (any time of day) 안녕 하세요
annyöng hase-yo
helmet (for road) 헬멧 helmed; crash
helmet 안전 헬멧 anjön helmed

help (assist) 도와요 towa-yo; help! 도와 주세요! towa juse-yo!; please help me fill out this form 이 사항에 써 넣을 것을 도와 주세요 i sahang-e ssö nöhül gösl towa juse-yo; can you help me with my luggage? 짐 좀 운반 해 주시겠어요? chim chom unban he jushigessö-yo?; could you help me? 나를 도와 주시겠어요? narl towa jushigessö-yo?; I'm afraid we can't help you 미안 합니다만, 도울 수가 없어요 mi-an hamnidaman, to-ul suga öbsö-yo; thank you for your help 도와 줘서 고맙습니다 towa chwösö komabsmnida; is there anyone who can help? 누구 도와줄 사람 있어요? nugu towajul saram issö-yo?

helpful 도움이 되는 to-umi dwenün; that was helpful 그 것은 도움이 됐어요 kü gösn to-umi dwessö-yo

helping (serving) 그릇 krd; one helping (of food) 한 그릇 han krd; may I have a second helping? 한 그릇 더 주시겠어요? han krd tö jushigessö-yo?

hemorrhoids 치질 ch-hijil

hepatitis 간염 kanyöm

her 그 여자 kü yöja; her husband 그의 남편 k-e namp-hyön; with her 그 여자와 같이 kü yöjawa kat-hi; that is her bag 그 것은 그 여자 의 가방에요 kü gösn kü yöja e kabang-e-yo; it is for her 그 여자에게 줄 것이에요 kü yöja-ege chul göshi-e-yo; I'm worried about her 그녀를 걱정 해요 knyörl kögjöng he-yo; could you send it to her? 그 여자에게 보내 주시겠어요? kü yöja-ege pone chushigessö-yo?

herbs (spice) 향료 hyang-ryo; (medicine) 약초 yagch-ho

here 여기 yögi; here is a gift for you 선물이에요 sönmuri-e-yo; here is my card 제 명함이에요 che myöng-ami-e-yo; come here 이리 오세요 iri ose-yo;

from here to the ocean 여기서부터 바다까지 yögisöbut-hö padag-gaji; I'm here as a tourist 관광하러 왔어요 kwan-gwang-arö wassö-yo; right here 바로 여기에 paro yögi-e; over here 여기로 yögiro; what's happening here? 여기는 무슨 일이 일어나요? yöginün musn iri iröna-yo?; is he here? 그는 여기에 있어요? knün yögi-e issö-yo?; please sign here 여기에 서명 해 주세요 yögi-e sömyöng he juse-yo; please stop here 여기서 멈추어 주세요 yögisö mömch-hu-ö juse-yo; while I'm here 내가 여기에 있을 때 nega yögi-e issl dde; is it around here? 이 근처에 있어요? i gnch-hö-e issö-yo?; I just got here 나는 이제 도착 했어요 nanün ije toch-hag hessö-yo; I'm in pain here 여기가 아퍼요 yögiga ap-hö-yo; may I sit here? 여기에 앉아도 좋아요? yögi-e anjado choha-yo?; please put it down here 그것을 여기에 내려놔 주세요 kgösl yögi-e neryönwa juse-yo

hero 영웅 yöng-ung

herring 청어 ch-höng-ö

hers 그 여자의 kü yöja-e

hey! 이봐요! ibwa-yo!

hi! 안녕 하세요 annyöng hase-yo

hibiscus 무궁화 mugung-wa

hiccups 딸꾹질 ddalg-gugjil

hide 숨어요 sumö-yo

high 높은 nop-hün

highchair 아기용 의자 agi-yong eja

highland 고지 koji

highlighter (for face) 하이라이트 ha-ira-it-hü

highway 고속도로 kosogdoro; interstate highway 국도 kugdo

hike (see also WALK) 하이킹 가요 ha-ik-hing ka-yo

hiking 하이킹 ha-ik-hing

hill 언덕 öndög; at the bottom of the hill 언덕의 밑에 öndöge mit-he; at the top of the hill 언덕 꼭대기에 öndög ggogdegi-e

hilly 언덕이 많은 öndögi manün

him 그 사람 kü saram; look at him 그
를 좀 봐요 krl chom pwa-yo; that is
for him 그 사람에게 줄 것이에요 kü
saramege chul göshi-e-yo; will you
ask him? 그에게 물어 봐 주시겠어요? k-
ege murö pwa jushigessö-yo?; I work
with him 그와 함께 일 하고 있어요
kwa hamg-ge il hago issö-yo; when
can I see him? 언제 뵐 수 있을까요?
önje pwel su isslg-ga-yo?; I gave that
to him 그것을 그에게 드렸어요 kgösl
k-ege tryössö-yo

hip 엉덩이 öng-döng-i

hire 고용 해요 ko-yong he-yo

his 그 사람의 kü sarame

historian 역사가 yögsaga

history 역사 yögsa; the history of
Korea 한국 역사 han-gug yögsa

hit 쳐요 ch-hyö-yo; that guy hit me
그 사람은 나를 때렸어요 kü saramn
narl dderyössö-yo

hit record 유명 한 레코오드 yumyöng
han rek-ho-odü

hitchhike 차좀 대워 달라고 해요 ch-
hajom tewö tallago he-yo

hitchhiker 히치하이커 hich-hiha-ik-hö

hobby 취미 ch-hwimi

hockey 하키 hak-hi

hold (take) 쥐어요 chwi-ö-yo; could
you hold my place? 내 자리를 봐
주시겠어요? ne charirl pwa jushigessö-
yo?; hold the line, please 끊지 마세요
gglch-hi mase-yo

hole 구멍 kumöng

holiday 휴일 hyu-il; public holiday 공
휴일 kong-yu-il

Holland 네덜란드 nedöllandü

home 집 chib; (in my country)
고향에(서) kohyang-e(sö); at home
집에(서) chibe(sö); he goes home
tomorrow 내일 집으로 돌아가요 ne-il
chibro toraga-yo; at my home 내 집에

ne chibe; I'm staying home tonight 오
늘 밤은 집에 있어요 onl pamn chibe
issö-yo; nobody is at home 아무도
집에 없어요 amudo chibe öbsö-yo; may
I take you home? 댁까지 태워다
드릴까요? tegg-gaji t-hewöda trilg-ga-
yo?; I want to go home 집에 돌아가고
싶어요 chibe toragago ship-hö-yo

home address 집 주소 chib chuso

homemade 집에서 만든 chibesö mandn

homesickness 향수병 hyang-subyöng

hometown 고향 kohyang

honest 정직한 chöng-jik-han

honestly? 정말이에요? chöng-mari-e-yo?

honey 꿀 ggul

honeymoon 신혼 여행 shinon yöheng

Hong Kong 홍콩 hong-k-hong

hood (auto) 본네트 ponnet-hü

hop: hop in! (to car) 타세요! t-hase-
yo!

hope 희망 hemang; I hope so 그렇기를
바래요 krök-hirl pare-yo; I hope it
will clear up 날씨가 맑으면 좋겠어요
nalshiga malgmyön chok-hessö-yo; I
hope you enjoy it 마음에 드셨으면
좋겠어요 ma-me tshyössmyön chok-
hessö-yo; I hope that ... ...면
좋겠어요 ...myön chok-hessö-yo

horizon 지평선 chip-hyöng-sön

horn (auto) 크락션 k-hüragshyön

horrible 무시무시한 mushimushihan

hors d'oeuvre 칵테일 음식 k-hagt-he-il
ümshig

horse 말 mal

horse race 경마 kyöng-ma

horseradish 서양고추냉이 sö-yang-goch-
huneng-i

hose (tube) 호스 hosü

hospital 병원 pyöng-wön

hospitality 환대 hwande

hostel 호스텔 host-hel; youth hostel 유
스호스텔 yushost-hel; I'm staying at
the youth hostel 유스호스텔에 묵어요
yushost-here mugö-yo

Pronounce: a father; e let; i machine; o note; ö löng; u rude; ü fürther

hot 더운 tö-un; (spicy) 매운 me-un;
boiling hot 매우 더운 me-u tö-un; less
hot (spicy) 적게 매운 chögge me-un;
too hot 너무 더워요 nömu töwö-yo;
it's so hot 매우 더워요 me-u töwö-yo;
there is no hot water 뜨거운 물이
나오지 않아요 ddgö-un muri na-oji
anö-yo
hot chocolate 코코아 k-hok-ho-a
hot dog 핫도그 haddogü
hot pepper 고추 koch-hu
hot springs 온천 onch-hön
hot-water bottle 탕파 t-hang-p-ha
hotel (Western style) 호텔 hot-hel;
(Korean style) 여관 yögwan; the hotel
is pretty ordinary 그 호텔에 특별한
것이 아무것도 없어요 kü ot-here t-
hügbyöran göshi amugöddo öbsö-yo;
our hotel 우리의 호텔 uri-e hot-hel;
this hotel 이 호텔 i ot-hel; at the
hotel 호텔에(서) hot-here(sö); the best
hotel in town 시내에서 제일 좋은 호텔
shine-esö che-il chohün hot-hel;
please call another hotel for me 다른
호텔에 전화 좀 걸어 주세요 tarn hot-
here chönwa chom körö juse-yo; a
better than average hotel 보통 이상 의
호텔 pot-hong isang e hot-hel; a less
than average hotel 보통 이하 의 호텔
pot-hong iha e hot-hel; the name of
the hotel 호텔의 이름 hot-here irm;
would you send it to my hotel? 내
호텔로 배달 해 주시겠어요? ne hot-
hello pedal he jushigessö-yo?
hotel bus 호텔 버스 hot-hel pösü
hotel clerk 호텔 안내원 hot-hel
annewön
hour 시간 shigan; rush hour 러시아워
röshi-awö; business hours 영업 시간
yöng-öb shigan; half an hour before
반시간 전에 panshigan chöne; a half
hour 반 시간 pan shigan; in an hour
한 시간 후에 han shigan hu-e; a
quarter hour 십오분 shibobun; less

than an hour 한시간 이하 hanshigan
iha; what's the price per hour? 한
시간에 얼마에요? han shigane ölma-e-
yo?
house 집 chib; Blue House (Presidential
Palace) 청와대 ch-höng-wade;
boarding house 하숙집 hasugjib; the
house specialty 명물 myöng-mul; their
house 그 사람들 의 집 kü saramdl e
chib
housecoat 실내복 shilnebog
housekeeper 가정부 kajöng-bu
housewares 가정용품 kajöng-yong-p-
hum
housewife 주부 chubu
how 어떻게 öd-dök-he; how are you
doing? 안녕 하십니까 annyöng
hashimnig-ga; how much do you
charge? 얼마를 청구하세요? ölmarl ch-
höng-guhase-yo?; how much does it
come to? 얼마 드리면 되지요 ölma
trimyön dweji-yo; how do I contact
...? ...과 어떻게 연락 해요? ...gwa
öd-dök-he yönrag he-yo?; how far is
it from ... to ...? ...부터 ...까지
얼마나 멀라요? ...but-hö ...ggaji
ölmana mölla-yo?; how about a
drink? 술 한잔 어때요? sul hanjan öd-
de-yo?; how about going for a drive?
드라이브 하는게 어때요? tra-ibü hanün-
ge öd-de-yo?; how much is it to ...?
...까지 얼마에요? ...ggaji ölma-e-
yo?; how do you feel today? 오늘은
기분이 어때요 onrn kibuni öd-de-yo;
how are you? -- fine 안녕 하세요? --
예, 덕분에 annyöng hase-yo? - ye,
tögbune; how can I get to ...?
...에는 어떻게 가면 돼요? ...enün öd-
dök-he kamyön dwe-yo?; how did
that happen? 어떻게 일어났어요? öd-
dök-he irönassö-yo?; how many?
(things / people) 몇 개 / 분 myöt ke
/ bun; how many times? 몇 번? myöt
pön?; how nice! 정말 좋군요! chöng-

mal chok-hunyo!; how long does it last? 얼마나 계속돼요? ölmana kyesogdwe-yo?; how old are you? 나이가 몇살이에요? na-iga myöt-hsari-e-yo?; how is this pronounced? 이것을 어떻게 발음 해요? igösl öd-dök-he parm he-yo?; how often do the buses run? 버스는 몇분마다 있어요? pösnün myödp-hunmada issö-yo?; how do you say ... in Korean? ...을 한국말로 어떻게 말 해요 ...l han-gungmallo öd-dök-he mal he-yo; how was it? -- so-so 어땠어요? -- 그저 그랬어요 öd-dessö-yo? - kjö kressö-yo; how do you write it? 어떻게 써요? öd-dök-he ssö-yo?; would you show me how to do it? 옳은 방법을 가르쳐 주시겠어요? orn pang-böbl karch-hyö jushigessö-yo?

however: however you'd like 좋을 대로 chohül tero

humid 습기 있는 sbgi innün; it's humid 습기가 있어요 sbgiga issö-yo

humidity 습기 sbgi

humor 유모어 yumo-ö

hungry 폐가 고픈 p-hega kop-hün; I'm hungry 배가 고파요 pega kop-ha-yo

hurry (to rush) 서둘러요 södullö-yo; hurry up! 서둘러요! södullö-yo!; no need to hurry 서두를 필요는 없어요 södurl p-hiryonün öbsö-yo

hurt (to ache) 아파요 ap-ha-yo; I'm hurt 내가 다쳤어요 nega tach-hyössö-yo; is anyone hurt? 부상자가 있어요? pusang-jaga issö-yo?

husband (my) 남편 namp-hyön; her husband 그의 남편 k-e namp-hyön; did you see my husband? 제 남편을 보셨어요? che namp-hyönl poshyössö-yo?

hydrofoil 수중 익선 sujung igsön

I

I (often omitted in Korean!) 나 na; I don't have much time 시간이 별로 없어요 shigani pyöllo öbsö-yo; I don't know yet 아직은 모르겠어요 ajign morgessö-yo; I don't understand Korean 한국말을 몰라요 han-gungmarl molla-yo; I have indigestion 소화불량 이에요 sohwabullyang-i-e-yo; I speak a little Korean 한국말을 좀 해요 han-gungmarl chom he-yo; I feel ill 몸이 불편 해요 momi pulp-hyön he-yo; I don't like that 나는 그것을 좋아 하지 않어요 nanün kgösl choha haji anö-yo

ice 얼음 örm; with ice 얼음을 넣어 örml nöhö

ice cream 아이스 크림 a-isü k-hürim; a vanilla ice cream 바닐라 아이스크림 한개 panilla a-isk-hürim han-ge

ice-cream cone 콘 아이스크림 k-hon a-isk-hürim

iced coffee 아이스 커피 a-isü k-höp-hi

idea 생각 seng-gag; good idea! 좋은 생각 chohün seng-gag

ideal 이상적인 isang-jögin

identity card 신분 증명서 shinbun chüng-myöng-sö

idiot 바보 pabo

if ... 만일 ...면 manil ...myön; if we can 만일 할수 있으면 manil halsu issmyön; if you should come to America 만일 미국에 가보면 manil miguge kabomyön; if you find them 만일 찾으면 manil ch-hajmyön; if you can 만일 주실 수가 있으면 manil chushil suga issmyön; if not 않으면 anmyön; if it's sunny 날씨가 좋으면 nalshiga chohümyön; even if ... 만일 ... 더라도 manil ... törado; mind if I smoke? 담배 피워도 좋아요? tambe p-hiwödo choha-yo?

ignition 점화장치 chömwajang-ch-hi

ill 병든 pyöng-dn; seriously ill 심각하게 병든 shimgag hage pyöng-dn

illegal 불법의 pulböbe

illegible 읽기 어려운 ilgi öryö-un; it's illegible 읽을 수가 없어요 ilgl suga öbsö-yo

illness 병 pyöng

imagination 상상력 sang-sang-ryög

imitation (artificial) 모조품 mojop-hum

immediately 즉시 chügshi

immigration 이민 imin

impatient 참을 수 없는 ch-haml su ömnün

import (buy) 수입 해요 su-ib he-yo

important 중대한 chung-dehan; it's quite important 매우 중대 해요 me-u chung-de he-yo

imported 수입 한 su-ib han

imports 수입 품 su-ib p-hum

impossible 불가능한 pulganüng-an

impressive 인상적인 insang-jögin

improve 좋아져요 chohajyö-yo

improvement 개선 kesön

in (with verbs of existence; see also INSIDE) ...에 ...e; (with verbs of action) ...에서 ...esö; in New York 뉴욕에(서) nyu-yoge(sö); in an hour 한 시간 후에 han shigan hu-e; in English 영어로 yöng-öro; in Korean 한국 말로 han-gug mallo; they live in Korea 한국에서 살어요 han-gugesö sarö-yo; is it included in the price? 그것이 값에 포함 됐어요? kgöshi kabse p-hoham dwessö-yo?

in-law 사돈 sadon

incense 향 hyang

inch 인치 inch-hi

include 포함 해요 p-hoham he-yo; is everything included? 전부 들어 있어요? chönbu trö issö-yo?; does the rate include milage? 계산에 주행 거리가 포함 돼요? kyesane chuheng köriga p-hoham dwe-yo?; does the price of this film include processing? 이 가격에는 현상료도 포함되어 있어요? i gagyögenün hyönsang-ryodo p-hohamdwe-ö issö-yo?

including ... ...도 넣어서 ...do nöhösö

income (money) 수입 su-ib

inconvenient 불편한 pulp-hyönan

increase (growth) 증가 chüng-ga

indecent (ill-bred) 버릇 없는 pörd ömnün; indecent behavior 추잡한 행동 ch-hujap-han heng-dong

independent 독립한 togrip-han

India 인도 indo

Indian (adjective) 인도 의 indo e; (person) 인도 사람 indo saram; West Indian (adjective) 서인도 제도의 sö-indo chedo-e

indicator (auto) 계기판 kyegip-han

indies: West Indies 서인도 제도 sö-indo chedo

indigestion 소화 불량 sohwa pullyang; I have indigestion 소화불량이에요 sohwabullyang-i-e-yo

Indonesia 인도네시아 indoneshi-a

indoors 실내에 shilne-e

industrious 부지런 한 pujirön han

industry (business) 산업 sanöb

inedible: it's inedible 먹을 수 없어요 mögl su öbsö-yo

inefficient (bad service) 서비스가 나쁜 söbisga nab-bn

inexpensive 싼 ssan

infected 감염 된 kamyöm dwen

infection 감염 kamyöm

infectious 전염하는 chönyömanün

inflammation 연소 yönso

inflation 인플레이 inp-hülle-i

influence 영향 yöng-yang

inform 알려 줘요 allyö chwö-yo

informal 자연스러운 cha-yönsrö-un

information 안내 anne; tourist

information office 관광 안내소 kwan-gwang anneso

information desk 안내창구 annech-hang-gu

information office 안내소 anneso

ingredients 성분 söng-bun

inhabitant 주민 chumin

injection 주사 chusa

injured 다친 tach-hin; he's been badly injured 그는 심하게 다쳤어요 knün shimage tach-hyössö-yo

injury 상처 sang-ch-hö

inn (Korean) 여관 yögwan

innocent 순수한 sunsuhan; (not guilty) 죄가 없는 chwega ömnün

inquiries: directory inquiries 전화 번호 안내 chönwa pöno anne

insect 벌레 pölle

insect bite 벌레 물 pölle mulm; do you have something for insect bites? 벌레물린데 좋은 약 있어요? pöllemullinde chohün yag issö-yo?

insect repellent 방충제 pang-ch-hung-je

insecticide 살충제 salch-hung-je

insert (verb) 끼워요 ggiwö-yo

inside 안에 ane; may I take pictures inside? 안에서 사진을 찍어도 돼요? anesö sajinl jjigödo dwe-yo?

insignia 훈장 hunjang

insomnia 불면증 pulmyönjng

inspection 검열 kömyöl; customs inspection 통관 t-hong-gwan

instant coffee 인스턴트 커피 inst-hönthü k-höp-hi

instead 그 대신에 kü deshine; instead of ... ... 대신에 ... teshine

instruction (lessons) 교육 kyo-yug

insulin 인슐린 inshyullin

insult (insolence) 모욕 mo-yog

insurance 보험 pohöm; comprehensive insurance 종합 보험 chong-ab pohöm; group insurance 단체 보험 tanch-he pohöm; life insurance 생명 보험 seng-myöng pohöm

insurance policy 보험 증서 pohöm chüng-sö

intellectual (person) 지적인 chijögin

intelligent 지적인 chijögin

intend: I intend to sue 고소 하겠어요 koso hagessö-yo

intentional 고의의 ko-e-e

interest (enjoyment) 재미 chemi; points of interest 명소 myöng-so

interesting 재미 있는 chemi innün; that's most interesting 그것은 매우 재미 있어요 kgösn me-u chemi issö-yo; it looks very interesting 재미있어 보여요 chemi-issö po-yö-yo

intermission 휴식 시간 hyushig shigan

international 국제적인 kugjejögin; international telephone call 국제 전화 kugje chönwa

international driver's license 국제 운전 면허증 kugje unjön myönöjng

interpret 통역 해요 t-hong-yög he-yo

interpreter 통역 할 사람 t-hong-yög hal saram

intersection (4-way) 네거리 negöri

interstate highway 국도 kugdo

into ... ...에 들어 ...e trö; he's really into fitness 그는 보건 체조에 열심이에요 knün pogön ch-hejo-e yölshimi-e-yo; could you change this into won? 이것을 원화로 바꿔 주시겠어요? igösl wönwaro pag-gwö jushigessö-yo?; which bus can I take into town? 도시로 가려면 어느 버스를 타야 해요? toshiro karyömyön önü pösrl t-ha-ya he-yo?

introduce 소개 해요 soge he-yo; introduce oneself 인사 해요 insa he-yo; please introduce yourself 인사 하세요 insa hase-yo; will you introduce me to them? 저분들을 좀 소개해 주시겠어요? chöbundrl chom sogehe jushigessö-yo?

introduction 소개 soge

invalid (document, etc) 무효한

muhyohan; (disabled person) 불구자 pulguja

invention 발명 palmyŏng

invitation 초대 ch-hode

invite 초대 해요 ch-hode he-yo; I'd like to invite you to dinner 저녁 식사에 초대 하겠어요 chŏnyŏg shigsa-e ch-hode hagessŏ-yo

iodine 옥도정기 ogdojŏng-gi

Iran 이란 iran

Ireland 아일랜드 a-illendü; Northern Ireland 북아일랜드 puga-illendü

Irish 아일랜드의 a-illend-e

Irishman 아일랜드 사람 a-illendü saram

Irishwoman 아일랜드 사람 a-illendü saram

iron (substance) 철 ch-höl;

iron (verb) 다려요 taryö-yo; (appliance) 다리미 tarimi; would you iron these for me? 이것을 다려 주시겠어요? igösl taryö jushigessö-yo? is (often not translated!) (이)에요 (i)e-yo; is camping allowed here? 여기에서 캠프를 해도 되요? yögi-esö k-hemp-hürl hedo dwe-yo?; is it contagious? 전염이 돼요? chönyömi dwe-yo?; is it crowded? 사람이 많아요? sarami mana-yo?; is it done? 다 됐어요? ta dwessö-yo?; is there a curfew? 통행금지가 있어요? t-hong-eng-gmjiga issö-yo?; is there a program in English? 영어로 된 프로그램 있어요? yöng-öro dwen p-hürogrem issö-yo?; is there a sale today? 오늘 할인 판매 해요? onl harin p-hanme he-yo?; is there a scenic route? 경치 좋은 길이 있어요? kyöng-ch-hi chohün kiri issö-yo?; is there an English translation of ...? ...을 영어로 번역 한 것이 있어요? ...l yöng-öro pönyög han göshi issö-yo?

island 섬 söm

isolated 고립 된 korib dwen

Israel 이스라엘 isra-el

it: it looks very interesting 재미있어

보여요 chemi-issö po-yö-yo; it really was delicious 맛있게 먹었어요 mashidge mögössö-yo; it itches 가렵게 해요 karyöbge he-yo; is it ...? (이)에요? (i)e-yo?; that's it (that's right) 맞었어요 majössö-yo

Italy 이탈리아 it-halli-a

itch 가려워요 karyöwö-yo

itinerary 스케줄 sk-hejul

ivory 상아 sang-a

J

jack (auto) 잭 cheg

jacket 자켓 chak-hed; dinner jacket 턱시도 t-högshido; life jacket 구명 자켓 kumyöng chak-hed; sport jacket 스포츠 자켓 sp-hoch-hü chak-hed

jade 옥 og

jam 잼 chem; traffic jam 교통 체증 kyot-hong ch-hejng

janitor 수위 suwi

January 일월 irwöl

Japan 일본 ilbon

Japan sea 동해 tong-e

Japanese (adjective) 일본 의 ilbon e; (person) 일본 사람 ilbon saram; (language) 일본어 ilbonö

jazz 째즈 jjejü

jazz club 재즈 클럽 chejü k-hüllöb

jealous 샘이 많은 semi manün; she's jealous 그는 샘이 많아요 knün semi mana-yo

jeans 청바지 ch-höng-baji

jellyfish 해파리 hep-hari

jet lag 제트기 피로 chet-hügi p-hiro; I've got jet lag 제트기 피로를 앓고 있어요 chet-hügi p-hirorl alk-ho issö-yo

jetty 방파제 pang-p-haje

jewelry 보석 posög

jewelry store 보석상 posögsang
Jewish 유태인의 yut-he-ine
job 일 il
jog (to run) 조깅 해요 choging he-yo
jogging 조깅 choging; I do jogging 조깅 해요 choging he-yo
join: would you join us? (go with) 함께 가 주시겠어요? hamg-ge ka jushigessö-yo?; (sit with) 함께 앉아 주시겠어요? hamg-ge anja jushigessö-yo?; where can I join the tour? 관광을 어디서부터 할 수 있어요? kwan-gwang-l ödisöbut-hö hal su issö-yo?
joint (of body) 관절 kwanjöl
joke 농담 nong-dam; you must be joking! 농담이시겠지요 nong-damishigedji-yo
Jordan 요르단 yordan
journey 여행 yöheng; have a nice journey! 잘 다녀오세요 chal tanyö-ose-yo
judge (person) 판사 p-hansa
jug 항아리 hang-ari
juice 쥬스 chyusü; fruit juice 과일 쥬스 kwa-il chyusü; grapefruit juice 그레이프프루트 쥬스 kre-ip-hüp-hürut-hü chyusü; lime juice 라임 쥬스 ra-im chyusü; orange juice 오렌지 쥬스 orenji chyusü; pineapple juice 파인애플 쥬스 p-ha-inep-hül chyusü; tomato juice 토마토 쥬스 t-homat-ho chyusü
July 칠월 ch-hirwöl
junction (railroad station) 갈아 타는 역 kara t-hanün yög; (intersection) 교차점 kyoch-hajöm; (interchange) 인터체인지 int-höch-he-inji
June 유월 yuwöl
junk (garbage) 폐물 p-hemul; (ship) 정크선 chöng-k-hüsön; (poor quality goods) 하찮은 것 hach-hanün göd
just (exactly) 바로 paro; just let me get dressed 옷을 좀 입겠어요 osl chom ibgessö-yo; just for fun 장난삼아

chang-nansama; just a little 조금만 주세요 chogmman chuse-yo; just a second! 잠깐만요! chamg-ganmanyo!; just a trim please (hair) 대충 다듬어 주세요 tech-hung tadmö juse-yo; that's just the problem 그게 바로 문제란 말이에요. kge paro munjeran mari-e-yo; that's just as good 그것 만큼 좋아요 kgöd man-k-hüm choha-yo; I'm just looking 그저 구경 하는 거에요 kjö kugyöng hanün kö-e-yo; one just like this 이와 같은 것 iwa kat-hün göd; I'll just watch 보기만 하겠어요 pogiman hagessö-yo; I was just going to go 나는 막 가려고 했어요 nanün mag karyögo hessö-yo; please give me just a little 조금만 주십시오 chogmman chushibshi-o

K

karat (diamond) 캐러트 k-heröt-hü;
karat (gold) 케이 k-he-i
keep (hold) 가지고 있어요 kajigo issö-yo; keep the change 거스름 돈은 가지세요 gösrm tonün kajise-yo; keep quiet! 가만히 계세요! kamani kyese-yo!; it keeps me awake 그것이 나를 잠 못 들게 해요 kgöshi narl cham mod tlge he-yo; let's keep in touch 계속 연락 해요 kyesog yönrag he-yo
kerosene 등유 tng-yu
ketchup 케챂 k-hech-hyap
kettle 주전자 chujönja
key 열쇠 yölswe; car keys 차 열쇠 ch-ha yölswe; I left my key in the room 열쇠를 방에 놓고 문을 잠갔어요 yölswerl pang-e nok-ho munl chamgassö-yo; it's the wrong key 틀린 열쇠에요 t-hüllin yölswe-e-yo
kid (child) 아이 a-i; I'm not kidding 농

담이 아니에요 nong-dami ani-e-yo
kidneys 신장 shinjang
kill 죽여요 chugyö-yo
killer: fly killer 파리약 / 스프레이 p-hari-yag / sp-hüre-i
kilo(gram) 킬로그램 k-hillogrem
kilometer 킬로미터 k-hillomit-hö
kimchee 김치 kimch-hi; kimchee doesn't agree with me. 김치는 내 몸에 안 맞아요. kimch-hinün ne mome an maja-yo.; cucumber kimchee 오이소박이 o-isobagi; radish kimchee 깍두기 ggagdugi
kimchee stew 김치 찌개 kimch-hi jjige
kin: next of kin 가까운 가족 kag-ga-un kajog
kind (kindly) 친절 한 ch-hinjöl han; what kind of 무슨 musn; what kind of (precious) stone is that? 저것은 무슨 보석이에요? chögösn musn posögi-e-yo?; that's very kind of you 친절히 해주셔서 감사합니다 ch-hinjöri hejushyösö kamsahamnida; a different kind of ... 다른 종류의 ... tarn chong-ryu-e ...
kindergarten 유치원 yuch-hiwön
king 왕 wang
kipper 훈제한 청어 hunjehan ch-höng-ö
kisaeng (Korean geisha) 기생 kiseng
kiss (verb) 키스 해요 k-hisü he-yo
kitchen 부엌 pu-ök
kitchen towel 행주 heng-ju
kitchenette 간이 부엌 kani pu-ök
kite 연 yön
kite flying 연날리기 yönnalligi
kiwi (fruit) 키위 k-hiwi
Kleenex (tm) 클리넥스 k-hüllinegsü
knee 무릎 murp; below the knee 무릎 아래에 murp are-e
knife (dinner) 나이프 na-ip-hü; (to cut) 칼 k-hal
knitting 뜨개질 ddegejil
knock (sound) 노크 nok-hü; I've

knocked my head 머리를 부딪쳤어요 mörirl pudijch-hyössö-yo; she's been knocked over 그는 때려 눕혀졌어요 knün dderyö nup-hyöjyössö-yo
knot (tied) 매듭 medb
know 알아요 ara-yo; we know each other 우리는 서로 알아요 urinün söro ara-yo; I don't know this area 그 근처를 몰라요 kü gnch-hörl molla-yo; we don't know her 그 여자를 몰라요 kü yöjarl molla-yo; I don't know yet 아직은 모르겠어요 ajign morgessö-yo; we don't know what to do 어찌 해야 좋을지 모르겠어요 öj-ji he-ya chohülji morgessö-yo; I don't know where he is 그가 어디에 있는지 몰라요 kga ödi-e innünji molla-yo; I'll let you know 알려 주겠어요 allyö chugessö-yo; would you let us know? 알려 주시겠어요? allyö jushigessö-yo?
knowledge 지식 chishig
Korea 한국 han-gug; North Korea 북한 puk-han; South Korea 남한 naman; made in Korea 한국제 han-gugje; the history of Korea 한국 역사 han-gug yögsa; they live in Korea 한국에서 살아요 han-gugesö sarö-yo; I really love Korea 한국을 정말 좋아 해요 han-gugl chöng-mal choha he-yo; we bought it in Korea 한국에서 샀어요 han-gugesö sassö-yo
Korean (adjective) 한국 의 han-gug e; (person) 한국 사람 han-gug saram; (language) 한국말 han-gungmal; Korean breakfast 한식 아침 식사 hanshig ach-him shigsa; Korean writing 한글 han-gl; in Korean characters 한글로 han-gllo; in Korean 한국 말로 han-gug mallo; the Korean language 한국어 han-gugö; the Korean people 한국 사람 han-gug saram; he speaks Korean fluently 그는 한국말을 유창하게 해요 knün han-gungmarl yuch-hang-age he-yo; a traditional

Korean meal 전통적 한국식 식사 chönt-hong-jög han-gugshig shigsa; I don't understand Korean 한국말을 몰라요 han-gungmarl molla-yo; I can't read Korean 한글을 읽을 수가 없어요 han-grl ilgl suga öbsö-yo; are there Western or Korean meals? 음식은 양식이에요, 한식이에요? ümshign yang-shigi-e-yo, hanshigi-e-yo?; I speak a little Korean 한국말을 좀 해요 han-gungmarl chom he-yo; could you teach us Korean? 한국어를 가르쳐 주시겠어요? han-gugörl karch-hyö jushigessö-yo?; I want to improve my Korean 내 한국 말을 향상 시키고 싶은데요 ne han-gug marl hyang-sang shik-higo ship-hünde-yo; how do you say ... in Korean? ...을 한국말로 어떻게 말 해요 ...l han-gungmallo öd-dök-he mal he-yo

Korean backgammon 윷 yuch
Korean bedding 이부자리 ibujari
Korean card game 화투 hwat-hu
Korean checkers 바둑 padug
Korean chess 장기 chang-gi
Korean clothing 한복 hanbog
Korean fencing 검도 kömdo
Korean style food 한식 hanshig
Korean style room 온돌 방 ondol pang
Korean War 한국 전쟁 han-gug chönjeng
Korean wrestling 씨름 sshirm
Kuwait 쿠웨이트 k-huwe-it-hü
Kwangju Incident 광주 사태 kwang-ju sat-he

*

L

label 라벨 rabel
labor 노동 nodong
laces (shoes) 구두 끈 kudu ggn
lack (not have) 없어요 öbsö-yo
lacquer ware 칠기 ch-hilgi
ladies room 여자 화장실 yöja hwajang-shil
lady 숙녀 sungnyö; ladies and gentlemen! 여러분 yöröbun
lake 호수 hosu
lamb (meat) 새끼양 고기 seg-gi-yang kogi
lamp 램프 remp-hü
lampshade 램프의 갓 remp-hü-e kad
land (soil) 땅 ddang
lane (highway) 차선 ch-hasön
language 말 mal; obscene language 속어 sogö; the Korean language 한국어 han-gugö; the English language 영어 yöng-ö
language course 어학 과정 öhag kwajöng
large (size) 큰 k-hün; extra large 엑스라지 egsraji; three times as large as ... ...보다 세 배로 커요 ...boda se pero k-hö-yo; I'd like the money in large bills 큰 돈으로 주세요 k-hün tonro chuse-yo
laryngitis 후두염 hudu-yöm
lass 소녀 sonyö
last (latest) 최후의 ch-hwehu-e; last night 어젯밤 öjedbam; last month 지난 달 chinan tal; last time 지난 번에 chinan pöne; at last 마침내 mach-himne; when is the last bus? 마지막 버스는 언제 있어요? majimag pösnün önje issö-yo?
last name 성 söng

late 늦은 njn; it's rather late 매우 늦어졌어요 me-u njöjyössö-yo; because it's getting late 늦어지기 때문에 njöjigi ddemune; is the train late? 열차가 지연 돼요? yölch-haga chi-yön dwe-yo?; please don't be late 늦지 말아 주세요 njji marö juse-yo; I'll be back late 늦 게 들어 오겠어요 ndge trö ogessö-yo; now it's too late 지금은 너무 늦어졌어요 chigmn nömu njöjyössö-yo; I usually get up late 나는 보통 늦게 일어나요 nanün pot-hong ndge iröna-yo

lately 최근 ch-hwegn

later 나중에 najung-e; see you later 나 중에 뵙겠어요 najung-e pwebgessö-yo; we'll be back later 나중에 돌아오겠어요 najung-e tora-ogessö-yo; is there a later flight than that? 그 보다 더 늦은 비행기가 있어요? kü boda tö njn piheng-giga issö-yo?

latest 최신의 ch-hweshine

laugh (verb) 웃어요 usö-yo; (noun) 웃 음 usm; it's nothing to laugh about 웃을 것 없어요 usl göd öbsö-yo

laundromat 셀프 서비스 세탁소 selp-hü söbisü set-hagso

laundry (wash) 빨래 bballe; (building) 세탁소 set-hagso; this laundry isn't mine 이 빨래는 내 것이 아니에요 i bballenün ne göshi ani-e-yo; is my laundry ready? 내 빨래가 다 되었어요? ne bballega ta dwe-össö-yo?; where can I hang my laundry? 세탁물을 어디서 널면 돼요? set-hangmurl ödisö nölmyön dwe-yo?

lavatory 화장실 hwajang-shil

law 법 pöb

lawn 잔디 chandi

lawyer 변호사 pyönosa

laxative 변비약 pyönbi-yag

lay (see also LIE) 놓아요 noha-yo

lazy 게으른 ke-rn

lead: where does this road lead to? 이건

어디 가는 길이지요 igön ödi kanün kiriji-yo

leader: group leader 그룹 대표자 krub tep-hyoja

leaf 잎 ip; autumn leaves 단풍 tanp-hung

leaflet 리플렛 rip-hülled; are there any leaflets on ...? ...에 관한 리플렛 있어요? ...e kwanan rip-hülled issö-yo?

leak 새는 물 senün mul; the roof leaks 지붕이 새요 chibung-i se-yo

learn 배워요 pewö-yo; I'd like to learn to waterski 수상 스키를 배우고 싶은데요 susang sk-hirl pe-ugo ship-hünde-yo

lease (rent) 임대 해요 imde he-yo

least: at least 30 적어도 삼십이에요 chögödo samshibi-e-yo; not in the least 천만에요 ch-hönmane-yo

leather 가죽 kajug

leave 떠나요 ddöna-yo; leave us alone! 제발 혼자 있게 해 주십시오! chebal honja idge he jushibshi-o!; we leave tomorrow 내일 떠나요 ne-il ddöna-yo; he left his bag here 백을 여기에 놓고 갔어요 pegl yögi-e nok-ho kassö-yo; please leave the windows open 창문을 열어 두어 주세요 ch-hang-munl yörö tu-ö juse-yo; we'll leave it up to you 당신의 판단에 맡기겠어요 tang-shine p-handane madk-higessö-yo; I must leave early 일찌기 떠나야 해요 ilj-jigi ddöna-ya he-yo; let's not leave yet 아 직 가지 말아요 ajig kaji mara-yo; would you leave a message for ... ...한테 말씀 좀 전해 주시겠어요? ...ant-he malsm chom chöne jushigessö-yo?; must I leave a deposit? 선금을 내야 돼요? sön-gml ne-ya dwe-yo?; may I leave my valuables here? 귀중품을 여기서 맡겨도 좋아요? kwijung-p-huml yögisö madk-hyödo choha-yo?; when does it leave? 언제 출발 해요? önje ch-hulbal he-yo?;

there isn't much left 많이 남지 않았어요 mani namji anassö-yo; when does he leave? 언제 떠나요? önje ddöna-yo?; there is hardly any money left 돈이 거의 남지 않았어요 toni kö-e namji anassö-yo

Lebanon 레바논 rebanon

lecture 강의 kang-e

leeks 부추 puch-hu

left 왼쪽 wenj-jog; turn left 왼쪽으로 가세요 wenj-jogro kase-yo; please part my hair on the left 가름마를 왼쪽으로 해 주세요 karmmarl wenj-jogro he juse-yo

left over (remaining) 남아 있는 nama innün

left wing (political) 좌익 chwa-ig

left-handed 왼손잡이 wensonjabi

leg 다리 tari

legal 법률(의) pöbryul(e)

leisure 여가 yöga

lemon 레몬 remon; bitter lemon 쓴 레몬 ssn remon

lemon lime soda 사이다 sa-ida

lemon tea 레몬을 탄 홍차 remonl t-han hong-ch-ha

lemonade 레모네이드 remone-idü

lend 빌려 줘요 pillyö chwö-yo; can you lend a hand? 나를 도와 주시겠어요? narl towa jushigessö-yo?; would you lend me a ...? ... 좀 빌려 주시겠어요? ... chom pillyö jushigessö-yo?

length 길이 kiri

lens 렌즈 renjü; telephoto lens 망원 렌즈 mang-wön renjü; wide-angle lens 광각 렌즈 kwang-gag renjü; zoom lens 줌 렌즈 chum renjü; contact lenses 콘 택트 렌즈 k-hont-hegt-hü rensü; hard lenses 하드 렌즈 hadü renjü; soft contact lens 소프트 콘택트 렌즈 sop-hüt-hü k-hont-hegt-hü renjü

lens cap 렌즈 뚜껑 renjü ddug-gyöng

lentils 렌즈콩 renjk-hong

lesbian 레즈비언 rejbi-ön

less 이하 iha; less hot (spicy) 적게 매운 chögge me-un; a less than average hotel 보통 이하 의 호텔 pot-hong iha e hot-hel

lesson 학과 haggwa

let (do) 하게 해요 hage he-yo; let me try it 내가 해 볼께요 nega he polg-ge-yo; let me go! 놓아 줘! noha chwö!; let's go now 자 지금 가요 cha chigm ka-yo; just let me get dressed 옷을 좀 입겠어요 osl chom ibgessö-yo; please let me off at ... ...에서 내려 주세요 ...esö neryö juse-yo; would you let us know? 알려 주시겠어요? allyö jushigessö-yo?

letter (note) 편지 p-hyönji; (character) 글자 klja; letter of introduction 소개장 sogejang; I'll write you a letter 편지 하겠어요 p-hyönji hagessö-yo

letter box 우체통 uch-het-hong

lettuce 상추 sang-ch-hu

lever 지렛대 chiredde

liable (responsible) 책임이 있는 ch-hegimi innün

librarian 도서관 직원 tosögwan chigwön

library 도서관 tosögwan

license 면허 myönö; driver's license 운 전 면허증 unjön myönöjng; international driver's license 국제 운전 면허증 kugje unjön myönöjng

license plate 번호판 pönop-han

lid 뚜껑 ddug-göng

lie (tell lies) 거짓말 해요 köjinmal he-yo; I want to go lie down 누우러 가고 싶어요 nu-urö kago ship-hö-yo

life 인생 inseng; night life 밤의 유흥 pame yuhüng; he saved my life 그는 나를 살렸어요 knün narl sallyössö-yo

life belt 구명띠 kumyöng-ddi

life insurance 생명 보험 seng-myöng pohöm

life jacket 구명 자켓 kumyöng chak-hed

lifeboat 구명정 kumyöng-jöng

Pronounce: a father; e let; i machine; o note; ö löng; u rude; ü further

lifeguard 인명 구조원 inmyöng kujowön

lift: I'll give you a lift home 차로
집까지 데려 다 드리겠어요 ch-haro
chibg-gaji teryö ta trigessö-yo; would
you give me a lift? 나를 태워
주시겠어요? narl t-hewö jushigessö-yo?

light 빛 pich; (electric) 전등 chöndng;
(not heavy) 가벼운 kabyö-un; fog
light 안개등 an-gedng; the light was
on 불은 켜져 있었어요 purn k-hyöjyö
issössö-yo; something light, please 뭐
간단 한 걸로 주세요 mwö kandan han
köllo chuse-yo; traffic light 교통
신호등 kyot-hong shinodng; parking
lights 주차등 chuch-hadng; got a
light? (cigarette) 불을 좀 빌려
주시겠어요? purl chom pillyö
jushigessö-yo?; the warning light is
on 위험 신호가 켜져요 wihöm shinoga
k-hyöjyö-yo; past the lights 신호를
지나서 shinorl chinasö; will you put
the light out? 불을 꺼 주시겠어요? prl
ggö jushigessö-yo?

light bulb 전구 chön-gu; I need a new
light bulb 새 전구 하나 주세요 se
chön-gu hana juse-yo

light meter 노출계 noch-hulgye

lightening 번개 pön-ge

lighter (cigarette) 라이터 ra-it-hö

lighthouse 등대 tng-de

like: we'd like to go dancing 춤 추러
가고 싶은데요 ch-hum ch-hurö kago
ship-hünde-yo; I'd like some Western
food 양식을 먹고 싶은데요 yang-shigl
möggo ship-hünde-yo; I'd like a ...
...를 원 해요 ...rl wön he-yo; I'd
like to ... ...고 싶은데요 ...go ship-
hünde-yo; he likes it 좋아 해요 choha
he-yo; I like to swim 나는 수영을
좋아 해요 nanün su-yöng-l choha he-
yo; I like it a lot 매우 좋아 해요 me-
u choha he-yo; I like this one the
most 이것이 제일 좋아요 igöshi che-il
choha-yo; however you'd like 좋을

대로 chohül tero; would you like to
dance? 춤을 추시겠어요? ch-huml ch-
hushigessö-yo?; I don't like either of
them 그 어느 쪽도 마음에 들지 않아요
kü önü jjogdo ma-me tlji anö-yo; I
don't like that 나는 그것을 좋아 하지
않아요 nanün kgösl choha haji anö-
yo; I really like ... ...를 아주 좋아
해요 ...rl aju choha he-yo; we don't
like it 좋아 하지 않아요 choha haji
anö-yo; like hell it is! 그럴리가
없어요! krölliga öbsö-yo!; I don't feel
like doing it 하고 싶지 않아요 hago
shibch-hi anö-yo; what is it like? 어
때요? öd-de-yo?

likely (probably) 아마 ama; it seems
likely to rain 비가 올 것 같아요 piga
ol göd kat-ha-yo

lime juice 라임 쥬스 ra-im chyusü

limit: age limit 연령 제한 yönryöng
chehan; speed limit 속도 제한 sogdo
chehan; weight limit 무게 제한 muge
chehan

line 선 sön; (queue) 열 yöl; the line
was busy 통화 중이었어요 t-hong-wa
chung-i-össö-yo; clothes line 빨래줄
bballejul; hold the line, please 끊지
마세요 gglch-hi mase-yo; there was a
long line 긴 줄이 있었어요 kin churi
issössö-yo; would you drop me a
line? 연결 해 주시겠어요? yön-gyöl he
jushigessö-yo?

linen 린네르 rinnerü

linguist (polyglot) 외국어에 능한 사람
wegugö-e nüng-an saram

lining 안감 an-gam

lip 입술 ibsul

lip brush 립 부러쉬 rib puröswi

lip gloss 립글로스 ribgllosü

lip salve 입술 크림 ibsul k-hürim

lipstick 립스틱 ribst-hig

liqueur 리큐르 rik-hyurü

liquor 술 sul

liquor store 술집 suljib

Pronounce: a father; e let; i machine; o note; ö löng; u rude; ü fürther

list 리스트 rist-hü; wine list 포도주 리스트 p-hodoju rist-hü

listen 들어요 trö-yo

liter 리터 rit-hö; a half liter 반 리터 pan rit-hö

literature 문학 munag; classical literature 고전 문학 kojön munag; modern literature 현대 문학 hyönde munag

litter (garbage) 쓰레기 ssregi

little 작은 chagn; very little for me, please 나에게 아주 조금만 주세요 na-ege aju chogmman chuse-yo; it's a little too big 조금만 작았으면 좋겠어요 chogmman chagassmyön chok-hessö-yo; it's a little cold today 오늘은 조금 추워요 onrn chogm ch-huwö-yo; only a little 조금만 chogmman; I'm a little better 조금 나아졌어요 chogm na-ajyössö-yo; that's a little expensive 조금 비싸요 chogm pissa-yo; I speak a little Korean 한국말을 좀 해요 han-gungmarl chom he-yo; I'll wait a little longer 조금 더 기다리겠어요 chogm tö kidarigessö-yo; may I taste a little? 조금 맛봐도 좋아요? chogm madbwado choha-yo?

live 살어요 sarö-yo; I live in Chicago 시카고에서 살어요 shik-hago-esö sarö-yo; they live in Korea 한국에서 살어요 han-gugesö sarö-yo; they live together 함께 살고 있어요 hamg-ge salgo issö-yo; where do you live? 어디서 살고 있어요? ödisö salgo issö-yo?

liver 간 kan

lizard 도마뱀 tomabem

loaf (of bread) 덩어리 töng-öri

lobby 로비 robi; shall we go into the lobby? 로비에 들어 갈까요? robi-e trö kalg-ga-yo?

lobster 바닷 가재 padad kaje

local 지방의 chibang-e; a local newspaper 지방 신문 chibang shinmun

local call 시내 전화 shine chönwa

lock (noun) 자물쇠 chamulswe; I locked myself out of the room 나도 모르게 방문을 잠겨버렸어요 nado morge pang-munl chamk-hyöböryössö-yo

locker 로커 rok-hö

lollipop 막대기 사탕 magdegi sat-hang

London 런던 röndön; I'm from London 런던에서 왔어요 röndönesö wassö-yo

lonely 쓸쓸 한 sslsl han; are you lonely? 쓸쓸 하세요? sslsl hase-yo?

long 긴 kin; how long have you been here? 여기 오신지 얼마나 되셨어요? yögi oshinji ölmana dweshyössö-yo?; how long does it last? 얼마나 계속돼요? ölmana kyesogdwe-yo?; a long time 오랫 동안 ored tong-an; so long! 안녕! annyöng!; that happened long ago 훨씬 이전에 일어난 일이에요 hwölshin ijöne irönan iri-e-yo; for how long is it valid? 유효 기간은 얼마 동안이에요? yuhyo kiganün ölma tong-ani-e-yo?; it wasn't a long time ago 오래전 일이 아니에요 orejön iri ani-e-yo; there was a long line 긴 줄이 있었어요 kin churi issössö-yo; he shouldn't take long 틀림 없이 오래 않을 거에요 t-hüllim öbshi ore anl kö-e-ö-yo; is it a long way to ...? ...까지 멀어요? ...ggaji mörö-yo?; do I have to wait long? 오래 기다려야 돼요? ore kidaryö-ya dwe-yo?

long distance call 장거리 전화 chang-göri chönwa

long underwear 내복 nebog

look (see) 봐요 pwa-yo; look for 찾아요 ch-haja-yo; look at him 그를 좀 봐요 krl chom pwa-yo; that looks good (to eat) 그것은 맛있게 보여요 kgösn mashidge po-yö-yo; he looks tired 피로해 보여요 p-hirohe po-yö-yo; we're looking for ... ...를 찾어요 ...rl ch-hajö-yo; can I take a look? 좀 보여 주시겠어요? chom po-yö jushigessö-yo?; I want to go and look

around 가서 답사를 하고 싶은데요 kasö tabsarl hago ship-hünde-yo
loose (unfastened) 풀린 p-hullin
lose 잃어버려요 iröböryö-yo; I've lost ... ...를 잃어버렸어요 ...rl iröböryössö-yo; I'm lost 길을 잃어버렸어요 kirl iröböryössö-yo; I want to lose weight 나는 체중을 줄이고 싶은데요 nanün ch-hejung-l churigo ship-hünde-yo
lost and found 분실물 취급소 punshilmul ch-hwigbso
lot: a whole lot 많이 mani; quite a lot 꽤 많은 ggwe manün; I feel a lot better 많이 좋아졌어요 mani chohajyössö-yo; he's had a lot to drink 많이 마셨어요 mani mashyössö-yo; I'll buy the whole lot 모두 사겠어요 modu sagessö-yo; this place has changed a lot 이곳에 모습이 많이 바뀌었군요 igose mosbi mani pag-gwi-ödgunyo; I used to swim a lot 수영을 자주 했었어요 su-yöng-l chaju hessössö-yo
lotion 로션 roshyön; body lotion 보디 로션 podi roshyön; hand lotion 핸드 로션 hendü roshyön; setting lotion 세트용 로션 set-hü-yong roshyön; suntan lotion 선탠 크림 sönt-hen k-hürim
lottery: national lottery 주택 복권 chut-heg poggwön
lotus 연 yön
loud 시끄러운 shig-grö-un; the music is too loud 음악은 너무 시끄러워요 ümagn nömu shig-gröwö-yo
lounge (lobby) 로비 robi; (waiting room) 대합실 tehabshil
lousy 더러운 törö-un
love 사랑 해요 sarang he-yo; I love you 당신을 사랑 해요 tang-shinl sarang he-yo; I really love Korea 한국을 정말 좋아 해요 han-gugl chöng-mal choha he-yo

lovely 훌륭 한 hullyung han
low (inexpensive) 싼 ssan; (not high) 낮은 najn; low gear 저속 기어 chösog ki-ö
lozenges: throat lozenges 인후 정제 inu chöng-je
LP 엘피 elp-hi
luck 운 un; good luck! 행운을 빕니다! heng-unl pimnida!; tough luck! 불운 purun; that's my luck! 제기랄 또 글렸어요! chegiral ddo kllyössö-yo!
luggage 짐 chim; hand luggage 수화물 suhwamul; can you help me with my luggage? 짐 좀 운반 해 주시겠어요? chim chom unban he jushigessö-yo?
lump (a growth) 혹 hog
lunar calendar 음력 ümryög
lunch 점심 chömshim; box lunch 도시락 toshirag
lungs 폐 p-hye
luxurious 사치스러운 sach-hisrö-un
luxury 사치 sach-hi

M

machine 기계 kigye; answering machine 자동 응답기 chadong üng-dabgi; cash machine 현금 자동 지급기 hyön-gm chadong chigbgi; ticket machine 차표 자동 판매기 ch-hap-hyo chadong p-hanmegi; vending machine 자동 판매기 chadong p-hanmegi; washing machine 세탁기 set-haggi
macho 사내다운 saneda-un
mackerel 고등어 kodng-ö
mad (insane) 미친 mich-hin; (angry) (see also ANGRY) 성난 söng-nan
madam 부인 pu-in; thank you, ma'am 고맙습니다, 부인 komabsmnida, pu-in
Madam President 대통령 부인 tet-hong-ryöng pu-in

magazine 잡지 chabji

magnifying glass 돋보기 todbogi

mahjong game 마작 majag

maid 파출부 p-hach-hulbu

maiden name 여성의 결혼 전의 성 yösöng-e kyöron chöne söng

mail 우편물 up-hyönmul; express mail 속달 sogdal; registered mail 등기 우편 tng-gi up-hyön; could you mail this for me? 이것을 부쳐 주시겠어요? igösl puch-hyö jushigessö-yo?; is there another mail delivery? 우체부가 오늘 또 와요? uch-hebuga onl ddo wa-yo?; could you forward my mail? 내 편지를 부쳐 주시겠어요? ne p-hyönjirl puch-hyö jushigessö-yo?

mailbox 우체통 uch-het-hong

mailman 우체부 uch-hebu

main 주요 한 chu-yo han; on the main floor 일층에 ilch-hüng-e; off the main road 본 길에(서) pon kire(sö)

main attractions 가장 볼만 한 구경 거리 kajang polman han kugyöng köri

main road 큰 길 k-hün kil

major (important) 중요 한 chung-yo han; what is your major (subject)? 무슨 과목을 전공 하세요? musn kwamogl chön-gong hase-yo?

majority 다수 tasu

make 만들어요 mandrö-yo; made in Korea 한국제 han-gugje; make a mistake 잘못 해요 chalmod he-yo; please make the arrangements 준비를 해 주십시오 chunbirl he jushibshi-o; that make no sense 그건 말이 안 돼요 kgön mari an dwe-yo; do you make it yourself? 직접 만들어요? chigjöb mandrö-yo?; it's well made 잘 만든 것이에요. chal mandn göshi-e-yo; may I make a telephone call? 전화를 걸어도 좋아요? chönwarl körödo choha-yo?; I want to make an appointment 약속 시간을 정하고 싶은데요 yagsog shiganl chöng-ago ship-hünde-yo

make-up 화장 hwajang

make-up remover pads 화장 지우는 패드 hwajang chi-unün p-hedü

Malaysia 말레이지아 malle-iji-a

Malaysian (adjective) 말레이지아 의 malle-iji-a e; (person) 말레이지아 사람 malle-iji-a saram

male 남 nam

male chauvinist 남성 우월주의자 namsöng uwölju-eja

mall: pedestrian mall 차 없는 곳 ch-ha ömnün kod

man 남자 namja; the man in the blue shirt 푸른 샤쓰를 입는 사람 p-hurn shyassrl imnün saram; that man 그 남자 kü namja

management 관리 kwanri

manager 지배인 chibe-in; is the manager around? 여기 지배인은 있어요? yögi chibe-inün issö-yo?; call the manager! 지배인에게 오라고 해줘! chibe-inege orago hejwö!

Manhattan (drink) 맨하탄 menat-han

manicure 매니큐어 menik-hyu-ö

manner (method) 방법 pang-böb

manners 예의 ye-e

mansion 저택 chöt-heg

manufacture (make) 제조 해요 chejo he-yo

manufacturer (factory) 공장 kong-jang

manuscript 원고 wön-go

many 많은 manün; many women 많은 여자 manün yöja; many people 많은 사람 manün saram; how many? (things / people) 몇 개 / 분 myöt ke / bun; how many times? 몇 번? myöt pön?

map 지도 chido; city map 시내 지도 shine chido; this map doesn't show it 이 지도에 없어요 i jido-e öbsö-yo; road map 도로 지도 toro chido; street map 지도 chido; please draw a map for me 약도 좀 그려 주세요 yagdo chom kryö juse-yo; can you show me where we are on this map? 이 지도에서 우리가 있는 곳을 가리킬 수 있어요? i jido-esö uriga innün kosl karik-hil su issö-yo?

maple 단풍 tanp-hung

marble (material) 대리석 terisög

March 삼월 samwöl

margarine 마가린 magarin

marijuana 마리화나 marihwana

mark (spot) 얼룩 öllug; would you please mark it on the map? 지도에 표시 해 주시겠어요? chido-e p-hyoshi he jushigessö-yo?

market (marketplace) 시장 shijang; fish market 수산물 시장 susanmul shijang; overseas market 해외 시장 hewe shijang; the American market 미국 시장 migug shijang; I'd like to see the market 시장을 보고 싶어요 shijang-l pogo ship-hö-yo

marmalade 마멀레이드 mamölle-idü

marry 결혼 해요 kyöron he-yo;

married 결혼 한 kyöron han; I'm married 결혼 했어요 kyöron hessö-yo; are you married? 결혼 했어요? kyöron hessö-yo?

martial arts 태권도 t-hegwöndo

martini 마티니 mat-hini

marvelous! 멋진데 mödjinde; it was a marvelous meal 훌륭 한 식사였어요 hullyung han shigsa-yössö-yo

mascara 마스카라 mask-hara

mask 탈 t-hal; face mask (diving) 수중 마스크 sujung mask-hü

mask dance-drama 탈춤 t-halch-hum

mass (church) 미사 misa; I want to go to mass 미사에 가고 싶은데요 misa-e kago ship-hünde-yo

massage 맛사지 massaji

masseur 안마사 anmasa

mast 돛대 todt-he

masterpiece 명작 myöng-jag

mat (straw) 돗자리 todjari; place mat 접시받침 chöbshibadch-him

match (fire) 성냥 söng-nyang; (sports) 경기 kyöng-gi; is the match on television? 텔레비전에 시합이 있어요? t-hellebijöne shihabi issö-yo?; please give me some matches 성냥 좀 주세요 söng-nyang chom chuse-yo; have you got anything to match this? 이것에 어울리는 것이 있어요? igöse ö-ullinün göshi issö-yo?

material (cloth) 천 ch-hön

matinee 낮 공영 nad kong-yöng

matter (business) 일 il; printed matter 인쇄물 inswemul; it doesn't matter 상관 없어요 sang-gwan öbsö-yo; a private matter 개인적인 일 ke-injögin il

mattress (Korean style) 요 yo; (Western style) 매트레스 met-hüresü; air mattress 고무 침대 komu ch-himde

maximum 최대 ch-hwede

May 오월 owöl

may: may we use the bathroom? 화장실을 써도 좋아요? hwajang-shirl ssödo choha-yo?; may I introduce ...? ...을 소개 하겠어요 ...l soge hagessö-yo; may I go with you? 함께 가도 좋아요? hamg-ge kado choha-yo?; may I take you home? 댁까지 태워다 드릴까요? tegg-gaji t-hewöda trilg-ga-yo?; may we? (해도) 좋아요? (edo) choha-yo?; may I order now? 주문 해도 좋아요? chumun hedo choha-yo?; may I see? 나 좀 보여 주시겠어요? na chom po-yö jushigessö-yo?; may I smoke? 담배를 피워도 좋아요? tamberl p-hiwödo choha-yo?; may I speak with ...? (on phone) ...를 좀 바꿔 주세요? ...rl chom pag-gwö juse-yo?; may we use ...? ...를 써도 좋아요? ...rl ssödo choha-yo?; you may 괜찮아요 kwench-hana-yo; you may not 안 되는데요. an dwenünde-yo.; I may (must) not drink 마셔서는 안 돼요 mashyösönün an dwe-yo

maybe 아마 ama; maybe not 그렇지 않을
지도 모르지요 kröch-hi anl chido
morji-yo
mayonnaise 마요네즈 ma-yonejü
mayor 시장 shijang
me 나를 narl; me too 나도 nado; that
is for me 나에게 줄 것이에요 na-ege
chul göshi-e-yo; are there any
messages for me? 나한테 무슨 연락이
있어요? nahant-he musn yönragi issö-
yo?
meal 식사 shigsa; evening meal 저녁
chönyög; are meals included? 식사가
포함되어 있어요? shigsaga p-
hohamdwe-ö issö-yo?; a light meal 가
벼운 식사 kabyö-un shigsa; when is
meal time? 식사 시간이 어떻게 돼요?
shigsa shigani öd-dök-he dwe-yo?; a
traditional Korean meal 전통적 한국식
식사 chönt-hong-jög han-gugshig
shigsa; it was a marvelous meal 훌륭
한 식사였어요 hullyung han shigsa-
yössö-yo
meal cost 식비 shigbi
mean: what does she mean? 그의 말씀은
무슨 뜻이에요? k-e malsmn musn
ddshi-e-yo?; what does this word
mean? 이 말은 무슨 뜻이에요? i marn
musn ddshi-e-yo?
measles 홍역 hong-yög; German
measles 풍진 p-hung-jin
measure (verb) 재요 che-yo; tape
measure 줄자 chulja; can you measure
my size? 싸이즈 좀 재 주시겠어요? ssa-
ijü chom che chushigessö-yo?
measurements 치수 ch-hisu
meat 고기 kogi; this meat is spoiled 이
고기는 상했어요 i goginün sang-essö-
yo; this meat is burned 이 고기는 너무
탔어요 i goginün nömu t-hassö-yo
mechanic 정비공 chöng-bigong; auto
mechanic 자동차 정비공 chadong-ch-ha
chöng-bigong; is there a mechanic
here? 여기 정비공 있어요? yögi chöng-

bigong issö-yo?
medical treatment 치료 ch-hiryo
medicine 약 yag; cough medicine 기침
약 kich-himyag; I'm taking this
medicine 이 약을 먹고 있어요 i yagl
möggo issö-yo
medium (adjective) 중간의 chung-gane;
(clothes) 미디움 midi-um
medium rare (meat) 보통으로 설구운
pot-hong-ro sölgu-un
medium-sized 중형의 chung-yöng-e
meet 만나요 manna-yo; they meet in
the bar 빠에서 만나요 bba-esö manna-
yo; let's meet again 또 만나요 ddo
manna-yo; pleased to meet you 처음
뵙겠어요 ch-hö-m pwebgessö-yo; till
we meet again 그럼 다시 또 만날 때
까지 kröm tashi ddo mannal dde ggaji;
I'm sure we'll meet again 또 만나뵙게
되겠지요 ddo mannabwebge dwegedji-
yo; when shall we meet? 언제
만날까요? önje mannalg-ga-yo?
meeting (conference) 회의 hwe-e
meeting place 회의장 hwe-ejang
melon 참외 ch-hamwe
member 회원 hwewön; I want to
become a member 회원이 되고 싶은데요
hwewöni dwego ship-hünde-yo
memorandum 메모 memo
men 남자들 namjadl
mention (refer to) 언급 해요 ön-gb he-
yo; don't mention it 천만에요 ch-
hönmane-yo
menu 메뉴 menyu; fixed menu 정식
chöng-shig; the menu, please 메뉴 좀
주시겠어요 menyu chom chushigessö-
yo
merchant 상인 sang-in
mess 혼란 honran
message 멧세지 messeji; would you
leave a message for ... ...한테 말씀
좀 전해 주시겠어요? ...ant-he malsm
chom chöne jushigessö-yo?
messenger 배달인 pedarin

metal (material) 금속 kmsog
meter (about 3 feet) 미터 mit-hö;
 exposure meter 노출계 noch-hulgye;
 light meter 노출계 noch-hulgye
method 방법 pang-böb
metro (train) 지하철 chihach-höl
Mexico 멕시코 megshik-ho
mezzanine 이층 앞쪽 ich-hüng apjjog
microwave oven 전자 렌지 chönja renji
middle 가운데 ka-unde; in the middle
 한가운데에 han-ga-unde-e
might (do) 할 지도 몰라요 hal chido
 molla-yo
migraine 편두통 p-hyöndut-hung
milage 마일수 ma-ilsu; unlimited
 milage (for car rental) 무제한의 거리
 mujehane köri; does the rate include
 milage? 계산에 주행 거리가 포함 돼요?
 kyesane chuheng köriga p-hoham
 dwe-yo?
mild (bland) 부드러운 pudrö-un;
 (weather) 온화 한 onwa han
mile 마일 ma-il
military (adjective) 육군의 yuggune
milk 우유 u-yu; powdered milk 분유
 punyu; coffee with milk 프림을 탄
 커피 p-hüriml t-han k-höp-hi; tea
 with milk 우유를 탄 홍차 u-yurl t-han
 hong-ch-ha; a carton of milk 우유
 한팩 u-yu hanp-heg; do you have any
 milk? 우유 있어요? u-yu issö-yo?
milk shake 밀크 셰이크 milk-hü shyeik-hü
millimeter 밀리미터 millimit-hö
millionaire 백만 장자 pengman chang-ja
mind: mind if I smoke? 담배 피워도
 좋아요? tambe p-hiwödo choha-yo?;
 never mind 걱정 마세요 kögjöng mase-
 yo; would you mind this bag for me?
 이 가방을 맡아 주시겠어요? i gabang-l
 mat-ha jushigessö-yo?; I changed my
 mind 생각을 고쳤어요 seng-gagl koch-
 hyössö-yo
mine (my thing) 내 것 ne göd; have

one of mine 나의 것을 부탁 해요 na-e
 gösl put-hag he-yo; this laundry isn't
 mine 이 빨래는 내 것이 아니에요 i
 bballenün ne göshi ani-e-yo
mineral water 미네랄 워터 mineral wöt-
 hö
minimum (adjective) 최소 한 ch-hweso
 han
minister (clergyman) 목사 mogsa;
 Prime Minister 국무 총리 kungmu ch-
 hong-ri
minority 소수 sosu
mint (peppermint) 박하 pak-ha
minus 마이너스 ma-inösü; minus 5
 degrees 영하 오도 yöng-a odo
minute 분 pun
mirror 거울 kö-ul; rearview mirror 백미
 러 pengmirö; sideview mirror 사이드
 미러 sa-idü mirö
Miss 미스 misü; Miss Samuels 미스
 새뮤엘즈 misü semyu-eljü
miss: I miss you 보고 싶어요 pogo
 ship-hö-yo; I missed the bus 버스를
 놓쳤어요 pösrl noch-hyössö-yo; ... is
 missing ...이 있지 않아요 ...i idji
 anö-yo; nothing is missing 없는 것이
 없어요 ömnün göshi öbsö-yo; one is
 missing 하나가 없어요 hanaga öbsö-yo
missionary 선교사 sön-gyosa
mist 안개 an-ge
mistake 실수 shilsu; make a mistake 잘
 못 해요 chalmod he-yo; correct me
 when I make a mistake 실수 하면 고쳐
 주세요 shilsu hamyön koch-hyö juse-
 yo
misunderstanding 오해 ohe
mixture 혼합물 honammul
modern 현대의 hyönde-e
modern art gallery 현대 미술관 hyönde
 misulgwan
modern literature 현대 문학 hyönde
 munag
moisturizer (cream) 모이스쳐 크림 mo-
 isch-hyö k-hürim

Pronounce: a father; e let; i machine; o note; ö löng; u rude; ü fürther

moment 순간 sun-gan; wait just a moment 잠깐 기다려 주세요 chamg-gan kidaryö juse-yo

monastery 수도원 sudowön

Monday 월요일 wöryo-il; Monday through Friday 월요일부터 금요일까지 wöryo-ilbut-hö kmyo-ilg-gaji; Monday of next week 다음 주 월요일 ta-m chu wöryo-il; next Monday 이번 월요일 ibön wöryo-il

money 돈 ton; the money hasn't gotten here yet 돈은 아직 오지 않았어요 tonün ajig oji anassö-yo; all my money 내 모든 돈 ne modn ton; I'd like the money in large bills 큰 돈으로 주세요 k-hün tonro chuse-yo; a lot of money 많은 돈 manün ton; I have no money 돈이 없어요 toni öbsö-yo; do you accept American money? 미국 돈을 받으세요? migug tonl padse-yo?; I'm saving up my money 저금 하고 있어요 chögm hago issö-yo; where can I exchange money? 돈을 어디에서 바꿔요? tonl ödi-esö pag-gwi-yo?; would you give me my money back? 돈을 돌려 주시겠어요? tonl tollyö jushigessö-yo?

monk (Buddhist) 스님 snim

monkey wrench 스패너 sp-henö

monotonous 단조로운 tanjoro-un

month 달 tal; one month 일개월 ilgewöl; three months 삼개월 samgewöl; this month 이번 달 ibön tal; next month 다음 달 ta-m tal; last month 지난 달 chinan tal; for two months 이개월간 igewölgan; in two months 이개월 후에 igewöl hu-e; I wrote to you last month 지난 달에 편지를 보냈어요 chinan tare p-hyönjirl ponessö-yo

monument 기념물 kinyömmul

moon 달 tal; full moon 보름달 pormdal

moon viewing 달놀이 talnori

more 더 tö; more than 20 이십 이상

ishib isang; much more, please 더 많이 주세요 tö mani chuse-yo; no more 이제 그만 ije kman; much more 더욱 많이 tö-ug mani; no more than ... ... 이하 ... iha; nothing more, thanks 이제 됐어요 ije dwessö-yo; a little more 조금 더 주세요 chogm tö juse-yo; it needs more salt 소금이 더 필요 해요 sogmi tö p-hiryo he-yo; it's worth more than that 그 이상의 가치가 있어요 kü isang-e kach-higa issö-yo; please give us more water 물을 더 주세요 murl tö juse-yo; there is no more 더 없어요 tö öbsö-yo; I don't want to spend more than ... won ...원 이상은 쓰고 싶지 않아요 ...wön isang-n ssgo shibch-hi ana-yo; could you give me some more? 더 주시겠어요? tö jushigessö-yo?

morning 아침 ach-him; tomorrow morning 내일 아침 ne-il ach-him; yesterday morning 어제 아침 öje ach-him; in the morning 아침에 ach-hime; early in the morning 아침 일찍이 ach-him ilj-jigi; he left this morning 오늘 아침 그는 떠났어요 onl ach-him knün ddönassö-yo; first thing in the morning 아침이 되면 우선 ach-himi dwemyön usön

mosque 회교 사원 hwegyo sawön

mosquito 모기 mogi

mosquito net 모기장 mogijang

most (majority) 대부분 tebubun; most hotels 대부분의 호텔 tebubune hot-hel; that's most interesting 그것은 매우 재미 있어요 kgösn me-u chemi issö-yo

mother 어머니 ömöni

mother country 모국 mogug

motor 모터 mot-hö

motor scooter 스쿠터 sk-hut-hö

motorbike 오토바이 ot-hoba-i

motorboat 모터보트 mot-höbot-hü

motorist 운전자 unjönja

mountain 산 san; beyond the mountain

산 저편에 san chöp-hyöne
mouse 쥐 chwi
moustache 코수염 k-hosu-yöm
mouth 입 ib
move 움직여요 umjigyö-yo; don't move
움직이지 마세요 umjigiji mase-yo; can
we move to another table? 다른
테이블로 옮겨 주시겠어요? tarn t-he-
ibllo olgyö jushigessö-yo?; a very
moving tune 매우 감동적인 선율 me-u
kamdong-jögin sönyul
movie 영화 yöng-wa; thriller movie 공
포 영화 kong-p-ho yöng-wa; war
movie 전쟁 영화 chönjeng yöng-wa;
what time does the movie begin? 영화
는 몇 시에 시작 돼요 yöng-wanün
myöt shi-e shijag dwe-yo
movie camera 영화 카메라 yöng-wa k-
hamera
movie theater 영화관 yöng-wagwan
Mr ... 미스터 mist-hö; Mr Kim 미스터
김 mist-hö kim; please page Mr. ...
미스터 ...-를 찾어 주세요 mist-hö
...-rl ch-hajö juse-yo; poor old Mr.
Kim! 불쌍 한 미스터 김 pulsang han
mist-hö kim; this is Mr. Smith
speaking 스미스에요 smis-e-yo; would
you give this to Mr ...? 이것을
미스터 ...에게 주시겠어요? igösl mist-
hö ...ege chushigessö-yo?
Mrs 부인 pu-in; Mrs Jones 존스 부인
chonsü pu-in
Ms ... 미즈 mijü; Ms Johnson 미즈
존슨 mijü chonsn
much 많은 manün; much more, please
더 많이 주세요 tö mani chuse-yo;
much more 더욱 많이 tö-ug mani; as
much as possible 될 수 있는 대로 많이
dwel su innün tero mani; how much
is it? 얼마 에요? ölma e-yo?; too
much 너무 많이 nömu mani; not so
much cream! 크림을 그렇게 많이 넣으면
안 돼요! k-hüriml krök-he mani
nöhümyön an dwe-yo!; half as much

반 만큼 pan man-k-hüm; half as
much again 한배 반 hanbe pan; there
isn't much left 많이 남지 않았어요
mani namji anassö-yo; is it much
further? 더 멀어요? tö mörö-yo?; not
that much 그렇게 많지 않어요 krök-he
manch-hi anö-yo; twice as much 두배
의 분량 tube-e punryang; thank you
so much 감사 합니다 kamsa hamnida;
isn't that a bit too much? 그것은 좀
지나쳤죠 kgösn chom chinach-hyödjyo
mud 진흙 chinlg
muffler (auto) 소음기 so-mgi
mug (rob) 습격 해요 sbgyög he-yo;
I've been mugged 나는 습격 됐어요
nanün sbgyög dwessö-yo
mumps 이하선염 ihasönyöm
mural 벽화 pyök-hwa
muscle 근육 knyug
museum 박물관 pangmulgwan
mushroom 버섯 pösöd
music 음악 ümag; classical music 고전
음악 kojön ümag; country music 칸츄
리 뮤직 k-hanch-hyuri myujig;
farmer's music (Korean) 농악 nong-ag;
the music is too loud 음악은 너무
시끄러워요 ümagn nömu shig-gröwö-
yo; pop music 팝송 p-habsong
musical (play) 뮤지칼 myujik-hal
musician 음악가 ümagga
mussels 홍합 hong-ab
must (do) 해야 해요 he-ya he-yo; must
we pay now? 지금 요금을 치려야 돼요?
chigm yogml ch-hiryö-ya dwe-yo?;
must he stay in bed? 집에서 누워
있어야 돼요? chibesö nuwö issö-ya
dwe-yo?; I must be going now 나는
지금 가는 것이 좋아요 nanün chigm
kanün göshi choha-yo; I must leave
early 일찌기 떠나야 해요 ilj-jigi ddöna-
ya he-yo; you must be joking! 농담이
시겠지요 nong-damishigedji-yo; you
must apply in writing 서류 신청을
해야 돼요 söryu shinch-höng-l he-ya

dwe-yo; I really must go 정말로 가야
해요 chöng-mallo ka-ya he-yo
mustache 콧 수염 k-hod su-yöm; please
trim my mustache 코밑수염 좀 다듬어
주세요 k-homit-hsu-yöm chom tarmö
juse-yo
mustard 겨자 kyöja
mutton 양 고기 yang kogi
my 내 ne;
my my! (surprise) 어마! öma!
Myanmar (Thailand) 태국 t-hegug
myself 나 자신 na chashin; I'm going
by myself 나는 혼자 가요 nanün honja
ka-yo; can I cook for myself? 직접 해
먹어도 돼요? chigjöb he mögödo dwe-
yo?
mystery (play) 추리극 ch-hurigüg
myth 신화 shinwa

N

nail (fingers) 손톱 sont-hob;
(carpentry) 못 mod
nail clippers 손톱 깎이 sont-hob ggag-
gi
nail file 손톱 다듬는 줄 sont-hob
tadmnün chul
nail polish 매니큐어 menik-hyu-ö
nail polish remover 매니큐어 지우개
menik-hyu-ö chi-uge
nail scissors 손톱 가위 sont-hob kawi
naked 벌거벗은 pölgöbösn
name 이름 irm; last name 성 söng;
maiden name 여성의 결혼 전의 성
yösöng-e kyöron chöne söng; the
name of the hotel 호텔의 이름 hot-
here irm; what's the name? 이름이
무엇이에요? irmi mu-öshi-e-yo?;
please write your name and phone
number 성함과 전화 번호를 좀 써 주세요
söng-amgwa chönwa pönorl chom ssö

juse-yo; I reserved a room in the
name of ... ...의 이름으로 방을 예약
해 두었어요 ...e irmro pang-l ye-yag
he tu-össö-yo
name card 명함 myöng-am
nap 낮잠 najjam; she's napping 낮잠
자고 있어요 najjam chago issö-yo
napkin (dinner) 냅킨 nebk-hin; sanitary
napkin 생리대 seng-ride
narrow 좁은 chobn
nasty 나쁜 nab-bn; (injury) 심 한 shim
han
nation 국가 kugga
national 국민의 kungmine
national park 국립 공원 kugrib kong-
wön
nationality 국적 kugjög
natural 자연의 cha-yöne
naturally (of course) 물론 mullon
nature (outdoors) 자연 cha-yön
nausea 메스꺼움 mesg-gö-um
near 가까운 kag-ga-un; near ...
...근처에 ...gnch-hö-e; where's the
nearest ...? 가장 가까운 ...는 어디
있어요 kajang kag-ga-un ...nün ödi
issö-yo; do you stop near ...? ...
근처에서 멈추세요? ... knch-hö-esö
mömch-huse-yo?
nearby 가까운 kag-ga-un; nearby the
hotel 호텔 근처에 hot-hel knch-hö-e;
is there a place to stay nearby? 요근처
에 숙박 할 만한 데가 있어요? yognch-
hö-e sugbag hal manan tega issö-yo?
nearly 거의 kö-e; we're nearly finished
거의 끝났어요 kö-e kt-hnassö-yo
neat (orderly) 깔끔 한 ggalg-gm han;
(drink) 순수 한 sunsu han
necessary 필요 한 p-hiryo han; is ...
necessary? ...을 필요가 있어요? ...l p-
hiryoga issö-yo?; it isn't necessary 필
요는 없어요 p-hiryonün öbsö-yo; is it
really necessary? 정말로 필요 해요?
chöng-mallo p-hiryo he-yo?
necessity 필수품 p-hilsup-hum

neck 목 mog
necklace 목걸이 moggöri
necktie 넥타이 negt-ha-i
need 필요 해요 p-hiryo he-yo; we need rooms for three people 세사람 방이 필요 해요 sesaram pang-i p-hiryo he-yo; I need some fresh air 신선 한 공기가 필요 해요 shinsön han konggiga p-hiryo he-yo; I need a doctor 의사가 필요 해요 esaga p-hiryo he-yo; no need to hurry 서두를 필요는 없어요 södurl p-hiryonün öbsö-yo; it needs more salt 소금이 더 필요 해요 sogmi tö p-hiryo he-yo; no need 필요 없어요 p-hiryo öbsö-yo; I need to rest 쉬고 싶은데요 swigo ship-hünde-yo; I need a good sleep 정말로 자야겠어요 chöng-mallo cha-yagessö-yo; I don't need anything 아무 것도 필요 없어요 amu göddo p-hiryo öbsö-yo; do I need ...? ...가 필요 해요? ...ga p-hiryo he-yo?; I don't need any ... ...가 필요 없어요 ...ga p-hiryo öbsö-yo
needle 바늘 panl; knitting needles 뜨개 바늘 ddgebanl
negative (photo) 원판 wönp-han
negotiate 협상 해요 hyöbsang he-yo
neighbor 이웃 사람 i-ud saram
neighborhood 동네 tong-ne
neither: neither of them (people) 어떤 사람도 아니에요 öd-dön saramdo ani-e-yo; (things) 어떤 것도 아니에요 öd-dön göddo ani-e-yo; neither ... nor ... ...도 ...도 아니에요 ...do ...do ani-e-yo
nephew 조카 chok-ha
nerve: what nerve! 참 뻔뻔스럽기도 하군! ch-ham bbönb-bönsröbgido hagun!
nervous 신경적인 shin-gyöng-jögin; a nervous breakdown 신경 쇠약 shin-gyöng swe-yag
net (for fishing) 어망 ömang; (sports)

네트 net-hü; mosquito net 모기장 mogijang
neutral (gear) 중립 (기어) chung-rib (gi-ö)
never 결코 ... 아니에요 kyölk-ho ... ani-e-yo; never mind 걱정 마세요 kögjöng mase-yo; she never laughs 그 는 결코 웃지 않아요 knün kyölk-ho udji anö-yo; I have never been here before 여기에 와 본 적이 없어요 yögi-e wa pon chögi öbsö-yo
new 새로운 sero-un; a new bulb 새 전구 se chön-gu; would you put new soles on these shoes? 이 구두에 새 창을 대어 주시겠어요? i gudu-e se ch-hang-l te-ö jushigessö-yo?; would you put a new zipper on? 새 지퍼로 갈아 주시겠어요? se chip-höro kara jushigessö-yo?
New Year 새해 sehe; New Year's Eve 망 년 mang-nyön; New Year's Day 설날 sölnal
New York 뉴욕 nyu-yog
New Zealand 뉴질랜드 nyujillendü; New Zealander 뉴질랜드 사람 nyujillendü saram
news 뉴스 nyusü; the latest news 최신 뉴스 ch-hweshin nyusü
newspaper 신문 shinmun; a local newspaper 지방 신문 chibang shinmun
newsstands 신문 판매대 shinmun p-hanmede
next 다음 ta-m; next to the church 교 회의 옆에 kyohwe-e yöp-he; next month 다음 달 ta-m tal; next time 다 음 번에 ta-m pöne; next year 내년 nenyön; the next day 다음 날 ta-m nal; the next boat from ... ...에서부터 다음 의 배 ...esöbut-hö ta-m e pe; the next street 다음 길 ta-m kil; until next week 다음주까지 ta-mjug-gaji; please sit next to me 내 곁에 앉아주십시오 ne kyöt-he anjajushibshi-o; Monday of next week

다음 주 월요일 ta-m chu wöryo-il; it's on the next corner 다음 번 모퉁이에 있어요 ta-m pön mot-hung-i-e issö-yo
next door (at neighbor's) 이웃에 i-use
next of kin 가까운 가족 kag-ga-un kajog
nice (good) 좋은 chohün; (delicious) 맛있는 mashinnün; how nice! 정말 좋군요! chöng-mal chok-hunyo!; a nice lazy vacation 한가한 휴가 han-gahan hyuga; have a nice day! 잘 지내 세요 chal chine se-yo; it has a very nice taste 맛이 매우 좋아요 mashi me-u choha-yo
nickname 별명 pyölmyöng
niece 조카 chok-ha
night 밤 pam; good night (sleep well) 안녕히 주무세요 annyöng-i chumuse-yo; last night 어젯밤 öjedbam; per night 하루에 haru-e; for one night 하룻밤 harudbam; could you put me up for the night? 오늘 저녁 숙박 시켜 주시겠어요? onl chönyög sugbag shik-hyö jushigessö-yo?
night flight 야간 비행 yagan piheng
night life 밤의 유흥 pame yuhüng
nightcap (drink) 잠술 chamsul
nightclub 나이트 클럽 na-it-hü k-hüllöb
nightgown 잠옷 chamod
nightie 잠옷 chamod
nightmare 악몽 angmong; it's a real nightmare (i.e. vacation) 악몽 같아요 angmong kat-ha-yo
no (not yes) 아니요 ani-yo; no fried food 튀긴것은 안돼요 t-hwigin-gösn andwe-yo; no need to hurry 서두를 필요는 없어요 södurl p-hiryonün öbsö-yo; no later than Tuesday 화요일까지 hwa-yo-ilg-gaji; no more 이제 그만 ije kman; no smoking 금연 kmyön; no, thanks 괜찮어요 kwench-hanö-yo; no chance! 안 돼요! an dwe-yo!; no problem! 괜찮아요 kwench-hyana-yo; no, thank you 아니 괜찮습니다 ani

kwench-hansmnida; it's no good 안돼 요 andwe-yo; it's no joke 농담이 아니에요 nong-dami ani-e-yo; oh no! 아이구! a-igu!; I have no cash 현금이 없어요 hyön-gmi öbsö-yo; long time no see! 오랜만이에요! orenmani-e-yo!; there is no more 더 없어요 tö öbsö-yo no one 아무도 ...-지 않어요 amudo ...-ji anö-yo
nobody 아무도 ...-지 않어요 amudo ...-ji anö-yo; nobody is at home 아무 도 집에 없어요 amudo chibe öbsö-yo; there was nobody 아무도 없었어요 amudo öbsössö-yo
noise 잠음 chabm; there's a knocking noise from the engine 엔진이 노킹 해요 enjini nok-hing he-yo
noisy 시끄러운 shig-grö-un
nonalcoholic (soft drink) 알코홀을 함유하지 않는 alk-hohorl hamyuhaji annün
none (people) 아무도 ...-지 않어요 amudo ...-ji anö-yo; (things) 아무 것도 ...-지 않어요 amu göddo ...-ji anö-yo; I have none 없어요 öbsö-yo
nonsense 넌센스 nönsensü; that's nonsense! 바보 같은 소리야 pabo kat-hün sori-ya
nonsmoking (section) 금연의 kmyöne
nonstop (direct) 직행 chik-heng; is it nonstop? 직행 해요? chik-heng he-yo?
noodles 국수 kugsu
noon 정오 chöng-o; around noon 정오 경 chöng-o kyöng
nor: neither ... nor ... ...도 ...도 아니에요 ...do ...do ani-e-yo
normal 정상의 chöng-sang-e
north 북쪽 pugj-jog; to the north 북쪽 으로 pugj-jogro
North Korea 북한 puk-han
northeast 북동쪽 pugdong-jjog
Northern Ireland 북아일랜드 puga-illendü
northwest 북서쪽 pugsöj-jög

Pronounce: a father; e let; i machine; o note; ö löng; u rude; ü further

Norway 노르웨이 norwe-i
nose 코 k-ho; broken nose 부러진 코
puröjin k-ho; I've got a nose bleed 코
피가 나요 k-hop-higa na-yo
not -지 않어요 -ji anö-yo; not bad! 괜
찮아요 kwench-hyana-yo; not ... but
... ... 아니고 ... ... anigo ...; not
just now 지금은 안돼요 chigm andwe-
yo; not many 많지 않은 manch-hi
anün; not that much 그렇게 많지
않어요 krök-he manch-hi anö-yo; not
that one 그것이 아니에요 kgöshi ani-e-
yo; not in the least 천만에요 ch-
hönmane-yo; not now 지금은 안 돼요
chigmn an dwe-yo; not these, but
those 이것이 아니고, 그곳이에요 igöshi
anigo, kgoshi-e-yo; not till
Wednesday 수요일에야 비로소 su-yo-
ire-ya piroso; not yet 아직도 ajigdo;
afraid not 미안 합니다만, 그렇지 않어요
mi-an hamnidaman, kröch-hi anö-yo;
absolutely not (that is wrong) 전혀
아네요 chönyö anye-yo; certainly not!
어림도 없어요 örimdo öbsö-yo; if not
않으면 anmyön; maybe not 그렇지
않을 지도 모르지요 kröch-hi anl chido
morji-yo; I'm not sure 확실치 않어요
hwagshilch-hi anö-yo; it's not true 정
말 아니에요 chöng-mal ani-e-yo;
why not? 왜 안 되지요? we an dweji-
yo?; you may not 안 되는데요. an
dwenünde-yo.; of course not 물론
그렇지 않어요 mullon kröch-hi anö-
yo; I hope not 그렇지 않기를 바래요
kröch-hi ank-hirl pare-yo; it was not
--it was so! 그렇지 않어요 -- 아니요,
그래요 kröch-hi anö-yo - ani-yo, kre-
yo
note (money) 짜리 jjari; (letter) 편지
p-hyönji
notebook 공책 kong-ch-heg
nothing 아무것도 ...-지 않어요
amugöddo ...-ji anö-yo; nothing
else, thanks 다른 것은 필요 없어요,

고맙습니다 tarn gösn piryo öbsö-yo,
komabsmnida; nothing more, thanks
이제 됐어요 ije dwessö-yo; nothing
special 평범 한 p-hyöng-böm han
notions 잡화 chap-hwa
novel 소설 sosöl; a novel by Yi
Kwang-su 이광수 의 소설 igwang-su e
sosöl
novelist 소설가 sosölga
November 십이월 shibiwöl
now 지금 chigm; now it's too late 지금
은 너무 늦어졌어요 chigmn nömu
njöjyössö-yo; not just now 지금은
안돼요 chigmn andwe-yo; let's go
now 자 지금 가요 cha chigm ka-yo;
must we pay now? 지금 요금을 치려야
돼요? chigm yogml ch-hiryö-ya dwe-
yo?; may I order now? 주문 해도
좋아요? chumun hedo choha-yo?; I
must be going now 나는 지금 가는
것이 좋아요 nanün chigm kanün göshi
choha-yo
nowadays 요즈음 yoj-m
nowhere 아무데도 ...않어요 amudedo
...anö-yo
number (numeral) 숫자 sudja;
registration number 등록 번호 tng-rog
pöno; telephone number 전화 번호
chönwa pöno; what is the telephone
number? 전화 번호는 몇 번이에요?
chönwa pönonün myöt pöni-e-yo?; I
think I have the wrong number 번호를
잘못 건 것 같군요 pönorl chalmod kön
göd kadk-hunyo
nurse 간호사 kanosa
nursery (for children) 탁아소 t-hagaso
nut 호두 hodu; (for screw) 너트 nöt-hü
nutrasweet (tm) (aspartame sweetener)
뉴트라 스위트 nyut-hüra swit-hü
nutrition 영양 yöng-yang
nylon 나일론 na-illon

O

oak 참나무 ch-hamnamu
oatmeal 오트밀 ot-hümil
obnoxious (offensive) 싫은 shirn
obscene language 속어 sogö
obvious 명백한 myöng-bek-han
obviously 명백 하게 myöng-beg hage
occasionally 이따금 id-dagm
Occident 서양 sö-yang
Occidental (Western) 서양의 sö-yang-e
occupation 직업 chigöb
occupied 사용중 sa-yong-jung
ocean 바다 pada; Pacific Ocean 태평영
t-hep-hyöng-yöng; from here to the
ocean 여기서부터 바다까지 yögisöbut-
hö padag-gaji
o'clock -시 -shi
October 시월 shiwöl
octopus (small) 낙지 nagji
odd (strange) 이상 한 isang han; (not
even) 홀수 holsu
of ... ...의 ...e; I'm sick and tired
of... ...에 진저리 나요 ...e chinjöri
na-yo
off: getting off! 내려요! neryö-yo!;
10% off 십 퍼센트 할인 shib p-hösent-
hü harin; take off (clothes) 벗어요
pösö-yo; I fell off my bike 자전거에서
떨어졌어요 chajön-gö-esö ddöröjyössö-
yo; in the off season 한산기에 hansan-
gi-e; see someone off 마중 해요
majung he-yo; please let me off at
... ...에서 내려 주세요 ...esö neryö
juse-yo; where do I get off? 어디서
내려요? ödisö neryö-yo?; would you
switch it off? 꺼 주시겠어요? ggö
jushigessö-yo?
off-season 한산기(의) hansan-gi(e)
offend 화나게 해요 hwanage he-yo;

don't be offended 기분 나쁘게 생각
마세요 kibun nab-bge seng-gag mase-
yo
office (rooms) 사무실 samushil; box
office 매표소 mep-hyoso; information
office 안내소 anneso; post office 우체
국 uch-hegug; ticket office 매표구
mep-hyogu; tourist information office
관광 안내소 kwan-gwang anneso; I
work in an office 사무실에서 일 해요
samushiresö il he-yo
officer (policeman) 경관 kyöng-gwan
official (person) 관리인 kwanri-in
often 종종 chong-jong; how often do
the buses run? 버스는 몇분마다 있어요?
pösnün myödp-hunmada issö-yo?;
such things often happen 그런 일은
자주 일어나요 krön irn chaju iröna-yo
oh! (in surprise) 어이구 ö-igu; oh my
gosh! 어마! öma!; oh no! 아이구! a-
igu!
oil (lubrication) 오일 o-il; (cooking)
기름 kirm; sesame oil 참기름 ch-
hamgirm; suntan oil 선탠 오일 sönt-
hen o-il; it's leaking oil 오일이 새요
o-iri se-yo
oil painting 유화 yuhwa
oil pressure 유압 yu-ab
ointment 연고 yön-go; do you have an
ointment for burns? 화상에 듣는 약
있어요? hwasang-e tnnün yag issö-yo?
okay 좋아요 choha-yo; (may I?) 해도
좋아요? hedo choha-yo?; I'm okay 나
는 여전 해요 nanün yöjön he-yo; is
it okay to smoke? 담배를 피워도
좋아요? tamberl p-hiwödo choha-yo?
old (person) 늙은 nlgn; (object) 낡은
nalgn; poor old Mr. Kim! 불쌍 한
미스터 김 pulsang han mist-hö kim;
about 40 years old 약 마흔살 yag
mahünsal; she is 55 years old 쉰 다섯
살이에요 swin tasöd sari-e-yo
old-fashioned 구식의 kushige
olives 올리브 ollibü

Pronounce: a father; e let; i machine; o note; ö löng; u rude; ü further

omelette 오믈렛 omlled

on ... ... 위에 ... wi-e; on average 평균 해서 p-hyöng-gyun hesö; on the balcony 발코니에 palk-honi-e; on the shore 해변에 hebyöne; on the coast 해안에 he-ane; on what date? 며칠에? myöt-hire?; on the second floor 이층에 ich-hüng-e; on foot 걸어서 körösö; on the hour 정각에 chöng-gage; on the left 왼쪽에 wenj-joge; on purpose 고의로 ko-ero; on the radio 라디오로 radi-oro; on the rocks (ice) 언 더 락 ön tö rag; on top of ... ... 위에 ... wi-e; on the weekend 주말에 chumare; on the corner 모퉁이에 mot-hung-i-e; come on! 자 가요! cha ka-yo!; I'm on the pill 피임약을 복용 해요 p-hi-imyagl pogyong he-yo; I've come on business 일 때문에 왔어요 il ddemune wassö-yo; that depends on ... ...에 달려 있어요 ...e tallyö issö-yo; the light was on 불은 켜져 있었어요 purn k-hyöjyö issössö-yo; this time it's on me 이번에는 내가 내겠어요 ibönenün nega negessö-yo; please put it on the table 테이블 위에 놓으세요 t-he-ibl wi-e nohüse-yo; please switch it on 켜 주시겠어요 k-hyö jushigessö-yo; may I try it on? 입어 봐도 좋아요? ibö pwado choha-yo?; the woman with the black skirt on 검은 스커트를 입는 사람 kömn sk-höt-hürl imnün saram

once (one time) 한번 hanbön; (earlier) 일찌기 ilj-jigi; once per year 일년에 한 번씩 ilnyöne han pönshig; at once 곧 kod; only once 한 번만 han pönman; drop by once in a while 가끔 들러 주세요 kag-gm tllö juse-yo

one 한 / 하나 / 일 han / hana / il; one year ago 일년 전에 ilnyön chöne; one day (once) 어느 날 önü nal; one for each of us 우리에게 각각 한개씩 uri-ege kaggag han-gesshig; one like

that 저것과 같은 것 chögödgwa kat-hün göd; one month 일개월 ilgewöl; just one 하나만 hanaman; the one next to that 그 옆에 있는 것 kü yöp-he innün göd; for one night 하룻밤 harudbam; have one of mine 나의 것을 부탁 해요 na-e gösl put-hag he-yo; that one 그것 kgöd; this one 이것 igöd; which one? 어느 쪽이에요? önü jjogi-e-yo?; a big one 큰 것 k-hün göd; the other one 다른 것 tarn göd; how much for one of them? 하나에 얼마에요? hana-e ölma-e-yo?; I'll take this one 이것으로 주세요 igösro chuse-yo; I forget which one it was 어느 쪽인지 잊어 버렸어요 önü jjoginji ijö pöryössö-yo; it's different from this one 이것과 달라요 igödgwa talla-yo

one-way ticket 편도표 p-hyöndop-hyo; a one-way ticket to... ...행 편도표 ...eng p-hyöndop-hyo

onion 양파 yang-p-ha

only ... ... 만 ... man; only a few 정말 조금 chöng-mal chogm; only me 나만 naman; only a little 조금만 chogmman; it's only 10 o'clock 겨우 열시에요 kyö-u yölshi-e-yo; it's only a scratch 그저 작은 상처에요 kjö chagn sang-ch-hö-e-yo; I think it comes to only 5000 won 겨우 오천원 정도 되리라 생각 해요 kyö-u och-hönwön chöng-do dwerira seng-gag he-yo

open (not closed) 연 yön;

open (verb) 열어요 yörö-yo; please open it 열어 보세요 yörö pose-yo; it doesn't open 안 열려요 an yöllyö-yo; when does it open? 언제 문을 여세요? önje munl yöse-yo?; please leave the windows open 창문을 열어 두어 주세요 ch-hang-munl yörö tu-ö juse-yo; will you still be open? 그때까지 문을 열거에요? kd-deg-gaji munl yölgö ye-yo?

opener: bottle opener 병따개 pyöng-ddage; can opener 캉통 따개 k-hang-t-

hong ddage
opening ceremony 개막식 kemagshig
opera 오페라 op-hera
operation (surgery) 수술 susul
operator (telephone) 전화 교환수 chönwa kyohwansu; is there an operator who speaks English? 영어 하는 교환이 있어요? yöng-ö hanün kyohwani issö-yo?
opinion 의견 egyön
opponent 상대방 sang-debang
opportunity 기회 kihwe
opposite: opposite the theater 극장 맞은 편에 kgjang majn p-hyöne; the opposite (meaning) of ... ...의 반대말 ...e pandemal
optician 안경점 an-gyöng-jöm
optional 선택의 sönt-hege
or 또는 ddonün; either ... or ... ...든가 또는 ... ...dn-ga ddonün ...; are there Western or Korean meals? 음식은 양식이에요, 한식이에요? ümshign yang-shigi-e-yo, hanshigi-e-yo?
orange 오렌지 orenji
orange juice 오렌지 쥬스 orenji chyusü
orchestra 오케스트라 ok-hest-hüra; what is the orchestra playing? 오케스트라가 무슨 곡을 연주 해요? ok-hest-hüraga musn kogl yönju he-yo?
order 주문 해요 chumun he-yo; may I order now? 주문 해도 좋아요? chumun hedo choha-yo?; place an order 주무 해요 chumu he-yo; that's not what I ordered 그것은 내가 주문 한 것과 틀려요 kgösn nega chumun han gödgwa t-hüllyö-yo; this is out of order 이것이 고장 났어요 igöshi kojang nassö-yo
ordinary 보통의 pot-hong-e; an ordinary haircut 보통의 이발 해주세요 pot-hong-e ibal hejuse-yo; the hotel is pretty ordinary 그 호텔에 특별한 것이 아무것도 없어요 kü ot-here t-hügbyöran göshi amugöddo öbsö-yo
organization 조직 chojig

organize 계획 해요 kyehweg he-yo
Orient 동양 tong-yang
Oriental (Eastern) 동양의 tong-yang-e; (person) 동양인 tong-yang-in
original (inventive) 독창적인 togch-hang-jögin
other 다른 tarn; other than ... ... 외에 ... we-e; the other side of town 시내 반대쪽에 shine pandej-joge; I had no other choice 다른 방법이 없었어요 tarn pang-böbi öbsössö-yo; are there any other colors? 다른 색이 있어요? tarn segi issö-yo?; we know each other 우리는 서로 알아요 urinün söro ara-yo
otherwise 그렇지 않으면 kröch-hi anmyön
ouch! 아야! a-ya!
ought (do) 해야 해요 he-ya he-yo
ounce 온스 onsü
our 우리의 uri-e; our daughter 우리 딸 uri ddal; our granddaughter 우리 손녀 uri sonnyö; our grandson 우리 손자 uri sonja; our bags 우리의 가방 uri-e kabang; our son 우리 아들 uri adl
ours 우리의 uri-e
out 밖 pagg; out of breath 숨이 져서 sumi chyösö; out in the open 교외에 kyowe-e; out of the sun 그늘에 knre; come out 나와요 nawa-yo; it's out of order 고장 나요 kojang na-yo; we're out of cash 돈이 떨어 졌어요 toni ddörö chyössö-yo; watch out! 조심 해요! choshim he-yo!; worn out (tired) 피곤 한 p-higon han; he passed out 그는 기절 했어요 knün kijöl hessö-yo; to take out (food) 가지고 갈 ... kajigo kal ...; I've shut myself out 못 들어가게 되었어요 mod trögage dwe-össö-yo; may I invite you out with me? 나와 함께 외출 하시지 않겠어요? nawa hamg-ge wech-hul hashiji ank-hessö-yo?; will you put the light out? 불을 꺼 주시겠어요? prl ggö jushigessö-yo?

outdoors 문 밖에 mun pag-ge

outlet (electrical) 콘센트 k-honsent-hü

outline (summary, contours) 윤곽 yun-gwag

outside 밖에 pag-ge; a few kilometers outside of town 시내에서 몇 길로미터 떨어져(서) shine-esö myöt killomit-hö ddöröjyö(sö)

oven 오븐 obn; microwave oven 전자 렌지 chönja renji

over ... (above) ...위에 ...wi-e; over 200 이백 이상 ibeg isang; over there 저 기 chögi; it's over 끝났어요 ggt-hnassö-yo; left over (remaining) 남아 있는 nama innün; that gentleman / lady over there 저분 chöbun; she's been knocked over 그는 때려 눕혀졌어요 knün dderyö nup-hyöjyössö-yo; she's been run over 차 에 치었어요 ch-ha-e ch-hi-össö-yo

overcoat 외투 wet-hu

overcooked 너무 익은 nömu ign; it's overcooked 너무 익었어요 nömu igössö-yo

overexposed (picture) 노출 과다 한 noch-hul kwada han

overheat 과열 되요 kwa-yöl dwe-yo; it's overheating (auto) 과열 돼요 kwa-yöl dwe-yo

overnight 하룻밤 hardbam

overseas 해외 (의) hewe (e)

oversleep 늦잠 자요 njjam cha-yo

overweight (fat) 뚱뚱 한 ddung-ddung han; (baggage) 중량 초과의 chung-ryang ch-hogwa-e

owe 빚지고 있어요 pijjigo issö-yo

own (be owner) 소유에요 so-yu-e-yo; I'm on my own 혼자 있어요 honja issö-yo

owner 주인 chu-in

oxtail 쇠꼬리 sweg-gori

oyster 굴 kul

P

Pacific Ocean 태평영 t-hep-hyöng-yöng

pacifier (for babies) 고무 젖꼭지 komu chödg-gogji

pack (bags) 짐을 꾸려요 chiml gguryö-yo; face pack (cosmetic) 팩 p-heg; I'll go pack 가서 짐을 꾸리겠어요 kasö chiml ggurigessö-yo; the place was packed (crowded) 그곳이 초만원였어요 kgoshi ch-homanwönyössö-yo

package (parcel) 소포 sop-ho; did my package get here? 내 소포가 도착 했어요? ne sop-hoga toch-hag hessö-yo?

package tour 패키지 투어 p-hek-hiji t-hu-ö

packed lunch 도시락 toshirag

packet 갑 kab

paddy field 논 non

page (paper) 페이지 p-he-iji; please page Mr. ... 미스터 ...-를 찾어 주세요 mist-hö ...-rl ch-hajö juse-yo

pagoda 탑 t-hab

pain 아픔 ap-hüm; I'm in pain here 여 기가 아퍼요 yögiga ap-hö-yo

painful 아픈 ap-hün

painkiller 진통제 chint-hong-je

paint (noun) 페인트 p-he-int-hü

paintbrush (art) 그림붓 krimbud

painter (artist) 화가 hwaga

painting 그림 krim; oil painting 유화 yuhwa; I'm going to do painting 그림 을 그리겠어요 kriml krigessö-yo

pair of ... ... 두개 ... tuge; a pair of sandals 샌들 한 켤레 sendl han k-hyölle; a pair of shoes 구두 한 켤레 kudu han k-hyölle

pajamas 잠옷 chamod

Pakistan 파키스탄 p-hak-hist-han

Pakistani (adjective) 파키스탄의 p-hak-hist-hane; (person) 파키스탄 사람 p-hak-hist-han saram

pal 친구 ch-hin-gu; **pen pal** 펜팔 친구 p-henp-hal ch-hin-gu

palace (왕)궁 (wang)gung

pale (pallid) 창백 한 ch-hang-beg han; (color) 연 한 yön han; **he looks pale** 얼굴이 창백 해요 ölguri ch-hang-beg he-yo

pan: frying pan 프라이팬 p-hüra-ip-hen

pancake 팬케이크 p-hen-k-he-ik-hü

panic (horror) 공포 kong-p-ho

panties 팬티 p-hent-hi

pants (trousers) 바지 paji; (underpants) 팬티 p-hent-hi

panty girdle 팬티거들 p-hent-higödl

pantyhose 팬티 스타킹 p-hent-hi st-hak-hing

papaya 파파야 p-hap-ha-ya

paper 종이 chong-i; **toilet paper** 휴지 hyuji; **wrapping paper** 포장지 p-hojang-ji; **writing paper** 편지지 p-hyönjiji; **a sheet of paper** 종이 한 장 chong-i han chang

parachute 낙하산 nak-hasan

parallel 평행 한 p-hyöng-eng han

parallel to ... ...와 평행 한 ...wa p-hyöng-eng han

parasol 파라솔 p-harasol

pardon? 다시 한번 말씀 해 주시겠어요? tashi hanbön malsm he jushigessö-yo?

parents 부모님 pumonim

park (gardens) 공원 kong-wön; **amusement park** 유원지 yuwönji; **car park** 주차장 chuch-hajang; **national park** 국립 공원 kugrib kong-wön; **where can we park?** 어디에 주차 할 수 있어요? ödi-e chuch-ha hal su issö-yo?

parka 파카 p-hak-ha

parking brake 주차 브레이크 chuch-ha pre-ik-hü

parking lights 주차등 chuch-hadng

parking lot 주차장 chuch-hajang

parking place 주차장 chuch-hajang

parliament 의회 ehwe

parsley 파슬리 p-haslli

part (portion) 부분 pubun; **please part my hair on the left** 가름마를 왼쪽으로 해 주세요 karmmarl wenj-jogro he juse-yo; **spare part** 예비 부속품 yebi pusogp-hum

partner (friend) 상대자 sang-deja; (business) 동료 tong-ryo

party (troupe) 일행 ireng; (celebration) 파티 p-hat-hi; **dinner party** 만찬회 manch-hanwe; **farewell party** 송별회 song-byörwe; **search party** 수색대 susegde; **let's give a party** 파티를 해요 p-hat-hirl he-yo

pass (in mountain) 산길 san-gil; (overtake) 추월 해요 ch-huwöl he-yo; **boarding pass** 보딩 패스 poding p-hesü; **he passed out** 그는 기절 했어요 knün kijöl hessö-yo; **rail pass** 정기 패스 chöng-gi p-hesü; **she made a pass at me** 나에게 지분거렸어요 na-ege chibun-göryössö-yo

passable (traffic) 통행 할 수 있는 t-hong-eng hal su innün

passenger 승객 sng-geg

passport 여권 yögwön

past ... ... 지나서 ... chinasö; **past the lights** 신호를 지나서 shinorl chinasö; **may I get past?** 지나가도 돼요? chinagado dwe-yo?

pastry 생과자 seng-gwaja

pasture 목장 mogjang

patch (on clothes) 헝겊 조각 höng-göp chogag

pate' 파테 p-hat-he

path 길 kil

patience 인내 inne

patient (sick person) 환자 hwanja; **be patient** 참아 주세요 ch-hama juse-yo

patio 파티오 p-hat-hi-o

pattern 모형 mohyöng; **dress pattern** 무늬 mune

pavement 포장 p-hojang

pay 내요 ne-yo; **pay attention** 주의

해요 chu-e he-yo; pay the bill 계산 해요 kyesan he-yo; we'll pay in advance 선불 할게요 sönbul halge-yo; we'll pay in cash 현금으로 지불하겠어요 hyön-gmro chiburagessö-yo; I'll pay 내가 사겠어요 nega sagessö-yo; can I pay with dollars? 달러로 내도 돼요? tallöro nedo dwe-yo?; must we pay now? 지금 요금을 치려야 돼요? chigm yogml ch-hiryö-ya dwe-yo?; it has already been paid for 대금을 벌써 끝냈어요 tegml pölsö ggt-hnessö-yo

pay phone 공중 전화 kong-jung chönwa

payment 지불 chibul

peace (not war) 평화 p-hyöng-wa

peach 복숭아 pogsung-a

peanuts 땅콩 ddang-k-hong

pear 배 pe

pearl 진주 chinju

peas 완두 wandu

peasant 농부 nong-bu

pedal (noun) 페달 p-hedal; gas pedal 악셀 agsel

pedestrian 보행자 poheng-ja

pedestrian crossing 횡단 보도 hweng-dan podo

pedestrian mall 차 없는 곳 ch-ha ömnün kod

pen 펜 p-hen; ballpoint pen 볼펜 polp-hen; felt pen 펠트펜 p-helt-hüp-hen; have you got a pen? 펜이 있어요? p-heni issö-yo?; I write with a pen 펜으로 써요 p-henro ssö-yo

pen pal 펜팔 친구 p-henp-hal ch-hin-gu; do you want to be pen pals? 펜팔 하고 싶어요? p-henp-hal hago ship-hö-yo?

pencil 연필 yönp-hil; eyebrow pencil 눈썹 연필 nunsöb yönp-hil

penicillin 페니실린 p-henishillin

penknife 주머니칼 chumönik-hal

people 사람 saram; British people 영국 사람 yöng-gug saram; Chinese people 중국 사람 chung-gug saram; many people 많은 사람 manün saram; some people 어떤 사람들 öd-dön saramdl; young person 젊은이 chölmni; a room for two people 이 인용 방 i inyong pang

pepper (black) 후추 huch-hu; green pepper 피망 p-himang; hot pepper 고추 koch-hu

peppermint 박하 pak-ha

per ... ...에 ...e; per night 하루에 haru-e; per person 일인당 irindang; once per year 일년에 한 번씩 ilnyöne han pönshig; 3500 won per bottle 한병에 삼천 오백원 hanbyöng-e samch-hön obegwön

per cent 퍼센트 p-hösent-hü

perch 농어 nong-ö

perfect 완전 한 wanjön han; it's perfect 완벽 해요 wanbyög he-yo

performance (show) 공연 kong-yön

performer 출연자 ch-huryönja

perfume 향수 hyang-su

perhaps 아마 ama

period (season) 시기 shigi; (epoch) 시대 shide; (menstruation) 월경 wölgyöng

perm 파마 p-hama

permission 허가 höga

permit (a license) 허가 höga

persimmon 감 kam

person 사람 saram; per person 일인당 irindang; single person (unmarried) 미혼자 mihonja; the person who ... ...의 사람 ...e saram; person to person call 특정인 호출 전화 t-hügjöng-in hoch-hul chönwa; I don't know that person 그 사람을 몰라요 kü saraml molla-yo

person to person call 특정인 호출 전화 t-hügjöng-in hoch-hul chönwa

personal (private) 개인의 ke-ine; it's for my personal use 그것은 내가 쓰는

것이에요 kgösn nega ssnün göshi-e-yo
personal check 개인 수표 ke-in sup-hyo
Peru 페루 p-heru
pharmacy 약국 yaggug
pheasant 꿩 ggwöng
Philippines 필리핀 p-hillip-hin
phone 전화 chönwa; car phone 카 폰 k-ha p-hon; cellular phone 셀 방식 전화 sel pang-shig chönwa; pay phone 공중 전화 kong-jung chönwa; I'll phone you 당신에게 전화를 걸겠어요 tang-shinege chönwarl kölgessö-yo; please write your name and phone number 성함과 전화 번호를 좀 써 주세요 söng-amgwa chönwa pönorl chom ssö juse-yo
phonecard 텔레폰 카드 t-hellep-hon k-hadü
photograph (picture) 사진 sajin; could you take a photograph of me? 내 카메라로 사진 좀 찍어 주시겠어요? ne k-hameraro sajin chom jjigö jushigessö-yo?
photographer 사진사 sajinsa
photography studio 사진관 sajin-gwan
phrase 관용구 kwanyong-gu
phrase book 숙어집 sugöjib
pianist 피아니스트 p-hi-anist-hü
piano 피아노 p-hi-ano
pick up (fetch) 가지러 가요 kajirö ka-yo; when can I pick them up? 언제 가지러 갈까요 önje kajirö kalg-ga-yo
pickpocket 소매치기 somech-higi
picnic (outing) 소풍 sop-hung
picture 그림 krim; (photo) 사진 sajin; who painted that picture? 저 그림은 누가 그렸어요? chö krimn nuga kryössö-yo?; may I take your picture? 사진을 찍어도 될까요? sajinl jjigödo dwelg-ga-yo?
picture postcard 그림 엽서 krim yöbsö
pie 파이 p-ha-i; apple pie 사과 파이 sagwa p-ha-i; meat pie 미트 파이 mit-hü p-ha-i

piece 조각 chogag; a piece of cake (to eat) 케익 한조각 k-he-ig hanjogag; a piece of candy 캔디 한개 k-hendi hange
pier 부두 pudu
pig 돼지 dweji
pigeon 비둘기 pidulgi
pike 곤들매기 kondlmegi
pill 환약 hwanyag; sleeping pill 수면제 sumyönje
pillow 베개 pege
pillow case 베갓잇 pegashid
pimento 피망 p-himang
pin (noun) 핀 p-hin; safety pin 안전핀 anjönp-hin; bobby pins 머리핀 mörip-hin
pinball 핀볼 p-hinbol
pine 솔 sol
pineapple 파인애플 p-ha-inep-hül
ping pong 탁구 t-haggu
pink 분홍색 punong-seg
pint 파인트 p-ha-int-hü
pipe (tobacco) 파이프 p-ha-ip-hü; (water) 수도관 sudogwan
pipe cleaner 파이프 청소기 p-ha-ip-hü ch-höng-sogi
pipe tobacco 파이프 담배 p-ha-ip-hü tambe
piss (urine) 소변 sobyön; I need to take a piss 소변을 보고 싶어요 sobyönl pogo ship-hö-yo
pizza 피자 p-hija
place (location) 장소 chang-so; place an order 주문 해요 chumu he-yo; this place has changed a lot 이곳에 모습이 많이 바뀌었군요 igose mosbi mani paggwi-ödgunyo; favorite place (regular customer) 단골 tan-gol; meeting place 회의장 hwe-ejang; parking place 주차장 chuch-hajang; there's a parking place! 저기에 주차장 있어요! chögi-e chuch-hajang issö-yo!; could you hold my place? 내 자리를 봐 주시겠어요? ne charirl pwa jushigessö-

yo?

place mat 접시받침 chöbshibadch-him

plaid 격자 무늬 kyögja mune

plain (simple) 간단 한 kandan han; (no pattern) 무늬가 없는 munega ömnün

plan 계획 kyehweg

plane (airplane) 비행기 piheng-gi; when does the plane land? 언제 비행기가 착륙 해요? önje piheng-giga ch-hagryug he-yo?; when does the plane take off? 비행기는 언제나 이륙 해요 piheng-ginün önjena iryug he-yo; can I take a plane there? 비행기로 갈 수가 있어요? piheng-giro kal suga issö-yo?

plant 화초 hwach-ho

plastic 프라스틱 p-hürast-hig

plastic bag 비닐 봉투 pinil pong-t-hu

plate 접시 chöbshi; license plate 번호판 pönop-han; gold plated 금도금 kmdogm

platform 플랫폼 p-hülledp-hom; which platform is it? 어느 플랫폼이에요? önü p-hülledp-homi-e-yo?

platinum 백금 peggm

play (games, sports) 놀아요 nora-yo; (music) 연주 해요 yönju he-yo; (theatrical work) 연극 yön-güg; do you play cards? 카드 놀이를 하세요? k-hadü norirl hase-yo?; do you play golf? 골프 치세요? kolp-hü ch-hise-yo?; do you play tennis? 테니스 치세요? t-henisü ch-hise-yo?; shall we play table tennis? 탁구를 할까요? t-haggurl halg-ga-yo?

playboy 바람 둥이 param tung-i

playground 운동장 undong-jang; children's playground 어린이 놀이터 örini norit-hö

playwright 극작가 kgjagga

pleasant 쾌적한 k-hwejök-han

please (please do) 제발 chebal; please come again 또 오세요 ddo ose-yo; please find the word in this book 이

책에서 그 말을 찾아 주세요 i ch-hegesö kü marl ch-haja juse-yo; please introduce yourself 인사 하세요 insa hase-yo; please sign here 여기에 서명 해 주세요 yögi-e sömyöng he juse-yo; would you please ...? ...어 주시겠어요? ...ö jushigessö-yo?

pleasure 기쁨 kib-bm; with pleasure 기꺼이 kig-gö-i; it's a pleasure to do business with you 당신과 일을 같이 하게되서 기뻐요 tang-shin-gwa irl kat-hi hagedwesö kib-bö-yo

plenty 많음 manm; I've had plenty (to eat) 많이 먹었어요 mani mögössö-yo

plenty of ... 많은 ... manün ...

pliers 뻰찌 bbenj-ji

plug (electrical) 플러그 p-hüllögü; (stopper) 마개 mage; spark plug 점화 플러그 chömwa p-hüllögü

plug in (verb) 끼워요 ggiwö-yo

plum 자두 chadu

plumber 연관공 yön-gwan-gong

plus (math) 플러스 p-hüllösü

p.m. (after noon) 오후 ohu; at 6:00 p.m. 오후 여섯시에 ohu yösösshi-e

pneumonia 폐염 p-hye-yöm

pocket 주머니 chumöni

pocketbook (handbag) 손 가방 son kabang

pocketknife 주머니칼 chumönik-hal

point (indicate) 가리켜요 karik-hyö-yo; three point five 삼 점 오 sam chöm o; power point (electrical) 콘센트 k-honsent-hü

points of interest 명소 myöng-so

poisoning: food poisoning 식중독 shigjung-dog

poisonous 독이 있는 togi innün

Poland 폴란드 p-hollandü

police 경찰 kyöng-ch-hal

police station 파출소 p-hach-hulso

policeman 경관 kyöng-gwan; please ask that policeman over there 저기에 있는 경찰에게 물어보세요 chögi-e

Pronounce: a father; e let; i machine; o note; ö löng; u rude; ü fürther

innün kyöng-ch-harege muröbose-yo
policy: insurance policy 보험 증서 pohöm chüng-sö
polish (noun) 광내는 약 kwang-nenün yag;
polish (verb) 닦아요 tag-ga-yo; nail polish 매니큐어 menik-hyu-ö; nail polish remover 매니큐어 지우개 menik-hyu-ö chi-uge; shoe polish 구두약 kudu-yag; could you polish my shoes? 구두를 좀 닦아 주시겠어요? kudurl chom tag-ga jushigessö-yo?
polite 공손 한 kong-son han; polite language 정중한 말 chöng-jung-an mal
politician 정치가 chöng-ch-higa
politics 정치 chöng-ch-hi
polluted 오염 된 o-yöm dwen
pollution 오염 o-yöm
polyester 폴리에스텔 p-holli-est-hel
pond 연못 yönmod
pony 조랑말 chorang-mal
pool (swimming) 풀 p-hul; (billiards) 당구 tang-gu; children's pool 어린이 용 풀 örini-yong p-hul; indoor pool 실내 수영장 shilne su-yöng-jang
pool table 당구대 tang-gude
pooped: I'm pooped (very tired) 기진맥 진 해 졌어요 kijinmegjin he chyössö-yo
poor (impoverished) 가난 한 kanan han; (low quality) 열등 한 yöldng han
pop music 팝송 p-habsong
pop singer 유행가 가수 yuheng-ga kasu
popcorn 팝콘 p-habk-hon
Pope 로마 교황 roma kyohwang
popular 인기 있는 in-gi innün
population 인구 in-gu
porgy 도미 tomi
pork 돼지 고기 dweji kogi; sweet and sour pork 탕수육 t-hang-su-yug
porridge 죽 chug
port (haven) 항구 hang-gu
porter (doorman) 도어맨 to-ömen; (at

station) 짐꾼 chimg-gun; would you get me the porter? 짐꾼 좀 불러 주세요 chimg-gun chom pullö juse-yo
portrait 초상 ch-hosang
Portugal 포르투갈 p-hort-hugal
Portuguese language 포르투갈말 p-hort-hugalmal
posh (restaurant) 호화로운 hohwaro-un
position (location) 자리 chari; (employment) 일자리 iljari
possibility 가능성 kanüng-söng
possible 가능 한 kanüng han; as soon as possible 가능한 한 빨리 kanüng-an han bballi
post (the mail) 우편 up-hyön
post office 우체국 uch-hegug; beside the post office 우체국 옆에 uch-hegug yöp-he; where is the central post office? 중앙우체국 어디 있어요? chung-ang-uch-hegug ödi issö-yo?
postage 우편 요금 up-hyön yogm
postcard 엽서 yöbsö; picture postcard 그 림 엽서 krim yöbsö; New Year postcard 연하장 yönajang
poste restante 유치 우편 yuch-hi up-hyön
poster 포스터 p-host-hö
pot (pan) 남비 nambi
potable water 식수 shigsu
potato 감자 kamja; sauteed potatoes 살 짝 튀긴 감자 salj-jag t-hwigin kamja
potato chips 감자 튀김 kamja t-hwigim
potato salad 감자 샐러드 kamja sellödü
pottery 도자기 tojagi
pottery shop 도기 제조소 togi chejoso
pound (weight, British money) 파운드 p-ha-undü
pour (into glass) 부어요 pu-ö-yo; it's pouring (rain) 비가 퍼붓고 있어요 piga p-höbudgo issö-yo
powder (cosmetic) 분 pun; soap powder 가루 비누 karu pinu
powdered milk 분유 punyu
power 힘 him; electric power 전력

chönryög

power cut (electricity) 정전 chöng-jön

power point (electrical) 콘센트 k-honsent-hü

power station 발전소 paljönso

practice 연습 yönsb; I need the practice 연습이 필요 해요 yönsbi p-hiryo he-yo

prawns 중새우 chung-se-u

pray 기도 해요 kido he-yo

prefer 더 좋아요 tö choha-yo; I'd prefer boiled rice 밥이 더 좋아요 pabi tö choha-yo

preferably 차라리 ch-harari

pregnant 임신중인 imshinjung-in; she's pregnant 그는 임신부에요 knün imshinbu-e-yo

prepare 준비 해요 chunbi he-yo; can you show me how to prepare this? 이 것을 만드는 법을 가르쳐 주시겠어요? igösl mandnün pöbl karch-hyö jushigessö-yo?

prescription (for drug) 처방 ch-höbang

prescription drugstore 약제사 yagjesa

present (gift) 선물 sönmul; please accept this present 이 선물을 받아 주세요 i sönmurl pada juse-yo

president (company) 사장 sajang; (country) 대통령 tet-hong-ryöng; (university) 총장 ch-hong-jang; Madam President 대통령 부인 tet-hong-ryöng pu-in

press (clothes) 다림질 해요 tarimjil he-yo

pressure: oil pressure 유압 yu-ab; I have high blood pressure 나는 고혈압이 있어요 nanün kohyörabi issö-yo

pretty (beautiful) 예쁜 yeb-bn; they're pretty expensive 꽤 비싸요 ggwe pissa-yo; the hotel is pretty ordinary 그 호텔에 특별한 것이 아무것도 없어요 kü ot-here t-hügbyöran göshi amugöddo öbsö-yo

price 값 kabd; fixed price 정가 chöng-ga; cut the price 값을 깎아 줘요 kabsl

ggag-ga chwö-yo; did the price go up? 값이 올랐어요? kabshi ollassö-yo?; what's the admission price? 입장료는 얼마에요? ibjang-ryonün ölma-e-yo?; you've raised the price 값을 올리셨어요 kabsl ollishyössö-yo; can you give me a better price? 좀 싸게 해 주시겠어요? chom ssage he jushigessö-yo?

priest (Catholic) 신부 shinbu; (Buddhist) 스님 snim

Prime Minister 국무 총리 kungmu ch-hong-ri

print (pattern) 연속 무늬 yönsog mune; (woodblock) 판화 p-hanwa; please make one print of each 한 장씩 빼 주세요 han chang-sshig bbe chuse-yo

printed matter 인쇄물 inswemul

printer (for computer) 프린터 p-hürint-hö

prison 교도소 kyodoso

private 개인적인 ke-injögin

private room 별실 pyölshil

private school 사립 학교 sarib haggyo

prize 상품 sang-p-hum; (money) 상금 sang-gm

probably 대개 tege

problem 문제 munje; ethnic problem 인종 문제 injong munje; it's no problem 괜찮아요 kwench-hyana-yo; what's the problem? 무슨 일인가요? musn irin-ga-yo?; I'm having a problem with ... ...에 문제가 생겼어요 ...e munjega seng-gyössö-yo; that's just the problem 그게 바로 문제란 말이에요 kge paro munjeran mari-e-yo

processing: does the price of this film include processing? 이 가격에는 현상료도 포함되어 있어요? i gagyögenün hyönsang-ryodo p-hohamdwe-ö issö-yo?

producer (movies) 영화 제작자 yöng-wa chejagja

product 생산물 seng-sanmul; we are

very proud of this product 이 생산물을 자랑으로 여기고 있어요 i seng-sanmurl charang-ro yögigo issö-yo

professor 교수 kyosu

program (broadcast) 프로그램 p-hürogrem; (schedule) 예정표 yejöng-p-hyo; (theater, computer) 프로그램 p-hürogrem; **is there a program in English?** 영어로 된 프로그램 있어요? yöng-öro dwen p-hürogrem issö-yo?

promise (agreement) 약속 yagsog; **I promise** 약속 해요 yagsog he-yo; **do you promise?** 약속 해요? yagsog he-yo?

pronounce 발음 해요 parm he-yo; **how is this pronounced?** 이것을 어떻게 발음 해요? igösl öd-dök-he parm he-yo?

property (possession) 소유물 so-yumul; (real estate) 소유지 so-yuji

prostitute 매춘부 mech-hunbu

protect 보호 해요 poho he-yo

Protestant 신교도 shin-gyodo

proverb 속담 sogdam

province 도 to

provincial capital 도청 소재지 toch-höng sojeji

prunes 말린 오얏 mallin o-yad

public 공공의 kong-gong-e

public bath 공중목욕탕 kong-jung-mogyogt-hang

public holiday 공휴일 kong-yu-il

public rest room 공중 화장실 kong-jung hwajang-shil

pudding 푸딩 p-huding

pull 끌어요 ggrö-yo

pullover 풀오버 p-hurobö

pump (for liquid) 펌프 p-hömp-hü

punctual 시간을 엄수 하는 shiganl ömsu hanün

puncture (blowout) 빵꾸 bbang-ggu

puppet 인형 inyöng

pure (100%) 순수 한 sunsu han; **it was pure luck** 운이 좋았을 뿐이에요 uni chohassl bbuni-e-yo

purple 보라색 poraseg

purpose (intention) 의도 edo; **on purpose** 고의로 ko-ero

purse (money) 지갑 chigab; (pocketbook) 손 가방 son kabang

Pusan 부산 pusan

push 밀어요 mirö-yo; **don't push me in!** 떠밀고 들어가지 말아요! ddömilgo trögaji mara-yo!

push cart 손수레 sonsure

put (verb) 두어요 tu-ö-yo; **please put it on the table** 테이블 위에 놓으세요 t-he-ibl wi-e nohüse-yo; **could you put a patch on this?** 이것에 헝겊 조각을 대고 기워 주시겠어요? igöse höng-göp chogagl tego kiwö jushigessö-yo?; **would you put this in your safe?** 이것을 당신의 금고에 넣어 주시겠어요? igösl tang-shine kmgo-e nöhö jushigessö-yo?; **where shall I put ...?** ...를 어디다 둘까요? ...rl ödida tulg-ga-yo?

put in 넣어요 nöhö-yo

put onto 놓아요 noha-yo

Q

quail 메추리 mech-huri

quality 품질 p-humjil; **top quality** 최상품 ch-hwesang-p-hum

quarantine 격리 kyögri

quart 쿼트 k-hwöt-hü

quarter 사분 의 일 sabun e il; **a quarter hour** 십오분 shibobun

queen 여왕 yöwang

question 질문 chilmun; **excuse me, I'd like to ask a question** 실례지만, 말씀 좀 묻겠어요 shillyejiman, malsm chom mudgessö-yo

queue (noun) 줄 chul

quick (fast) 빠른 bbarn; **run, quick!** 빨

Pronounce: a father; e let; i machine; o note; ö löng; u rude; ü fürther

리 뛰어요! bballi ddwi-ö-yo!
quickly 빨리 bballi
quiet (tranquil) 조용 한 cho-yong han; **keep quiet!** 가만히 계세요! kamani kyese-yo!; **I'd like some peace and quiet** 조용한 것을 원 해요 cho-yong-an gösl wön he-yo
quinine 키니네 k-hinine
quite 꽤 ggwe; **quite by chance** 정말로 우연히 chöng-mallo u-yöni; **it's quite important** 매우 중대 해요 me-u chung-de he-yo; **they are quite different from each other** 서로 매우 달라요 söro me-u talla-yo

R

rabbi 랍비 rabbi
rabbit 토끼 t-hog-gi
rabies 광견병 kwang-gyönbyöng
race (horse) 경마 kyöng-ma; (car, foot) 경주 kyöng-ju
racket (sports) 라켓 rak-hed; **tennis racket** 테니스 라켓 t-henisü rak-hed
radiator (auto) 라지에터 raji-et-hö; (heater) 냉각기 neng-gaggi
radio 라디오 radi-o; (two way) 무전 mujön; **on the radio** 라디오로 radi-oro
radish 무우 mu-u
radish kimchee 깍두기 ggagdugi
rag (cloth) 걸레 kölle
rail pass 정기 패스 chöng-gi p-hesü
railroad 철도 ch-höldo
railroad crossing 철도 건널목 ch-höldo könnölmog
rain (noun) 비 pi; **it's raining** 비가 와요 piga wa-yo; **it seems likely to rain** 비가 올 것 같아요 piga ol göd kat-ha-yo
rain boots 장화 chang-wa
rainbow 무지개 mujige
raincoat 우비 ubi
rainy 비오는 pi-onün; **it's been rainy all week** 한주일 동안 비가 왔어요 hanju-il tong-an piga wassö-yo
rainy season 장마철 chang-mach-höl
raise (verb) 올려요 ollyö-yo; **you've raised the price** 값을 올리셨어요 kabsl ollishyössö-yo
raisins 건포도 könp-hodo
rape (violation) 강간 kang-gan
rare (scarce) 드문 tmun; (meat) 설구운 sölgu-un; **medium rare** (meat) 보통으로 설구운 pot-hong-ro sölgu-un; **the meat's too rare** 고기가 덜 익었어요 kogiga töl igössö-yo
rarely 희귀하게 hegwihage
rash (skin) 발진 paljin; **heat rash** 땀띠 ddamd-di
raspberries 나무딸기 namud-dalgi
rat 쥐 chwi
rate (exchange) 환율 hwanyul; **does the rate include milage?** 계산에 주행 거리가 포함 돼요? kyesane chuheng köriga p-hoham dwe-yo?; **what's the exchange rate?** 환율은 얼마에요? hwanyurn ölma-e-yo?
rather (quite) 꽤 ggwe
raw (meat) 날것 의 nalgöd e
razor 면도칼 myöndok-hal; **electric razor** 전기 면도기 chön-gi myöndogi
razor blades 면도날 myöndonal
reach (arrive) 도착 해요 toch-hag he-yo
read 읽어요 ilgö-yo
ready 준비가 된 chunbiga dwen; **we're not ready yet** 아직 준비 하지 않어요 ajig chunbi haji anö-yo; **is it ready?** 준비가 돼요? chunbiga dwe-yo?; **I'll go get ready** 준비 하러 가겠어요 chunbi harö kagessö-yo
real 실제의 shilje-e; **it's a real bargain** 싸게 팔아요 ssage p-hara-yo
real estate agent 부동산 업자 pudong-san öbja
really 정말 chöng-mal; **really?** 그래요?

kre-yo?; I'm really angry about it 나는 화가 많이 났어요 nanün hwaga mani nassö-yo; it's really annoying 몹시 귀찮게 해요 mobshi kwich-hyank-he he-yo; it's really beautiful 참 아름다워요 ch-ham armdawö-yo; I really like ... ...를 아주 좋아 해요 ...rl aju choha he-yo; it's really far away! 매우 멀어요! me-u mörö-yo!; you are really attractive 당신은 매우 매력적이군요 tang-shinün me-u meryögjögigunyo; it was really beautiful 매우 아름다웠어요 me-u armdawössö-yo

realtor 부동산 업자 pudong-san öbja

rear (the back) 뒤쪽 twij-jog

rearview mirror 백미러 pengmirö

reason (cause) 이유 i-yu; there's no reason 아무런 의의가 없어요 amurön e-ga öbsö-yo

reasonable (appropriate) 적당 한 chögdang han; (rational) 분별 있는 punbyöl innün; be reasonable 무리한 것을 말하지 마십시오 murihan gösl maraji mashibshi-o

receipt 영수증 yöng-sujng; please give me a receipt 영수증을 주세요 yöng-sujng-l chuse-yo

receive 받아요 pada-yo

recently 최근에 ch-hwegne

reception (in hotel) 접수부 chöbsubu; (a welcoming) 환영회 hwanyöng-we; the guy at reception 접수부에 있는 사람 chöbsubu-e innün saram

reception desk 접수부 chöbsubu

receptionist 응접계원 üng-jöbgyewön

recipe 조리법 choriböb

recognize 알아봐요 arabwa-yo; I didn't recognize you 당신을 알아보지 못 했어요 tang-shinl araboji mod hessö-yo

recommend (a person) 추천 해요 ch-huch-hön he-yo

reconfirm 재확인 해요 chehwagin he-yo

record (disc) 레코드 rek-hodü; hit record 유명 한 레코오드 yumyöng han rek-ho-odü;

record (verb) 녹음 해요 nogm he-yo

record player 전축 chönch-hug

record store 레코드 가게 rek-hodü kage

recorder: tape recorder 테이프 레코더 t-he-ip-hü rek-hodö

recover 회복 해요 hwebog he-yo

recovery 회복 hwebog

recreation 오락 orag

red 빨강색 bbalgang-seg; bright red 밝은 빨간색 palgn bbalganseg

red wine 붉은 포도주 pulgn p-hodoju

reduction (price) 할인 harin

referee 심판관 shimp-han-gwan

refined (person) 우아 한 u-a han

refreshing 상패 한 sang-k-hwe han

refrigerator 냉장고 neng-jang-go

refund 반환 panwan; will you give me a refund? 반환 해 주시겠어요? panwan he jushigessö-yo?

region 지방 chibang

register (verb) 등록 tng-rog; cash register 금전 등록기 kmjön tng-roggi

registered mail 등기 우편 tng-gi up-hyön

registration 등록 tng-rog

regular gasoline 보통 휘발유 pot-hong hwibaryu

relatives 친척 ch-hinch-hög

relaxing 휴식을 주는 hyushigl chunün; it's relaxing 휴식을 갖게 해요 hyushigl kadge he-yo

reliable 믿을 수 있는 midl su innün

religion 종교 chong-gyo

religious 종교적인 chong-gyojögin

religious service 예배 yebe; what time is the religious service? 예배는 몇시에 있어요? yebenün myöt-hshi-e issö-yo?; I want to attend the religious services today 오늘 예배에 참석 하고 싶은데요 onl yebe-e ch-hamsög hago ship-hünde-yo

remain 남아요 nama-yo

Pronounce: a father; e let; i machine; o note; ö löng; u rude; ü fürther

remember 기억 해요 ki-ög he-yo; I
don't remember 기억이 안 나요 ki-ögi
an na-yo
remote (far away) 먼 mön
remove 옮겨요 olgyö-yo
remover: make-up remover pads 화장
지우는 패드 hwajang chi-unün p-hedü;
nail polish remover 매니큐어 지우개
menik-hyu-ö chi-uge
rent (money for housing) 집세 chibse;
(lease) 빌려(줘)요 pillyö(jwö)yo; do
you rent bicycles here? 여기에 임대
자전거 있어요? yögi-e imde chajön-gö
issö-yo?; can I rent a car? 차를 빌릴
수가 있어요? ch-harl pillil suga issö-
yo?; do you rent them out? 빌려주세
요? pillyöjuse-yo?
rental: rental car 렌트카 rent-k-ha; car
rental 렌트카 rent-hük-ha
repair (fix) 수리 해요 suri he-yo; shoe
repair 제화점 chehwajöm; can you
repair it temporarily? 임시로 고칠 수
있어요? imshiro koch-hil su issö-yo?;
can it be repaired? 수리 할 수 있어요?
suri hal su issö-yo?
repair shop 정비소 chöng-biso
repeat 다시 해요 tashi he-yo; would
you repeat that? 다시 말씀 해
주시겠어요? tashi malsm he jushigessö-
yo?
repellent: insect repellent 방충제 pang-
ch-hung-je
replace 갈아요 kara-yo; will you
replace it? 바꿔 주시겠어요? pag-gwö
jushigessö-yo?
report (information) 보고 pogo; (verb)
보고 해요 pogo he-yo
representative (company) 대리인 teri-in
reputation 명성 myöng-söng
request (noun) 부탁 put-hag
rescue (save) 구조 해요 kujo he-yo
reservation 예약 ye-yag; we have
reservations 예약 했어요 ye-yag hessö-
yo; do you have our reservation? 예약

을 받으셨어요? ye-yagl padshyössö-
yo?; I don't have a reservation 예약
하지 않았어요 ye-yag haji anassö-yo;
I'd like to cancel my reservation 예약
을 취소하고 싶은데요 ye-yagl ch-
hwisohago ship-hünde-yo
reserve 예약 해요 ye-yag he-yo; please
reserve a table for two 두 사람 의
테이블을 예약 해주십시오 tu saram e t-
he-ibrl ye-yag hejushibshi-o
reserved seat 지정석 chijöng-sög
responsibility 책임 ch-hegim
responsible 책임이 있는 ch-hegimi
innün
rest (relaxation) 휴식 hyushig;
(remainder) 나머지 namöji; I need to
rest 쉬고 싶은데요 swigo ship-hünde-
yo
rest room 화장실 hwajang-shil
restaurant 레스토랑 / 식당 rest-horang /
shigdang; seafood restaurant 횟집
hwedjib; a local restaurant 지방 음식점
chibang ümshigjöm; do you know a
good restaurant? 좋은 음식점을 아세요?
chohün ümshigjöml ase-yo?
result (outcome) 결과 kyölgwa
retail sales 소매 some
retired 퇴직 한 t-hwejig han; I'm retired
퇴직 했어요 t-hwejig hessö-yo
retirement 은퇴 ünt-hwe
return (come back) 돌아 와요 tora wa-
yo; can I return this? 이것 좀 물러
주시겠어요? igöd chom mullö
jushigessö-yo?; could you return it?
그것을 돌려 주시겠어요? kgösl tollyö
jushigessö-yo?
reunification (of North & South Korea)
남북 통일 nambug t-hong-il
reverse gear 후진 기어 hujin ki-ö
revolting 메스꺼운 mesg-gö-un
rheumatism 류머티즘 ryumöt-hijm
rib (human) 갈비 뼈 kalbi bbyö; a
fractured rib 부러진 갈비 뼈 puröjin
kalbi bbyö

Pronounce: a father; e let; i machine; o note; ö löng; u rude; ü fürther

ribbon (ornament) 리본 ribon; (inked) 잉크 리본 ing-k-hü ribon

ribs (Korean style) 불갈비 pulgalbi; beef ribs 소갈비 sogalbi

rice (uncooked) 쌀 ssal; (boiled) 밥 pab; (fried) 볶음밥 pog-gmbab; I'd prefer boiled rice 밥이 더 좋아요 pabi tö choha-yo

rice bowl 밥 그릇 pab krd

rice cake 떡 ddög

rice field 논 non

rice wine 막걸리 maggölli

rich (person) 돈 많은 ton manün; (food) 맛좋은 madjohün

ride (verb) 타요 t-ha-yo; thanks for the ride 태워 주셔서 고맙습니다 t-hewö jushyösö komabsmnida; I got a ride 누가 태워다 줬어요 nuga t-hewöda chwössö-yo

ridiculous 바보 같은 pabo kat-hün; that's ridiculous 어리석은 말이에요 örisögn mari-e-yo

right (correct) 바른 parn; (direction) 바른쪽 parnj-jog; right here 바로 여기에 paro yögi-e; right away 곧 kod; right on time 정각에 chöng-gage; all right 좋아요 choha-yo; turn right 오른쪽으로 가세요 ornj-jogro kase-yo; that's absolutely right 완전히 옳으셔요 wanjöni orshyö-yo; that isn't right 그럴 리가 없어요 kröl riga öbsö-yo; it's just right 바로 맞었어요 paro majössö-yo; that's all right, thanks 괜찮어요 kwench-hyanö-yo; on the right 오른쪽 ornj-jog; it's not repaired right 확실히 수리 안 됐어요 hwagshiri suri an dwessö-yo; it's still not right 아직까지도 맞지 않아요 ajigg-gajido majji ana-yo

right of way (driving) 선행권 söneng-gwön

right wing (politics) 우익 u-ig

ring (for finger) 반지 panji; engagement ring 약혼 반지 yak-hon panji; wedding ring 결혼 반지 kyöron panji

rinse: cream rinse 린스 rinsü

rip-off (extortion) 착취 ch-hagch-hwi

ripe 잘 익은 chal ign

river 강 kang; by the river 강변에 kang-byöne

road 길 kil; main road 큰 길 k-hün kil; along the road 일을 따라 irl ddara; down the road further 길을 따라 훨씬 내려간 곳에 kirl ddara hwölshin neryögan kose; where does this road lead to? 이건 어디 가는 길이지요 igön ödi kanün kiriji-yo; is this the road to …? …으로 가는 길이에요? …ro kanün kiri-e-yo?; at the end of the road 길 끝에 kil ggt-he; in the middle of the road 길의 한가운데에 kire han-ga-unde-e; at the side of the road 길가에 kilga-e

road accident 교통 사고 kyot-hong sago

road map 도로 지도 toro chido

road sign 도로 표지 toro p-hyoji

roadside 길가 kilga

roadwork 로드워크 rodwök-hü

roast beef 로스트 비프 rost-hü pip-hü

rob (steal) 훔쳐요 humch-hyö-yo

robot 로보트 robot-hü

rock (stone) 바위 pawi; on the rocks (ice) 언 더 락 ön tö rag

rocky 바위로 된 pawiro dwen

rod: fishing rod 낚싯대 nag-gshidde

roll (bread) 롤 빵 rol bbang

roller skates 롤러 스케이트 rollö sk-he-it-hü

Roman Catholic 천주교의 ch-hönjugyo-e

romance 로맨스 romensü

romantic 낭만적인 nang-manjögin

roof 지붕 chibung; the roof leaks 지붕이 새요 chibung-i se-yo; sun roof (auto) 선 루프 sön rup-hü; on the roof 지붕 위에 chibung wi-e

room 방 pang; a room with a balcony

발코니가 있는 방 palk-honiga innün pang; a room with a bath 욕실이 달린 방 yogshiri tallin pang; dining room 식당 shigdang; double room 이인용 방 i-inyong pang; is room service available? 룸써비스가 있어요? rumsöbisga issö-yo?; private room 별실 pyölshil; a room for two nights 이틀 동안 묵을 방 it-hül tong-an mugl pang; twin room 침대 둘 있는 방 ch-himde tul innün pang; in my room 내 방에(서) ne pang-e(sö); Korean style room 온돌 방 ondol pang; a single room 일인용 방 irinyong pang; Western style room 침대 방 ch-him te pang; can we have another room? 다른 방을 주십시오 tarn pang-l chushibshi-o; please come into the room 방에 들어와 주세요 pang-e tröwa juse-yo; may we see the room? 방을 구경 해도 될까요? pang-l kugyöng hedo dwelg-ga-yo?; have you got a room? 방이 있어요? pang-i issö-yo?; what floor is the room on? 방이 몇 층에 있어요? pang-i myöt ch-hüng-e issö-yo?; we're not satisfied with the room 이 방으로 만족 하지 않어요 i bang-ro manjog haji anö-yo; please send breakfast to our room 아침 식사 방으로 갖다 주세요 ach-him shigsa pang-ro kadda juse-yo; will you take this to room 212? 이것을 이백 십이 호 실로 가져 가시겠어요 igösl ibeg shibi ho shillo kajyö kashigessö-yo; I went to the wrong room 방에 잘못 갔어요 pang-e chalmod kassö-yo; I left my key in the room 열쇠를 방에 놓고 문을 잠갔어요 yölswerl pang-e nok-ho munl chamgassö-yo

room service 룸 서비스 rum söbisü

rope 밧줄 padjul; tow rope 끄는 밧줄 ggnün padjul

rose 장미 chang-mi

Rose of Sharon 무궁화 mugung-wa

rose' (wine) 로제 roje

rough (rugged) 험 한 höm han

roughly (approximately) 거칠게 köch-hilge

roulette 룰렛 rulled

round (circular) 둥근 tung-gn; this is my round 이번에는 내가 내죠 ibönenün nega nejyo

round-trip ticket 왕복 차표 wang-bog ch-hap-hyo

route 길 kil; is there a scenic route? 경치 좋은 길이 있어요? kyöng-ch-hi chohün kiri issö-yo?; which is the best route? 어느 쪽이 제일 좋은 길이에요? önü jjogi che-il chohün kiri-e-yo?

rowboat 보트 pot-hü

rowing 조정 chojöng

rubber (substance) 고무 komu; (condom) 콘돔 k-hondom

rubber band 고무줄 komujul

rubbish (trash) 쓰레기 ssregi

rude 무례 한 murye han

rug 융단 yung-dan

ruins 유적 yujög

ruler (measure) 자 cha

rum 럼 röm

rum and coke 럼 앤 콕 röm en k-hog

rumor 소문 somun

run (hurry) 달려요 tallyö-yo; run, quick! 빨리 뛰어요! bballi ddwi-ö-yo!

rural 시골의 shigore

rush hour 러시아워 röshi-awö

Russia 러시아 röshi-a

Russian (adjective) 러시아의 röshi-a-e; (person) 러시아 사람 röshi-a saram; (language) 러시아 말 röshi-a mal

rye 호밀 homil; rye bread 호밀빵 homilb-bang

*

S

s: ...'s (the possessive) ...의 ...e
saccharine 사카린 sak-harin
sad 슬픈 slp-hün
saddle 안장 anjang
safe (secure) 안전 한 anjön han; have a
safe journey! 무사하시기를 빌어요!
musahashigirl pirö-yo!; is it safe
here? 이곳에 머무르는 것은 안전 해요?
igose mömurnün gösn anjön he-yo?;
is this safe to drink? 이것을 마셔도
안전 해요? igösl mashyödo anjön he-
yo?
safety pin 안전핀 anjönp-hin
sail (noun) 돛 toch
sailboat 보트 pot-hü
sailor 선원 sönwön
saint 성인 söng-in
salad 샐러드 sellödü; fruit salad 과일
사라다 kwa-il sarada; potato salad 감자
샐러드 kamja sellödü; side salad 추가주
문의 샐러드 ch-hugajumune sellödü
salad dressing 새러드 소스 serödü sosü
salami 살라미 sallami
salary 봉급 pong-gb
sale (sales event) 할인 판매 harin p-
hanme; retail sales 소매 some; is there
a sale today? 오늘 할인 판매 해요? onl
harin p-hanme he-yo?; it's not for
sale 팔 것이 아니에요 p-hal göshi ani-
e-yo
sales clerk 점원 chömwön
salmon 연어 yönö
salt 소금 sogm; I can't eat salt 나는
소금을 먹으면 안 되요 nanün sogml
mögmyön an dwe-yo; it needs more
salt 소금이 더 필요 해요 sogmi tö p-
hiryo he-yo
salty 짠 jjan

same 같은 kat-hün; the same as before,
please 전과 같은 것을 주세요 chön-gwa
kat-hün gösl chuse-yo; it's the same
thing 같은 것이에요 kat-hün göshi-e-
yo; enjoy yourself -- same to you 자
많이 즐기세요 -- 당신도요 cha mani
chülgise-yo - tang-shindo-yo; do you
have the same thing in white? 흰색으
로 같은 것이 있어요? hensegro kat-
hün göshi issö-yo?
sand 모래 more
sandals 샌들 sendl
sandwich 샌드위치 sendwich-hi
sandy 모래의 more-e
sanitary napkin 생리대 seng-ride
sarcastic 비꼬는 pig-gonün
sardines 정어리 chöng-öri
satire 풍자 p-hung-ja
satisfactory 만족 한 manjog han
Saturday 토요일 t-ho-yo-il
sauce 소스 sosü
saucepan 남비 nambi
saucer 받침 접시 padch-him chöbshi
sauna 사우나 sa-una
sausage 소시지 soshiji
save (rescue) 구해 내요 kuhe ne-yo;
(store up) 저축 해요 chöch-hug he-
yo; (be frugal) 절약 해요 chöryag he-
yo; he saved my life 그는 나를
살렸어요 knün narl sallyössö-yo; I'm
saving up my money 저금 하고 있어요
chögm hago issö-yo; could you save
my seat? 내 자리를 맡아 주시겠어요? ne
charirl mat-ha jushigessö-yo?
say 말 해요 mal he-yo; he said ... ...
라고 그는 말 했어요 ... rago knün mal
hessö-yo; he did not say anything 그
는 아무것도 말하지 않았어요 knün
amugöddo maraji anössö-yo; how do
you say ... in Korean? ...을 한국말로
어떻게 말 해요 ...l han-gungmallo öd-
dök-he mal he-yo; what did you say?
무엇이라고 말씀 했어요? mu-öshirago
malsm hessö-yo?

Pronounce: a father; e let; i machine; o note; ö löng; u rude; ü fürther

scallops 가리비 karibi
Scandinavian (person) 스칸디나비아 사람 sk-handinabi-a saram
scarf 목도리 mogdori
scarlet 주홍색 chuhong-seg
scene (setting) 배경 pegyöng
scenery 풍경 p-hung-gyöng
scenic: is there a scenic route? 경치 좋은 길이 있어요? kyöng-ch-hi chohün kiri issö-yo?
scent (perfume) 향수 hyang-su
schedule 스케줄 sk-hejul
scheduled flight 정기편 chöng-gip-hyön
school 학교 haggyo; (university) 대학 tehag; elementary school 국민 학교 kungmin haggyo; private school 사립 학교 sarib haggyo
science 과학 kwahag
science fiction film 공상 과학 영화 kong-sang kwahag yöng-wa
scientist 과학자 kwahagja
scissors 가위 kawi; nail scissors 손톱 가위 sont-hob kawi
scorcher: it's a real scorcher (weather) 굉장히 더운 날씨에요 kweng-jang-i tö-un nalshi-e-yo
score (in game) 득차 tgch-ha
scotch (whisky) 스카치 sk-hach-hi
Scotch tape (tm) 스카치 테이프 sk-hach-hi t-he-ip-hü
Scotland 스코틀랜드 sk-hot-hüllendü
Scottish 스코틀랜드의 sk-hot-hüllend-e
scrambled eggs 풀어서 한 계란 후라이 p-hurösö han kyeran hura-i
scratch (a cut) 작은 상처 chagn sang-ch-hö
scream (verb) 소리 쳐요 sori ch-hyö-yo
screen 스크린 sk-hürin; (folding screen) 병풍 pyöng-p-hung
screw (noun) 나사 nasa
screwdriver 드라이버 tra-ibö
scroll 두루마리 turumari
scrub brush 세탁솔 set-hagsol
scuba diving 스쿠버 다이빙 sk-hubö ta-ibing

sculptor 조각가 chogagga
sea 바다 pada; facing the sea 바다를 향해 padarl hyang he
sea air 바닷 공기 padad kong-gi
sea gull 갈매기 kalmegi
sea shell 바닷조개 padadjoge
seafood 해산 물 hesan mul
seafood restaurant 횟집 hwedjib
seal (personal stamp) 도장 tojang
search (look for) 찾어요 ch-hajö-yo; I've searched everywhere 구석 구석 찾아봤어요 kusög kusög ch-hajabwassö-yo
seashore 해변 hebyön; let's go to the seashore 우리 해변에 가요 uri hebyöne ka-yo
seasick 배멀미 난 pemölmi nan; I'm seasick 멀미가 나요 mölmiga na-yo
seaside 해변 hebyön; at the seaside 해변에 hebyöne
season 계절 kyejöl; rainy season 장마철 chang-mach-höl; in the busy season 최성기에 ch-hwesöng-gi-e; in the off season 한산기에 hansan-gi-e
seasoning 조미 chomi
seat 자리 chari; back seat 뒷자리 twidjari; reserved seat 지정석 chijöng-sög; window seat 창가 옆자리 ch-hang-ga yöbch-hari; no smoking seat 금연석 kmyönsög; could you save my seat? 내 자리를 맡아 주시겠어요? ne charirl mat-ha jushigessö-yo?; I think that is my seat 그 자리는 내 자리인 것 같아요 kü jarinün ne chari-in göd kat-ha-yo; I left my coat under the seat 좌석 밑에 코트를 놓고 내렸어요 chwasög mit-he k-hot-hürl nok-ho neryössö-yo
seat belt 좌석 벨트 chwasög pelt-hü
seaweed (toasted) 김 kim
secluded 한적한 hanjök-han
second (next) 두번째의 tubönj-je-e; (time) 초 ch-ho; second story 이층

ich-hüng; on the second floor 이층에 ich-hüng-e; just a second 잠깐만 chamg-ganman; I'll be back in a second 곧 돌아 오겠어요 kod tora ogessö-yo

second class 이등석 idng-sög

second class ticket 이등표 idng-p-hyo

second-hand 중고품의 chung-gop-hume

secret (noun) 비밀 pimil

secretary 비서 pisö

sedative 진정제 chinjöng-je

see 봐요 pwa-yo; see you later 나중에 뵙겠어요 najung-e pwebgessö-yo; see someone off 마중 해요 majung he-yo; see you then 그 때 뵙지요 kü dde pwebji-yo; see you tomorrow 내일 뵙겠어요 ne-il pwebgessö-yo; yes, I see 네, 알았어요 ne, arassö-yo; may we see the room? 방을 구경 해도 될까요? pang-l kugyöng hedo dwelg-ga-yo?; let's go see a movie 우리 영화 보러 가요 uri yöng-wa porö ka-yo; I didn't see that 그것을 보지 않았어요 kgösl poji anössö-yo; can we see the manager? 지배인을 만나 뵐 수 있어요? chibe-inl manna pwel su issö-yo?; may I see? 나 좀 보여 주시겠어요? na chom po-yö jushigessö-yo?; did you see my things? 내 것들을 보셨어요? ne göddrl poshyössö-yo?; when can I see him? 언제 뵐 수 있을까요? önje pwel su isslg-ga-yo?; I'd like to see the market 시장을 보고 싶어요 shijang-l pogo ship-hö-yo; long time no see! 오랜만이에요! orenmani-e-yo!; I also want to see the DMZ 휴전선도 보고 싶은데요 hyujönsöndo pogo ship-hünde-yo

seems that ... ...은 것 같아요 ...n göd kat-ha-yo

seldom 별로 ...지 않아요 pyöllo ...ji anö-yo

self-service 셀프서비스 selp-hüsöbisü

sell 팔아요 p-hara-yo; do you sell ...?

...를 팔아요 ...rl p-hara-yo

semester 학기 haggi

senator 상원 의원 sang-wön ewön

send 보내요 pone-yo; I'll send it by air 항공 우편으로 부치겠어요 hang-gong up-hyönro puch-higessö-yo; please send breakfast to our room 아침 식사 방으로 갖다 주세요 ach-him shigsa pang-ro kadda juse-yo; please send it to this address 이 주소로 부쳐 주세요 i jusoro puch-hyö juse-yo; could you send it to her? 그 여자에게 보내 주시겠어요? kü yöja-ege pone chushigessö-yo?; we want to send a telegram 전보를 치고 싶은데요 chönborl ch-higo ship-hünde-yo

senior citizen 노인 no-in

sensational (wonderful) 훌륭 한 hullyung han

sense: common sense 상식 sang-shig; where's your sense of humor? 유머는 어디에 갔어요? yumönün ödi-e kassö-yo?; that make no sense 그건 말이 안 돼요 kgön mari an dwe-yo

sensible 현명 한 hyönmyöng han

sensitive 민감 한 min-gam han

sentimental 감상적인 kamsang-jögin

Seoul 서울 sö-ul; downtown Seoul 서울의 중심가 sö-ure chung-shimga; I'm heading for Seoul 서울로 향 하고 있어요 sö-ullo hyang hago issö-yo; a book on Seoul 서울에 관 한 책 sö-ure kwan han ch-heg

separate 개개의 kege-e; could we get separate bills? 계산서를 따로따로 주시겠어요? kyesansörl ddarod-daro chushigessö-yo?

separately (individually) 따로 따로 ddaro ddaro

September 구월 kuwöl

Serbia 세르비아 serbi-a

serious (sincere) 진지 한 chinji han; (important) 중대 한 chung-de han; (severe) 지독 해요 chidog he-yo;

you're not serious! 진정은 아니겠지요! chinjöng-n anigedji-yo!

seriously 심각 하게 shimgag hage

servant 하인 ha-in

serve: do they serve meals? 식사가 나와요? shigsaga nawa-yo?; when is breakfast served? 아침 식사가 몇 시에 나와요? ach-him shigsaga myöt shi-e nawa-yo?

service 서비스 söbisü; religious service 예배 yebe; room service 룸 서비스 rum söbisü; the service was excellent 서비스가 훌륭 했어요 söbisga hullyung hessö-yo; is room service available? 룸 써비스가 있어요? rumsöbisga issö-yo?; this car needs servicing 이 차는 수리 해야 해요 i ch-hanün suri he-ya he-yo

service charge (restaurant) 봉사료 pongsaryo

service station 주유소 chu-yuso

serving: another serving 더 한 그릇 tö han krd; a half serving 반 정도 pan chöng-do

sesame oil 참기름 ch-hamgirm

set (noun) 한짝 hanj-jag; let's set a time 시간을 결정 해요 shiganl kyöljöng he-yo; the complete set 한 세트 han set-hü; could I have a shampoo and set? 샴푸 하고 세트 해 주시겠어요? shyamp-hu hago set-hü he jushigessö-yo?

setting lotion 세트용 로션 set-hü-yong roshyön

settle up 계산을 해요 kyesanl he-yo

several 몇개의 myödk-he-e

severe: a severe headache 악성의 두통 agsöng-e tut-hong

sew 꿰매요 ggweme-yo; would you sew this back on? 이것을 꿰매 달아 주시겠어요? igösl ggweme tara jushigessö-yo?

sex (gender) 성 söng; (sexual intercourse) 섹스 segsü

sexist 성차별의 söng-ch-habyöre

sexy 섹시 한 segshi han

shabby 초라 한 ch-hora han

shade 그늘 knl

shadow 그림자 krimja; eye shadow 아이 새도우 a-i shyedo-u

shake (tremble) 흔들려요 hündllyö-yo; milk shake 밀크 셰이크 milk-hü shyeik-hü

shall: shall we go into the lobby? 로비 에 들어 갈까요? robi-e trö kalg-ga-yo?; shall we ...? ... 할까요? ... halg-ga-yo?; shall we play table tennis? 탁구를 할까요? t-haggurl halg-ga-yo?; where shall we meet? 어디서 만날까요? ödisö mannalg-ga-yo; where shall I put ...? ...를 어디다 둘까요? ...rl ödida tulg-ga-yo?

shallow 얕은 yat-hün

shame (hard luck) 너무심한 일 nömushiman il; what a shame! 이게 무슨 창피냐! ige musn ch-hang-p-hinya!

shameful 수치스러운 such-hisrö-un

shampoo (noun) 샴푸 shyamp-hu; (verb) 머리를 감아요 mörirl kama-yo

share (verb) 같이 사용 해요 kat-hi sayong he-yo

shark 상어 sang-ö

sharp (knife) 잘 드는 chal tnün

shave (verb) 면도 해요 myöndo he-yo; would you give me a shave? 면도 좀 해 주시겠어요? myöndo chom he jushigessö-yo?

shaver 면도기 myöndogi

shaving cream 면도 크림 myöndo k-hürim

shaving socket 면도기 콘센트 myöndogi k-honsent-hü

shawl 숄 shyol

she 그 녀 kü nyö; she isn't an American 그녀는 미국 사람이 아니에요 knyönün migug sarami ani-e-yo; is she your friend? 그녀는 당신의 친구에요? knyönün tang-shine ch-hin-gu-e-yo?

sheep 양 yang

sheet 시트 shit-hü; a sheet of paper 종이 한 장 chong-i han chang; do you have the sheet music for ...? ...의 악보 있어요? ...e agbo issö-yo?

shelf 선반 sönban

shell 조가비 chogabi; sea shell 바닷조개 padadjoge

shellfish 조개 choge

shelter 피난처 p-hinanch-hö

sherbet 셔빗 shyöbid

sherry 세리 shyeri

shift: gear shift 기어 레버 ki-ö rebö

ship 배 pe; by ship 배로 pero

shirt 와이셔츠 wa-ishyöch-hü; tee shirt 티셔츠 t-hishyöch-hü; the man in the blue shirt 푸른 샤쓰를 입는 사람 p-hurn shyassrl imnün saram

shirtmaker 와이셔츠점 wa-ishyöch-hüjöm

shit! 제기 랄! chegi ral!

shiver 오한이 나요 ohani na-yo

shock (electrical) 감전 kamjön; I was shocked (surprise) 깜짝 놀랐어요 ggamj-jag nollassö-yo; he got an electric shock from the ... ...에서 감전 됐어요 ...esö kamjön dwessö-yo

shock absorber 완충기 wanch-hung-gi

shocking (outrageous) 지독 한 chidog han

shoe 구두 kudu; tennis shoes 테니스화 t-henishwa; training shoes 트레이닝 슈즈 t-hüre-ining shyujü; a pair of shoes 구두 한 켤레 kudu han k-hyölle; could you polish my shoes? 구두를 좀 닦아 주시겠어요? kudurl chom tag-ga jushigessö-yo?; should I take my shoes off? 구두를 벗을까요? kudurl pöslg-ga-yo?; would you put new soles on these shoes? 이 구두에 새 창을 대어 주시겠어요? i gudu-e se ch-hang-l te-ö jushigessö-yo?

shoe polish 구두약 kudu-yag

shoe repair 제화점 chehwajöm

shoe store 양화점 yang-wajöm

shoelaces 구두끈 kudug-gn

shooting (sport) 사격 sagyög

shop (store) 상점 sang-jöm; (verb) 쇼핑 해요 shyop-hing he-yo; antique shop 골동품상 koldong-p-humsang; gift shop 선물 가게 sönmul kaje; souvenir shop 선물 가게 sönmul kage; the shop across the street 길 건너편에 있는 상점 kil könnöp-hyöne innün sang-jöm; I'm going shopping 쇼핑 하러가겠어요 shyop-hing harögagessö-yo

shop window 점포의 진열장 chömp-ho-e chinyöljang

shopping 쇼핑 shyop-hing

shopping arcade 상가 sang-ga

shore 해안 he-an; on the shore 해변에 hebyöne

short 짧은 jjalbn; (brief) 간단 한 kandan han; (person) 키가 작은 k-higa chagn; you've short-changed me 나에게 거스름돈을 덜 주었어요 na-ege gösrmdonl töl chu-össö-yo; it's a short walk 걸어서 금방이에요 körösö kmbang-i-e-yo; don't cut it too short please 너무 짧게 깎지 마세요 nömu jjalge ggag-gji mase-yo

short circuit 쇼트 shyot-hü

shortcut 지름길 chirmgil

shorts (undershorts) 팬티 p-hent-hi

should (do) 해야 해요 he-ya he-yo; should I take my shoes off? 구두를 벗을까요? kudurl pöslg-ga-yo?; when should I give it back? 언제 돌려 주겠어요? önje tollyö chugessö-yo?; what should we do? 어떻게 해야 할까요? öd-dök-he he-ya halg-ga-yo?; you should have warned me! 나에게 알렸어야 했어요 na-ege allyössö-ya hessö-yo; he shouldn't take long 틀림 없이 오래 앉을 거에에요 t-hüllim öbshi ore anl kö-e-ö-yo; when should I come back? 언제 다시 올까요? önje tashi olg-ga-yo?; if you should come to America 만일 미국에 가보면 manil miguge kabomyön

shoulder 어깨 ög-ge; dislocated shoulder 탈구된 어깨 t-halgudwen ög-ge

shout (cry out) 외쳐요 wech-hyö-yo; you needn't shout! 소리 지를 필요는 없어요! sori chirl p-hiryonün öbsö-yo!

show (verb) 보여 줘요 po-yö chwö-yo; floor show 플로어쇼 p-hüllo-öshyo; variety show 버라이어티쇼 pöra-i-öt-hishyo; can you show me where we are on this map? 이 지도에서 우리가 있는 곳을 가리킬 수 있어요? i jido-esö uriga innün kosl karik-hil su issö-yo?; could you show me the way to do it? 하는 법을 가르쳐 주시겠어요? hanün pöbl karch-hyö jushigessö-yo?; can you show me how to prepare this? 이것을 만드는 법을 가르쳐 주시겠어요? igösl mandnün pöbl karch-hyö jushigessö-yo?; would you show me how to do it? 옳은 방법을 가르쳐 주시겠어요? orn pang-böbl karch-hyö jushigessö-yo?; this map doesn't show it 이 지도에 없어요 i jido-e öbsö-yo

shower (in bath) 샤워 shyawö

shower cap 샤워 모자 shyawö moja

showing (movie) 상영 sang-yöng

shrimps 새우 se-u

shrine 사당 sadang; New Year visit to a shrine 성묘 söng-myo

shrink 줄어들어요 churödrö-yo; it shrank 줄어들었어요 churödrössö-yo

shut (close) 닫어요 tadö-yo

shutter (camera) 셔터 shyöt-hö; (window) 빈지 pinji

shy 수줄어 하는 sujubö hanün

sick (ill) 병이 난 pyöng-i nan; I'm sick and tired of... ...에 진저리 나요 ...e chinjöri na-yo

sickness 병 pyöng

side 쪽 jjog; (party) 편 p-hyön; could you take it in at the side? 겨드랑쪽을

줄여 주시겠어요? kyödrang-jjogl churyö jushigessö-yo?

side dishes 반찬 panch-han

side street 골목 kolmog

sideburns 구렛나루 kurennaru

sideview mirror 사이드 미러 sa-idü mirö

sidewalk 인도 indo

sights (scenery) 명승지 myöng-sng-ji

sightseeing 관광 kwan-gwang; let's go sightseeing 우리가 구경하러 가요 uriga kugyöng-arö ka-yo

sign (a document) 싸인 해요 ssa-in he-yo; (on store, etc) 간판 kanp-han; please sign here 여기에 서명 해 주세요 yögi-e sömyöng he juse-yo; road sign 도로 표지 toro p-hyoji; where do we sign? 어디에 서명 해요? ödi-e sömyöng he-yo?

signal (noun) 신호 shino

signature 서명 sömyöng

signpost 도표 top-hyo

silence 침묵 ch-himmug

silk 비단 pidan; silk fabric 실크 shilk-hü

silk shop 주단 가게 chudan kage

silkworm 누에 nu-e

silly 어리석은 örisögn; don't act silly 어리석은 짓을 하지 마세요 örisögn chisl haji mase-yo

silver (substance) 은 ün; (of silver) 은의 ün e

silver foil 은박 ünbag

similar 비슷 한 pisd han

simple (easy) 쉬운 swi-un

simply (absolutely) 전혀 chönyö

since ... ...부터 ...but-hö; since I don't understand Korean 내가 한국말을 모르기 때문에 nega han-gungmarl morgi ddemune; since I arrived 여기에 온 이래 yögi-e on ire

sing 노래 해요 nore he-yo

Singapore 싱가폴 shing-gap-hol

singer 가수 kasu; pop singer 유행가 가수 yuheng-ga kasu

Pronounce: a father; e let; i machine; o note; ö löng; u rude; ü further

single 단 하나의 tan hana-e

single bed 일인용 침대 irinyong ch-himde

single person (unmarried) 미혼자 mihonja

sink (kitchen) 싱크대 shing-k-hüde

sirloin 소의 허릿고기 so-e höridgogi

sister (a man's older) 누나 nuna; (man's younger) 여동생 yödong-seng; (woman's older) 언니 önni; (woman's younger) 동생 tong-seng

sister-in-law (husband's sister) 시누이 shinu-i

sit 앉어요 anjö-yo; please sit next to me 내 곁에 앉아주십시오 ne kyöt-he anjajushibshi-o; let's sit inside 우리 안에 들어가 앉아요 uri ane tröga anja-yo; may I sit with you? 함께 앉아도 좋아요? hamg-ge anjado choha-yo?; may I sit outside? 밖에 앉어도 좋아요? pag-ge anjödo choha-yo?

site: camping site 캠핑장 k-hemp-hing-jang

situation 처지 ch-höji; it's a special situation 그것은 특별한 경우에요 kgösn t-hügbyöran kyöng-u-e-yo

size 사이즈 sa-ijü; can you measure my size? 싸이즈 좀 재 주시겠어요? ssa-ijü chom che chushigessö-yo?; are there any other sizes? 다른 사이즈가 있어요? tarn sa-ijga issö-yo?

skates: roller skates 롤러 스케이트 rollö sk-he-it-hü

sketch (drawing) 스케치 sk-hech-hi

ski (noun) 스키 sk-hi; (verb) 스키 타요 sk-hi t-ha-yo

ski boots 스키 부츠 sk-hi puch-hü

skid 미끄러져요 mig-gröjyö-yo

skin (of person) 피부 p-hibu

skin diving 스킨다이빙 sk-hinda-ibing

skinny 마른 marn

skirt 스커트 sk-höt-hü; the woman with the black skirt on 검은 스커트를 입는 사람 kömn sk-höt-hürl imnün saram

skull 두개골 tugegol; fractured skull 두개골 골절 tugegol koljöl

sky 하늘 hanl

skyscraper 마천루 mach-hönru

slack: the steering is slack 핸들이 헐렁해요 hendri höllöng he-yo

slacks 바지 paji

sleep (I sleep) 자요 cha-yo; (you sleep) 주무셔요 chumushyö-yo; sleep well! 안녕히 주무세요 annyöng-i chumuse-yo; I slept like a log 세상 모르고 잤어요 sesang morgo chassö-yo; I can't sleep 잠을 이루지 못 해요 chaml iruji mod he-yo; I'm going to sleep 나는 잠자겠어요 nanün chamjagessö-yo

sleeping car 침대간 ch-himdegan

sleeping pill 수면제 sumyönje

sleepy (drowsy) 졸리는 chollinün; (placid) 조용 한 cho-yong han; I'm sleepy 졸려요 chollyö-yo

sleeve 소매 some

slice 조각 chogag; two slices of bread 빵 두 조각 bbang tu chogag

slide (photo) 슬라이드 slla-idü

slim (thin) 가는 kanün

slip (underskirt) 슬립 sllib; I slipped (tripped) 헛디뎠어요 höddidyössö-yo

slippers 슬리퍼 sllip-hö

slippery 미끄러운 mig-grö-un

slow 느린 nrin

slowly 천천히 ch-hönch-höni; could you speak slowly? 천천히 말씀 해 주시겠어요? ch-hönch-höni malsm he jushigessö-yo?

small 작은 chagn; small (clothing size) 스몰 smol; I want to buy a small gift 작은 선물을 사고 싶어요 chagn sönmurl sago ship-hö-yo

small change 잔돈 chandon

smart (stylish) 산뜻 한 sand-düd han; (intelligent) 영리 한 yöng-ri han

smell (odor) 냄새 nemse; it smells bad

나쁜 냄새가 나요 nab-bn nemsega na-yo; such a nice smell! 참 냄새가 좋아요! ch-ham nemsega choha-yo!
smile (verb) 미소지어요 misoji-ö-yo
smoke (fumes) 연기 yön-gi; no smoking 금연 kmyön; no smoking seat 금연석 kmyönsög; I don't smoke 담배를 피우지 않어요 tamberl p-hi-uji anö-yo; may I smoke? 담배를 피워도 좋아요? tamberl p-hiwödo choha-yo?
smooth (not rough) 매끄러운 meg-grö-un
snack 간단 한 식사 kandan han shigsa
snack bar 스낵바 snegba
snake 뱀 pem
sneakers 운동화 undong-wa
snob 속물 songmul
snow (noun) 눈 nun; it's snowing 눈이 와요 nuni wa-yo
so (very) 매우 me-u; so long! 안녕! annyöng!; so do I 나도 그래요 nado kre-yo; afraid so 미안 합니다만, 그래요 mi-an hamnidaman, kre-yo; it's so annoying 정말 귀찮아요 chöng-mal kwich-hana-yo; not so much cream! 크림을 그렇게 많이 넣으면 안 돼요! k-hüriml krök-he mani nöhümyön an dwe-yo!; it's not so comfortable 그리 안락하지 않아요 kri anrak-haji ana-yo; I hope so 그렇기를 바래요 krök-hirl pare-yo; I suppose so 그렇게 생각 해요 krök-he seng-gag he-yo; is it so expensive? 그렇게나 빗싸요? krök-hena pissa-yo?; I think so 그렇게 생각 해요 krök-he seng-gag he-yo; I don't think so 그렇게 생각 하지 않아요 krök-he seng-gag haji anö-yo
soaked 젖은 chöjn
soap 비누 pinu; shaving soap 면도 비누 myöndo pinu
soap powder 가루 비누 karu pinu
sober (not drunk) 술 취 하지 않은 sul ch-hwi haji anün
soccer 축구 ch-huggu

socket (outlet) 콘센트 k-honsent-hü; shaving socket 면도기 콘센트 myöndogi k-honsent-hü
socks 양말 yang-mal
soda water 소다수 sodasu
sofa 소파 sop-ha
soft 부드러운 pudrö-un
soft contact lens 소프트 콘택트 렌즈 sop-hüt-hü k-hont-hegt-hü renjü
soft drink 청량 음료 ch-höng-ryang ümryo
soju (Korean vodka) 소주 soju
soju cup 소주잔 sojujan
soldier 군인 kunin
sole (on shoe) 구두창 kuduch-hang; (of foot) 발바닥 palbadag; would you put new soles on these shoes? 이 구두에 새 창을 대어 주시겠어요? i gudu-e se ch-hang-l te-ö jushigessö-yo?
solemn 엄숙 한 ömsug han
solid 튼튼 한 t-hünt-hün han
some (a little) 좀 chom; (things) 어떤 것 öd-dön göd; some of that cake, please 그 케익을 조금 주세요 kü k-heigl chogm chuse-yo; some other time, thanks 다음에 해 주세요 ta-me he juse-yo; some people 어떤 사람들 öd-dön saramdl; please bring some more bread 빵을 더 갖다 주세요 bbang-l tö kadda juse-yo; he's gotten some strange disease 그는 괴상한 병에 걸렸어요 knün kwesang-an pyöng-e köllyössö-yo; I'd like some Western food 양식을 먹고 싶은데요 yang-shigl möggo ship-hünde-yo; could we have some water? 물을 좀 주시겠어요? murl chom chushigessö-yo?; could you give me some? 좀 주시겠어요? chom chushigessö-yo?
someone (somebody) 누구 nugu; someone is sitting here 이 자리에 사람이 있어요 i jari-e sarami issö-yo; are you waiting for someone? 누구를

기다리고 계세요? nugurl kidarigo
kyese-yo?

something 무엇인가 mu-öshin-ga;
something to eat 무엇 좀 먹을 것 mu-
öd chom mögl göd; something else 그
밖에 무엇이 kü bag-ge mu-öshi;
something light, please 뭐 간단 한
걸로 주세요 mwö kandan han köllo
chuse-yo; there's something wrong
with ... ...에 어딘가 고장이 있어요
...e ödin-ga kojang-i issö-yo; is
there something wrong with it? 어디가
고장 났어요? ödiga kojang nassö-yo?;
do you have something to cure it? 치
료 할 것이 있어요? ch-hiryo hal göshi
issö-yo?

sometime 언젠가 önjen-ga

sometimes 가끔 kag-gm

somewhat (a little) 조금 chogm

somewhere 어디인지 ödi-inji;
somewhere else 그 밖에 어디에 kü bag-
ge ödi-e; somewhere not too touristy
어딘가 관광 개발 되지 않은 곳 ödin-ga
kwan-gwang kebal dweji anün kod;
let's try somewhere else 우리 다른 곳에
가 봐요 uri tarn kose ka pwa-yo

son 아들 adl; our son 우리 아들 uri adl

son-in-law 사위 sawi

song 노래 nore; folk songs 대중가요
tejung-ga-yo

soon 곧 kod; as soon as possible 가능한
한 빨리 kanüng-an han bballi; it's too
soon 너무 빨라요 nömu bballa-yo; will
it stop raining soon? 비가 곧 그칠까요?
piga kod kch-hilg-ga-yo?; he ought
to be here soon 그는 곧 도착 할
것이에요 knün kod toch-hag hal
göshi-e-yo

sore 아픈 ap-hün; it's sore 아파요 ap-
ha-yo

sorry! 유감이에요 yugami-e-yo; sorry
to bother you 폐를 끼쳐서 죄송 해요 p-
herl ggich-hyösö chwesong he-yo;
sorry I'm late 늦어 미안합니다 njö mi-

anamnida

sort 종류 chong-ryu

souffle 수플레 sup-hülle

sound (noise) 소리 sori

soup 국 kug; cold soup 냉면 neng-
myön

sour (acid) 신 shin

south 남쪽 namj-jog

South Africa 남 아프리카 nam ap-
hürik-ha

South African (adjective) 남 아프리카의
nam ap-hürik-ha-e

South America 남미 nammi; South
American person 남미 사람 nammi
saram

South Korea 남한 naman

southeast 남동 namdong

southwest 남서 namsö

souvenir 기념품 kinyömp-hum

souvenir shop 선물 가게 sönmul kage

soy sauce 간장 kanjang

spa 온천 onch-hön

space 공간 kong-gan

space heater 실내 남방기 shilne
nambang-gi

Spain 스페인 sp-he-in

spare part 예비 부속품 yebi pusogp-hum

spare tire 스페어 타이어 sp-he-ö t-ha-
i-ö

spark plug 점화 플러그 chömwa p-
hüllögü

speak (I speak) 말 해요 mal he-yo;
(you speak) 말씀 해요 malsm he-yo; I
speak a little Korean 한국말을 좀 해요
han-gungmarl chom he-yo; you speak
English very well 영어를 잘 해요
yöng-örl chal he-yo; could you speak
slowly? 천천히 말씀 해 주시겠어요? ch-
hönch-höni malsm he jushigessö-yo?;
can you speak English? 영어를 하세요?
yöng-örl hase-yo?; may I speak with
...? (on phone) ...를 좀 바꿔 주세요?
...rl chom pag-gwö juse-yo?

special 특별 한 t-hügbyöl han; it's a

special situation 그것은 특별한 경우에요 kgösn t-hügbyöran kyöng-u-e-yo; as a special case 예외로서 yewerosö; the food was nothing special 음식은 그저 그랬어요 ümshign kjö kressö-yo; are you doing anything special tonight? 오늘 저녁에 특별한 일 있어요? onl chönyöge t-hügbyöran il issö-yo?

specialist 전문가 chönmun-ga

specialty 전문 chönmun; local specialty 명물 myöng-mul; what is the specialty of the house? 이 집 전문이 뭐에요? i jib chönmuni mwö-e-yo?

spectator 구경꾼 kugyöng-ggun

speech 연설 yönsöl

speed (velocity) 속도 sogdo

speed limit 속도 제한 sogdo chehan

speedometer 속도계 sogdogye

spell: how is it spelled? 철자를 어떻게 써요? ch-höljarl öd-dök-he ssö-yo?

spend (time) 지내요 chine-yo; (money) (돈을) 써요 (donl) ssö-yo; I don't want to spend more than ... won ...원 이상은 쓰고 싶지 않아요 ...wön isang-n ssgo shibch-hi ana-yo

spice 향료 hyang-ryo

spicy 매운 me-un; it's very spicy (hot) 매우 매워요 me-u mewö-yo

spider 거미 kömi

spinach 시금치 shigmch-hi

splendid! 멋진데요! mödjinde-yo!

splinter 가시 kashi

spoiled (milk etc) 부패 한 pup-he han; it's spoiled 상 했어요 sang hessö-yo; won't it spoil? 썩지 않겠어요 ssögji ank-hessö-yo; this meat is spoiled 이 고기는 상했어요 i goginün sang-essö-yo

spoke (of wheel) 살 sal

spokesman 대변인 tebyönin

sponge 스폰지 sp-honji

sponsor 후원인 huwönin

spoon 숟가락 sudgarag

sport jacket 스포츠 자켓 sp-hoch-hü

chak-hed

sports 운동 undong; water sports 수상 스포츠 susang sp-hoch-hü

sportsman 운동 선수 undong sönsu

spot (speck) 점 chöm

sprain 삠 bbim; I've sprained my ... ...를 뺐어요 ...rl bbyössö-yo

spray (hair spray) 스프레이 sp-hüre-i; hair spray 헤어 스프레이 he-ö sp-hüre-i

spring (springtime) 봄 pom; (of machinery) 용수철 yong-such-höl; thermal spring 온천 onch-hön

square (open space) 광장 kwang-jang; a hundred square meters 백 평방 미터 peg p-hyöng-bang mit-hö

squash (sport) 스쿼시 테니스 sk-hwöshi t-henisü

squid 오징어 ojing-ö

stadium 운동장 undong-jang; baseball stadium 야구장 yagujang

staff (employees) 직원 chigwön

stage (theater) 무대 mude

stain (blot) 얼룩 öllug; can you get this stain out? 이 얼룩을 뺄 수 있어요? i öllugl bbel su issö-yo?

stainless steel 스텐레스 st-henresü

stairs 계단 kyedan

stale (rotten) 상 한 sang han

stall (die out) 꺼져요 ggöjyö-yo

stamp (for postage) 우표 up-hyo; commemorative stamp 기념 우표 kinyöm up-hyo

stand (verb) 서요 sö-yo; taxi stand 택시 승차장 t-hegshi sng-ch-hajang; I can't stand ... (can't take) ...를 참을 수 없어요 ...rl ch-haml su öbsö-yo

standard (adjective) 표준의 p-hyojune

standby (passenger) 공석을 대기하는 여행자 kong-sögl tegihanün yöheng-ja

star 별 pyöl; (movie star) 스타 st-ha

start (beginning) 시작 shijag; starting Tuesday 화요일부터 hwa-yo-ilbut-hö; at the start 처음에 ch-hö-me; it won't start 시동이 안 걸려요 shidong-i an köllyö-yo; what time does the tour start? 관광은 몇 시에 출발 해요? kwan-gwang-n myöt shi-e ch-hulbal he-yo?

starter (auto) 스타터 st-hat-hö

state (within country) 주 chu; (in Korea) 도 to; the States (USA) 미국 migug

station 역 yög; bus station 정류장 chöng-ryujang; central station 중앙역 chung-ang-yög; police station 파출소 p-hach-hulso; power station 발전소 paljönso; train station 기차역 kich-ha-yög

stationary store 문방구 munbang-gu

statue (동)상 (dong)sang

stay 묵어요 mugö-yo; I'm staying home tonight 오늘 밤은 집에 있어요 onl pamn chibe issö-yo; must he stay in bed? 집에서 누워 있어야 돼요? chibesö nuwö issö-ya dwe-yo?; I'd like to stay longer 좀더 있고 싶어요 chomdö idgo ship-hö-yo; I might want to stay another 4 days 나흘간 더 숙박 할 지도 몰라요 nahülgan tö sugbag hal chido molla-yo; is there a place to stay nearby? 요근처에 숙박 할 만한 데가 있어요? yognch-hö-e sugbag hal manan tega issö-yo?

steak 스테이크 st-he-ik-hü

steal 훔쳐요 humch-hyö-yo

steel: stainless steel 스텐레스 st-henresü

steep (slope) 가파른 kap-harn

steering 핸들 hendl; could you please check the steering? 핸들 좀 점검해 주세요? hendl chom chömgöme juse-yo?

steering wheel 핸들 hendl

step (stairs) 계단 kyedan

stereo 스테레오 st-here-o

stew (vegetable) 스튜 st-hyu; kimchee stew 김치 찌개 kimch-hi jjige

steward (airline) 스튜어드 st-hyu-ödü

stewardess 스튜어디스 st-hyu-ödisü

stick: walking stick 지팡이 chip-hang-i

sticky 끈적끈적 한 ggnjögg-gnjög han

sticky tape 접착 테이프 chöbch-hag t-he-ip-hü

still (yet) 아직 ajig; he's still sleeping 아직 자고 있어요 ajig chago issö-yo; I'm still a beginner 나는 아직 초보자에요 nanün ajig ch-hoboja-e-yo; I'm still at school 나는 아직 학생이에요 nanün ajig hagseng-i-e-yo; is she still alive? 아직 살아 있어요? ajig sara issö-yo?; does it still exist? 아직 남아 있어요? ajig nama issö-yo?

sting (be stung by insect) 쏘여요 sso-yö-yo

stink (odor) 악취 agch-hwi; it stinks 악취가 나요 agch-hwiga na-yo

stockings 스타킹 st-hak-hing

stolen 훔친 humch-hin; my bag has been stolen 지갑을 도둑맞았어요 chigabl todungmajassö-yo

stomach 배 pe; upset stomach 배탈 pet-hal; I have a stomach ache 배가 아파요 pega ap-ha-yo

stomachache 위통 wit-hong

stone (jewel) 보석 posög;

stone 돌 tol

stop (bus, streetcar) 정류장 chöng-ryujang; stop that! 그만 하세요! kman hase-yo!; bus stop 버스 정거장 pösü chöng-göjang; will it stop raining soon? 비가 곧 그칠까요? piga kod kch-hilg-ga-yo?; where is the stop for ...? ...에 가는 정거장은 어디 에요? ...e kanün chöng-göjang-n ödi e-yo?; please let me off at the next stop 다음 정류장에서 내려 주세요 ta-m chöng-ryujang-esö neryö juse-yo

stopover 단기 체재 tan-gi ch-heje

store (shop) 가게 kage; department store 백화점 pek-hwajöm; grocery store 식품점 shigp-humjöm; I hope that the store is open 상점이 열려 있으면 좋겠어요 sang-jömi yöllyö issmyön chok-hessö-yo

storm 폭풍 p-hogp-hung

story (of building) 층 ch-hüng; (tale)
이야기 i-yagi; three story pagoda 삼
층 탑 samch-hüng t-hab; that's a
different story 그 렇다면 말은 달라져요
kü röt-hamyön marn tallajyö-yo

stove 난로 nanro

straight (direct) 똑 바른 ddog parn;
straight through the city center 곧장,
시의 중심을 지나서 kodjang, shi-e
chung-shiml chinasö; go straight,
please 똑바로 가세요 ddogbaro kase-yo;
go straight? 똑바로 가요? ddogbaro ka-
yo?

straighten: will you straighten it out?
정리 해 주시겠어요? chöng-ri he
jushigessö-yo?

strange (unusual) 이상 한 isang han;
(unknown) 모르는 mornün; that's
strange 그것은 이상 해요 kgösn isang
he-yo; there's a strange smell 이상 한
냄새가 있어요 isang han nemsega issö-
yo; he's gotten some strange disease 그
는 괴상한 병에 걸렸어요 knün
kwesang-an pyöng-e köllyössö-yo; it
has a strange taste 이상 한 맛이 있어요
isang han mashi issö-yo

stranger 모르는 사람 mornün saram

strap (shoulder strap) 견장 kyönjang

straw mat 돗자리 todjari

strawberry 딸기 ddalgi

stream 시냇물 shinenmul

street 도로 toro; back street 뒷골목
twidgolmog; side street 골목 kolmog;
this street 이 길 i gil; across the street
길을 건너서 kirl könnösö; on a back
street 뒷골목에(서) twidgolmoge(sö)

street map 지도 chido

streetcar 전차 chönch-ha

strength (power) 힘 him

strike (labor inaction) 파업 p-ha-öb

string 끈 ggn

striped 줄무늬 chulmune

stripes 줄무늬 chulmune

stroke 뇌졸중 nwejoljung; heat stroke
일사병 ilsabyöng

stroll (outing) 산보 sanbo

stroller (for babies) 유모차 yumoch-ha

strong 센 sen

stuck 막힌 mak-hin

student 학생 hagseng; exchange student
교환 학생 kyohwan hagseng

studio: photography studio 사진관
sajin-gwan

study (learn) 공부 해요 kong-bu he-yo;
what are you studying? 무엇을 공부
해세요? mu-ösl kong-bu hese-yo?

stupid 어리석은 örisögn

style 스타일 st-ha-il; Korean style food
한식 hanshig; Korean style room 온돌
방 ondol pang; Western style food 양
식 yang-shig; Western style room 침
대 방 ch-him te pang

subject (of conversation) 화제 hwaje;
change the subject 화제를 바꿔요
hwajerl pag-gwö-yo

subscribe 구독 해요 kudog he-yo

subscription 구독 kudog

subtitles (English) 영어 자막 yöng-ö
chamag

suburb 교외 kyowe

subway (metro) 지하철 chihach-höl

success 성공 söng-gong

successful 성공 한 söng-gong han

such (a) 그런 krön; such a nice smell!
참 냄새가 좋아요! ch-ham nemsega
choha-yo!; such things often happen
그런 일은 자주 일어나요 krön irn
chaju iröna-yo

suddenly 갑자기 kabjagi

sue 고소 해요 koso he-yo

suede 쎄무 가죽 ssemu kajug

sugar 설탕 sölt-hang; coffee with sugar
설탕을 넣은 커피 sölt-hang-l nöhün k-
höp-hi; coffee without sugar 설탕을
넣지 않은 커피 sölt-hang-l nöch-hi
anün k-höp-hi

suggest 제의 해요 che-e he-yo

suit (men's) 남자 양복 namja yang-bog;
that suits me (arrangements) 그것은
편리 해요 kgösn p-hyönri he-yo

suitable (convenient) 편리 한 p-hyönri
han

suitcase 슈트케이스 shyut-hük-he-isü;
I'd like to check this suitcase in 이
가방을 좀 부쳐 주세요 i gabang-l chom
puch-hyö juse-yo

sukiyaki 스끼야끼 sg-gi-yag-gi

sulk 실쭉 해요 shilj-jug he-yo

summer 여름 yörm; in the summer 여름
에 yörme

sun 해 he; I can't take too much sun
나는 햇볕을 너무 쬐면 안돼요 nanün
hedbyöt-hül nömu jjwemyön andwe-
yo

sun block cream 선 블럭 크림 sön pllög
k-hürim

sun roof (auto) 선 루프 sön rup-hü

sunbathe 일광욕을 해요 ilgwang-yogl
he-yo

sunburn 볕에 탐 pyöt-he t-ham

sunburned 볕에 그을은 pyöt-he k-rn;
I'm sunburned all over 나는 온몸이
볕에 탔어요 nanün onmomi pyöt-he t-
hassö-yo; my arms are so sunburned 나
는 팔이 볕에 매우 탔어요 nanün pari
pyöt-he me-u t-hassö-yo

Sunday 일요일 iryo-il; except Sunday
일요일 외엔 iryo-il we-en

sunflower 해바라기 hebaragi

sunglasses 선글래스 sön-gllesü

sunrise 해돋이 hedodi; at sunrise 새벽
녘에 sebyög nyök-he

sunscreen 선스크린 sönsk-hürin

sunset 일몰 ilmol

sunshade 차양 ch-ha-yang

suntan 볕에 그을음 pyöt-he k-rm

suntan lotion 선탠 크림 sönt-hen k-
hürim

suntan oil 선탠 오일 sönt-hen o-il

suntanned 볕에 그을은 pyöt-he k-rn

super (gasoline) 고급 kogb

super express train 새마을호 sema-ro

superb 훌륭 한 hullyung han

supermarket 수퍼마켓 sup-hömak-hed

superstition 미신 mishin

supper 저녁 chönyög

supplement (charge) 추가 비용 ch-huga
pi-yong

suppose 상상 해요 sang-sang he-yo

suppository 좌약 chwa-yag

sure (certain) 확실 한 hwagshil han;
I'm sure we'll meet again 또 만나뵙게
되겠지요 ddo mannabwebge dwegedji-
yo; are you sure? 확실 하세요?
hwagshil hase-yo?; I'm absolutely sure
정말 확실 해요 chöng-mal hwagshil
he-yo; I'm not sure 확실치 않어요
hwagshilch-hi anö-yo

surgeon 외과 의사 wegwa esa

surgery (operation) 외과 wegwa

surname 성 söng

surprise (astonishment) 놀람 nollam

surprising 놀라운 nolla-un

sushi 생선초밥 seng-sönch-hobab

suspension (auto) 차대버팀 장치 ch-
hadeböt-him chang-ch-hi

swallow (gulp) 삼켜요 samk-hyö-yo

swearword 욕 yog

sweat (perspire) 땀 흘려요 ddam hüllyö-
yo; (perspiration) 땀 ddam; I'm
sweating bullets 따믈 몹시 흘렸어요
ddaml mobshi hüllyössö-yo

sweater 스웨터 swet-hö

sweatshirt 트레이닝 셔츠 t-hüre-ining
shyöch-hü

Sweden 스웨덴 sweden

sweet 단 tan; home sweet home 그리운
내 집이여 kri-un ne chibi-yö

sweetener (artificial) 스위트 swit-hü

sweets 감미료 kammiryo

swelling 종기 chong-gi

sweltering 매우 더운 me-u tö-un

swerve 비켜서 가요 pik-hyösö ka-yo

swim (verb) 수영 해요 su-yöng he-yo;

I like to swim 나는 수영을 좋아 해요 nanün su-yöng-1 choha he-yo; I used to swim a lot 수영을 자주 했었어요 su-yöng-1 chaju hessössö-yo; he's going for a swim 수영 하러 가요 su-yöng harö ka-yo

swim suit 수영복 su-yöng-bog

swimming 수영 su-yöng; is this beach safe for swimming? 이 해변에서 수영해도 안전 해요? i ebyönesö su-yöng-edo anjön he-yo?

swimming pool 수영장 su-yöng-jang

swimming suit 수영복 su-yöng-bog

swimming trunks 수영 팬츠 su-yöng p-hench-hü

switch (electrical) 스위치 swich-hi; please switch it on 켜 주시겠어요 k-hyö jushigessö-yo

Switzerland 스위스 swisü

swollen 부어오른 pu-ö-orn

symphony 교향악 kyohyang-ag

synagogue 유대교 교회 yudegyo kyohwe

synthetic 인조의 injo-e

syrup 시럽 shiröb

system 체계 ch-hegye

T

table 테이블 t-he-ibl; pool table 당구대 tang-gude; a corner table 구석 테이블 kusög t-he-ibl; please reserve a table for two 두 사람 의 테이블을 예약 해주십시오 tu saram e t-he-ibrl ye-yag hejushibshi-o; can we reserve a table for tonight? 오늘밤 테이블을 예약 해 주시겠어요? onlbam t-he-ibrl ye-yag he jushigessö-yo?; can we move to another table? 다른 테이블로 옮겨 주시겠어요? tarn t-he-ibllo olgyö jushigessö-yo?; please put it on the

table 테이블 위에 놓으세요 t-he-ibl wi-e nohüse-yo

table tennis 탁구 t-haggu

tablecloth 식탁보 shigt-hagbo

tablet 정제 chöng-je; cough tablets 정제 로 된 기침약 chöng-jero dwen kich-himyag

tackle: fishing tackle 낚시 도구 nag-gshi togu

Taekwondo (martial arts) 태권도 t-hegwöndo

tailor 양복점 yang-bogjöm

Taiwan 대만 teman

Taiwanese (adjective) 대만 의 teman e; (person) 대만 사람 teman saram

take (transportation) 타요 t-ha-yo; take lessons 강습을 받아요 kang-sbl pada-yo; take pictures 사진 찍어요 sajin jjigö-yo; please take this 이 것을 받아 주십시오 i gösl pada jushibshi-o; goodbye, take care! 안녕, 몸조심 하십시오! annyöng, momjoshim hashibshi-o!; I'll take this one 이것으 로 주세요 igösro chuse-yo; I'll take (buy) it 사겠어요 sagessö-yo; it'll take 5 hours 다섯 시간 걸려요 tasöd shigan köllyö-yo; to take out (food) 가지고 갈 ... kajigo kal ...; may I take a bath? 목욕을 해도 좋아요? mogyogl hedo choha-yo?; will you take care of it? (see to it) 준비를 해 주십시오 chunbirl he jushibshi-o; would you take a check? 수표를 받으세요? sup-hyorl padse-yo?; can I take a plane there? 비행기로 갈 수가 있어요? piheng-giro kal suga issö-yo?; can I take a look? 좀 보여 주시겠어요? chom po-yö jushigessö-yo?; may I take pictures inside? 안에서 사진을 찍어도 돼요? anesö sajinl jjigödo dwe-yo?; may I take you home? 댁까지 태워다 드릴까요? tegg-gaji t-hewöda trilg-ga-yo?; should I take my shoes off? 구두 를 벗을까요? kudurl pöslg-ga-yo?; he shouldn't take long 틀림 없이 오래 않을 거에어요 t-hüllim öbshi ore anl kö-e-ö-yo; will you take this to room 212? 이것을 이백 십이 호 실로 가져 가시겠어요 igösl ibeg shibi ho shillo kajyö kashigessö-yo; would you take me to the airport? 공항까지 데려다 주시겠어요? kong-ang-ggaji teryöda jushigessö-yo?; could you take it in at the side? 겨드랑쪽을 줄여 주시겠어요? kyödrang-jjogl churyö jushigessö-yo?; it will take one year 일 년간 걸려요 il nyön-gan köllyö-yo; how long does it take? 시간이 얼마나 걸리까요? shigani ölmana köllig-ga-yo?; what credit cards do you take? 어떤 크레딧 카드를 받아요? öd-dön k-hüredid k-hadrl pada-yo?

take off (clothes) 벗어요 pösö-yo

talcum powder 분 pun

talk (verb) 이야기 해요 i-yagi he-yo; don't talk fresh 건방지구나 könbang-jiguna; could you talk to them on the telephone for me? 내 대신에 그와 전화로 이야기 해 주시겠어요? ne teshine kwa chönwaro i-yagi he jushigessö-yo?

tall (stature) 키가 큰 k-higa k-hün; (high) 높은 nop-hün

tampons 탐폰 t-hamp-hon

tan (noun) 볕에 그을음 pyöt-he k-rm; I don't get a tan 볕에 그을을 수가 없어요 pyöt-he k-rl suga öbsö-yo

tangerine 귤 kyul

tank (auto) 탱크 t-heng-k-hü; gas tank 가스 탱크 kasü t-heng-k-hü

tap (faucet) 꼭지 ggogji

tape (cassette) 카세트 테이프 k-haset-hü t-he-ip-hü; (cellophane) 스카치 테이프 sk-hach-hi t-he-ip-hü; adhesive tape 접착 테이프 chöbch-hag t-he-ip-hü; insulating tape 절연용 테이프 chöryönyong t-he-ip-hü; Scotch tape (tm) 스카치 테이프 sk-hach-hi t-he-ip-

hü

tape measure 줄자 chulja

tape recorder 테이프 레코더 t-he-ip-hü rek-hodö

taste (flavor) 맛 mad; it tastes awful 맛이 아주 나빠요 mashi aju nab-bö-yo; may I taste a little? 조금 맛봐도 좋아요? chogm madbwado choha-yo?; it has a very nice taste 맛이 매우 좋아요 mashi me-u choha-yo

tasty (meal) 맛있는 mashinnün

tavern 술집 sljib

tax 세금 segm; airport tax 공항 세금 kong-ang segm

taxi 택시 t-hegshi; would you get a taxi for me? 택시를 불러 주시겠어요? t-hegshirl pullö jushigessö-yo?; where can I get a taxi? 택시를 어디서 타지요? t-hegshirl ödisö t-haji-yo?

taxi driver 택시 운전수 t-hegshi unjönsu

taxi stand 택시 승차장 t-hegshi sng-ch-hajang

tea 차 ch-ha; ginger tea 생강차 seng-gang-ch-ha; ginseng tea 인삼차 insamch-ha; green tea 녹차 nogch-ha; lemon tea 레몬을 탄 홍차 remonl t-han hong-ch-ha; black tea 홍차 hong-ch-ha; barley tea 보리차 porich-ha; could I get a cup of tea? 차 한 잔 주시겠어요? ch-ha han chan chushigessö-yo?

tea bag 티백 t-hibeg

tea room 다방 tabang

teach 가르쳐요 karch-hyö-yo; will you teach me some basic sentences? 기본적인 문장을 가르쳐 주시겠어요? kibonjögin munjang-l karch-hyö jushigessö-yo?; could you teach us Korean? 한국어를 가르쳐 주시겠어요? han-gugörl karch-hyö jushigessö-yo?; would you teach me to play paduk? 바둑 좀 가르쳐 주시겠어요? padug chom karch-hyö jushigessö-yo?

teacher 선생 sönseng

team 팀 t-him
teapot 찻 주전자 ch-had chujönja
tearoom 다방 tabang
technical 기술적인 kisuljögin
tee shirt 티셔츠 t-hishyöch-hü
teenager 틴에이저 t-hine-ijö
telegram 전보 chönbo
telephone 전화 chönwa; international
telephone call 국제 전화 kugje
chönwa; what is the telephone
number? 전화 번호는 몇 번이에요?
chönwa pönonün myöt pöni-e-yo?
telephone booth 공중 전화 박스 kong-
jung chönwa pagsü
telephone directory 전화 번호부 chönwa
pönobu
telephone number 전화 번호 chönwa
pöno
telephone operator 교 환 kyo hwan
telephoto lens 망원 렌즈 mang-wön
renjü
television 텔레비전 t-hellebijön; on
television 텔레비전으로 t-hellebijönro;
I want to watch television 텔레비전을
보고 싶은데요 t-hellebijönl pogo ship-
hünde-yo
tell 말 해요 mal he-yo; would you tell
her to call me back? 저에게 전화하라고
전해 주시겠어요? chö-ege
chönwaharago chöne jushigessö-yo?;
would you tell me how to get to the
city center? 중심가로 가는 길을 가르쳐
주시겠어요? chung-shimgaro kanün
kirl karch-hyö jushigessö-yo?; I can't
tell the difference 다른 점을 구별할
수가 없어요 tarn chöml kubyöral suga
öbsö-yo; can you tell me how to get
to ...? ...으로 가는 길을 가르쳐
주시겠어요? ...ro kanün kirl karch-
hyö jushigessö-yo?
temperature (air) 온도 ondo; (body) 체
온 ch-he-on; (a fever) 열 yöl; I
have a temperature 열이 있어요 yöri
issö-yo

temple (Buddhist) 절 chöl; Buddhist
temple 절 chöl; inside the temple 절
안에 chöl ane
temporarily 임시로 imshiro; can you
repair it temporarily? 임시로 고칠 수
있어요? imshiro koch-hil su issö-yo?
temporary 일시적인 ilshijögin
tempura 튀김 t-hwigim
tenant (renter) 세든 사람 sedn saram
tennis 테니스 t-henisü; do you play
tennis? 테니스 치세요? t-henisü ch-
hise-yo?
tennis ball 테니스 공 t-henisü kong
tennis court 테니스 코트 t-henisü k-
hot-hü
tennis racket 테니스 라켓 t-henisü rak-
hed
tennis shoes 테니스화 t-henishwa
tent 텐트 t-hent-hü
term (semester) 학기 haggi
terminal (bus) 버스 터미널 pösü t-
höminöl
terrace 테라스 t-herasü
terrible 무시무시 한 mushimushi han
terrific 훌륭 한 hullyung han
test (trial) 시험 shihöm; (try out) 시험
해요 shihöm he-yo
Thai language 타이말 t-ha-imal
Thailand 태국 t-hegug
than ... ...보다 ...boda; farther than
... ...보다 더 멀리 ...boda tö mölli;
less than an hour 한시간 이하
hanshigan iha; less than that 그것 이하
kgöd iha; more than 20 이십 이상
ishib isang; more than that 그것 이상
kgöd isang; other than ... ... 외에
... we-e; no more than ... ... 이하
... iha; is there a later flight than
that? 그 보다 더 늦은 비행기가 있어요?
kü boda tö njn piheng-giga issö-yo?;
I don't want to spend more than ...
won ...원 이상은 쓰고 싶지 않아요
...wön isang-n ssgo shibch-hi ana-yo
thank you 감사 합니다 kamsa hamnida;

thank you -- you're welcome 고맙습니다 -- 천만에요 komabsmnida - chhönmane-yo; thank you for your help 도와 줘서 고맙습니다 towa chwösö komabsmnida; thank you for your order 주문 하셔서 고맙습니다 chumun hashyösö komabsmnida; thank you so much 대단히 고맙습니다 tedani komabsmnida; no, thank you 아니 괜찮습니다 ani kwench-hansmnida

that 그(것) k(göd); that one 그것 kgöd; that's it (exactly) 맞았어요 majössö-yo; I hope that ... ...면 좋겠어요 ...myön chok-hessö-yo

the (often not translated) 그 kü

theater 극장 kgjang; movie theater 영화 관 yöng-wagwan; opposite the theater 극장 맞은 편에 kgjang majn p-hyöne

theft 도난 tonan

their (of people) 그 사람들 의 kü saramdl e

theirs 그 사람들 의 것 kü saramdl e göd

them 그 사람들 kü saramdl; (things) 그 것들 kgöddl; all of them 모두 modu; each of them (things) 각기 kaggi; neither of them (people) 어떤 사람도 아니에요 öd-dön saramdo ani-e-yo; I dislike all of them 아무것도 싫어요 amugöddo shirö-yo; please give me both of them 두개 다 주세요 tuge ta juse-yo; will you introduce me to them? 저분들을 좀 소개해 주시겠어요? chöbundrl chom sogehe jushigessö-yo?

then (therefore) 그러면 krömyön; see you then 그 때 뵙지요 kü dde pwebji-yo

there 거기 kögi; there was no answer 대답이 없었어요 tedabi öbsössö-yo; there was nobody there 저기에는 아무도 없었어요 chögi-enün amudo öbsössö-yo; there isn't much left 많이 남지 않았어요 mani namji anassö-yo; there is no more 더 없어요 tö öbsö-yo;

there is ... ...가 있어요 ...ga issö-yo; there you are (here it is) 있어요 yögi issö-yo; there are two of us 두 사람이에요 tu sarami-e-yo; is there anyone who can help? 누구 도와줄 사람 있어요? nugu towajul saram issö-yo?; are there places to eat here? 여기 음식점이 있어요? yögi ümshigjömi issö-yo?; are there any other colors? 다른 색이 있어요? tarn segi issö-yo?; is there any news? 무슨 별다른 일이 있어요? musn pyöldarn iri issö-yo?; over there 저기로 chögiro; he went there yesterday 어제 거기에 갔어요 öje kögi-e kassö-yo; is he there? 그는 있어요? knün issö-yo?; that gentleman / lady over there 저분 chöbun

thermal spring 온천 onch-hön

thermometer (for air) 온도계 ondogye; (for body) 체온계 ch-he-on-gye

thermos bottle 보온병 po-onbyöng

thermostat (auto) 온도 조절기 ondo chojölgi

these 이것들 igöddl; not these, but those 이것이 아니고, 그곳이에요 igöshi anigo, kgoshi-e-yo; will you give me these? 이것들을 주시겠어요? igöddrl chushigessö-yo?

they 그 사람들 kü saramdl; (things) 그 것들 kgöddl; they are different 서로 달라요 söro talla-yo; do they serve meals? 식사가 나와요? shigsaga nawa-yo?; when will they come? 그들은 언제 와요? kdrn önje wa-yo?; please let me know when they arrive 그들이 도착 하면 곧 알려 주십시오 kdri tochhag hamyön kod allyö jushibshi-o

thick 두꺼운 tug-gö-un; (stupid) 우둔 한 udun han

thief 도둑 todug

thigh 넓적다리 nöljögdari

thin (of people) 여윈 yöwin; (of things) 얇은 yalbn

thing 것 göd; the whole thing 전부 chönbu; it's the same thing 같은 것이에요 kat-hün göshi-e-yo; did you see my things? 내 것들을 보셨어요? ne göddrl poshyössö-yo?; do you have the same thing in white? 흰색으로 같은 것이 있어요? hensegro kat-hün göshi issö-yo?

think 생각 해요 seng-gag he-yo; I think my ankle is broken 발목이 부러진 것 같아요 palmogi puröjin göd kat-ha-yo; I think that ... ...은 것 같아요 ...n göd kat-ha-yo

third 세째 sej-je

thirsty 목이 마른 mogi marn

this 이(것) i(göd); this is out of order 이것이 고장 났어요 igöshi kojang nassö-yo; this one 이것 igöd; this is ... (I am ...) ...이에요 ...i-e-yo; does this belong to you? 이것은 당신의 것이에요? igösn tang-shine göshi-e-yo?

those 그것들 kgöddl

though ... ... 하지만 ... hajiman

thread (noun) 실 shil

thriller movie 공포 영화 kong-p-ho yöng-wa

throat 목구멍 moggumöng; strep throat 후두염 hudu-yöm; I have a sore throat 나는 목이 아파요 nanün mogi ap-ha-yo

throat lozenges 인후 정제 inu chöng-je

throttle (noun) 스로틀 srot-hül

through ... ...으로 ...ro; does it go through Kwangju? 광주를 경유 해요? kwang-jurl kyöng-yu he-yo?

through train 직통 열차 chigt-hong yölch-ha

throw (verb) 던져요 tönjyö-yo

thumb 엄지손가락 ömjison-garag

thumbtack 압핀 abp-hin

thunder (noun) 천둥 ch-höndung

thunderstorm 뇌우 nwe-u

Thursday 목요일 mogyo-il

ticket 표 p-hyo; one-way ticket 편도표 p-hyöndop-hyo; round-trip ticket 왕복 차표 wang-bog ch-hap-hyo; first class ticket 일등표 ildng-p-hyo; second class ticket 이등표 idng-p-hyo

ticket machine 차표 자동 판매기 ch-hap-hyo chadong p-hanmegi

ticket office 매표구 mep-hyogu

tide: ebb tide 썰물 ssölmul; what time is high tide? 몇 시에 만조가 돼요? myöt shi-e manjoga dwe-yo?

tie (necktie) 넥타이 negt-ha-i

tight (close fitting) 꼭 끼는 ggog gginün

tights 타이즈 t-ha-ich-hü

till: till we meet again 그럼 다시 또 만날 때 까지 kröm tashi ddo mannal dde ggaji; not till Wednesday 수요일에 야 비로소 su-yo-ire-ya piroso

time 시간 shigan; each time ... 그때마 다 kd-demada; long time no see! 오랜 만이에요! orenmani-e-yo!; this time it's on me 이번에는 내가 내겠어요 ibönenün nega negessö-yo; opening time 근무 시간 knmu shigan; it's time we were starting off 출발 할 시간이에요 ch-hulbal hal shigani-e-yo; what time does the movie begin? 영화 는 몇 시에 시작 돼요 yöng-wanün myöt shi-e shijag dwe-yo; what time is it? 지금 몇시에요? chigm myöt-hshi-e-yo?; seven times 일곱 번 ilgob pön; what time is the next train to ...? ...행 다음 열차가 몇 시에 있어요? ...eng ta-m yölch-haga myöt shi-e issö-yo?; a long time 오랫 동안 ored tong-an; some other time, thanks 다음 에 해 주세요 ta-me he juse-yo; let's set a time 시간을 결정 해요 shiganl kyöljöng he-yo; most of the time 대 개 tege; when is meal time? 식사 시간이 어떻게 돼요? shigsa shigani öd-dök-he dwe-yo?; this is the first time 이 번이 처음이에요 i böni ch-hö-mi-e-yo; I don't have much time 시간이

별로 없어요 shigani pyöllo öbsö-yo;
when was the last time you were in
New York? 최근 뉴욕에 계셨던 게
언제였어요? ch-hwegn nyu-yoge
kyeshyöddön ke önje-yössö-yo?; I
don't have the time 시간이 없어요
shigani öbsö-yo
timetable (schedule) 시간표 shiganp-hyo
tinfoil 은박지 ünbagji
tiny 작은 chagn
tip (gratuity) 팁 t-hib; is the tip
included? 값에는 팁이 보함 됐어요?
kabsenün t-hibi poham dwessö-yo?
tire (auto) 타이어 t-ha-i-ö; spare tire
스페어 타이어 sp-he-ö t-ha-i-ö; I've
got a flat tire 타이어에 바람이 빠졌어요
t-ha-i-ö-e parami bbajyössö-yo
tired 피로 한 p-hiro han; he looks tired
피로해 보여요 p-hirohe po-yö-yo; I'm
sick and tired of... ...에 진저리 나요
...e chinjöri na-yo
tiring 지치게 하는 chich-hige hanün
tissues 티슈 t-hishyu
title 제목 chemog
to ... (see also FOR) ...에 ...e; to
New York 뉴욕에 nyu-yoge; to your
health (toast) 당신의 건강을 위하여
축배 해요 tang-shine kön-gang-l
wiha-yö ch-hugbe he-yo; a one-way
ticket to... ...행 편도표 ...eng p-
hyöndop-hyo
toast (bread) 토스트 t-host-hü; (while
drinking) 건배 könbe; let's toast 축배
를 할까요 ch-hugberl halg-ga-yo
toasted seaweed 김 kim
tobacco 담배 tambe; pipe tobacco 파이
프 담배 p-ha-ip-hü tambe
tobacco shop 담배 가게 tambe kage
today 오늘 onl; it's windy today 오늘은
바람이 잘 불어요 onrn parami chal
purö-yo; a week from today 다음 주의
오늘 ta-m chu-e onl; how do you feel
today? 오늘은 기분이 어때요 onrn
kibuni öd-de-yo; you promised it for

today 오늘까지 해준다고 하셨는데요
onlj-jaji hejundago hashyönnünde-yo
toe 발가락 palgarag
together 함께 hamg-ge; they live
together 함께 살고 있어요 hamg-ge
salgo issö-yo
toilet (lavatory) 화장실 hwajang-shil;
the toilet won't flush 변기가
고장났어요 pyön-giga kojang-nassö-yo
toilet paper 휴지 hyuji
toilet water 향수 hyang-su
toiletries 화장품 hwajang-p-hum
toll (road fee) 통행료 t-hong-eng-ryo
tollgate 톨게이트 t-holge-it-hü
tomato 토마토 t-homat-ho
tomato juice 토마토 쥬스 t-homat-ho
chyusü
tomorrow 내일 ne-il; tomorrow
afternoon 내일 오후 ne-il ohu;
preferably not tomorrow 내일은 말고요
ne-irn malgo-yo
ton 톤 t-hon
toner (cosmetic) 토너 t-honö
tongue 혀 hyö
tonic water 토닉 워터 t-honig wöt-hö
tonight 오늘밤 onlbam; I'll see you
tonight! 오늘 밤에 뵙겠어요! onl pame
pwebgessö-yo!
tonsils 편도선 p-hyöndosön
too ... (excessively) 너무 ... nömu
...; (also) ... 도 ... to; me too 나도
에요 nado ye-yo; that's too bad! 참
안됐군요! ch-ham andwedgunyo!; it's
too big 너무 커요 nömu k-hö-yo; it's
too soon 너무 빨라요 nömu bballa-yo;
it's too hot today 오늘은 너무 더워요
onrn nömu töwö-yo; now it's too
late 지금은 너무 늦어졌어요 chigmn
nömu njöjyössö-yo; will you come
too? 당신도 함께 오시겠어요? tang-
shindo hamg-ge oshigessö-yo?
tool 도구 togu
tooth 이 i
toothache 치통 ch-hit-hong

Pronounce: a father; e let; i machine; o note; ö löng; u rude; ü fürther

toothbrush 치솔 ch-hisol
toothpaste 치약 ch-hi-yag
toothpick 이쑤시개 issushige
top 위 wi; on top of ... ... 위에 ...
wi-e; it's a long climb to the top 정
상까지 오르는데 오랫동안 걸려요
chöng-sang-ggaji ornünde oreddong-an
köllyö-yo
total (sum) 합계 habgye
totaled (completely destroyed) 완전히
부숴진 wanjöni puswöjin
touch (verb) 만져요 manjyö-yo
tough (meat) 질긴 chilgin
tour (sightseeing) 관광 kwan-gwang;
bus tour 버스 관광 pösü kwan-gwang;
package tour 패키지 투어 p-hek-hiji t-
hu-ö; sightseeing tour 관광 여행
kwan-gwang yöheng; do you have a
tour of ...? ... 의 관광이 있어요? ...
e kwan-gwang-i issö-yo?; what time
does the tour start? 관광은 몇 시에 출발
해요? kwan-gwang-n myöt shi-e ch-
hulbal he-yo?; where can I join the
tour? 관광을 어디서부터 할 수 있어요?
kwan-gwang-l ödisöbut-hö hal su
issö-yo?
tour guide 관광 안내원 kwan-gwang
annewön
tourism 관광 kwan-gwang
tourist 관광객 kwan-gwang-geg; I'm
here as a tourist 관광하러 왔어요
kwan-gwang-arö wassö-yo
tourist information office 관광 안내소
kwan-gwang anneso
touristy 관광 개발 된 kwan-gwang
kebal dwen
tournedos 투르느도 t-hurndo
tow 끌어요 ggrö-yo
tow rope 끄는 밧줄 ggnün padjul
tow truck 견인차 kyöninch-ha
towards ... ...를 향하여 ...rl hyang-a-
yö
towel 타올 t-ha-ol; kitchen towel 행주
heng-ju; could I have a bath towel?

목욕용 수건을 주시겠어요?
mogyogyong sugönl chushigessö-yo?
town 도시 toshi; the best hotel in
town 시내에서 제일 좋은 호텔 shine-esö
che-il chohün hot-hel; in the center
of town 중앙에 chung-ang-e; what's
going on in town? 시내 어디를 구경
가면 좋겠어요? shine ödirl kugyöng
kamyön chok-hessö-yo?; the other
side of town 시내 반대쪽에 shine
pandej-joge; a few kilometers outside
of town 시내에서 몇 길로미터
떨어져(서) shine-esö myöt killomit-hö
ddöröjyö(sö); let's take a walk around
the town 도시에 산책 나갈까요 toshi-e
sanch-heg nagalg-ga-yo; can you
give me a ride into town? 시내까지
태워 주시겠어요? shineg-gaji t-hewö
jushigessö-yo?
town hall (government) 시청 shich-
höng; (auditorium) 시민 회관 shimin
hwegwan
toy 장난감 chang-nan-gam; toy
department 완구부 wan-gubu
track 홈 hom
track and field 육상 yugsang
track suit 운동 선수의 보온복 undong
sönsu-e po-onbog
trade (foreign) 무역 mu-yög; (to
barter) 교환 해요 kyohwan he-yo
trade fair 무역 전시장 mu-yög
chönshijang
traditional 전통적인 chönt-hong-jögin;
traditional Korean dancing 전통 무용
chönt-hong mu-yong
traffic 교통 kyot-hong; traffic jam 교통
체증 kyot-hong ch-hejng
traffic circle 로터리 rot-höri
traffic cop 교통 순경 kyot-hong sun-
gyöng
traffic jam 교통 체증 kyot-hong ch-
hejng
traffic light 교통 신호등 kyot-hong
shinodng

Pronounce: a father; e let; i machine; o note; ö löng; u rude; ü fürther

tragedy (play) 비극 pigüg

trailer (for car) 트레일러 t-hüre-illö

train 기차 kich-ha; by train 기차로 kich-haro; express train 급행 kp-heng; through train 직통 열차 chigt-hong yölch-ha; is the train late? 열차가 지연 돼요? yölch-haga chi-yön dwe-yo?; super express train 새마을호 sema-ro; we're on the wrong train 열차를 잘못 탔어요 yölch-harl chalmod t-hassö-yo; what time is the next train to ...? ...행 다음 열차가 몇 시에 있어요? ...eng ta-m yölch-haga myöt shi-e issö-yo?

train station 기차역 kich-ha-yög

training shoes 트레이닝 슈즈 t-hüre-ining shyujü

tranquilizers 진정제 chinjöng-je

transfer (change trains, etc) 갈아 타요 kara t-ha-yo

transformer (electrical) 변압기 pyönabgi

translate 번역 해요 pönyög he-yo; would you translate that into English? 영어로 번역 하시겠어요? yöng-öro pönyög hashigessö-yo?

translation 번역 pönyög; is there an English translation of ...? ...을 영어로 번역 한 것이 있어요? ...l yöng-öro pönyög han göshi issö-yo?

translator 번역자 pönyögja

transmission (auto) 변속기 pyönsoggi; automatic transmission 오토매틱 ot-homet-hig; I have transmission trouble 변속기 의 고장이 있어요 pyönsoggi e kojang-i issö-yo

transportation 교통편 kyot-hong-p-hyön

travel 여행 해요 yöheng he-yo; overseas travel 해외 여행 hewe yöheng

travel agency 여행사 yöheng-sa

travel alarm clock 여행용 알람 시계 yöheng-yong allam shigye

traveller 여행자 yöheng-ja

tray 쟁반 cheng-ban

treatment (medical) 치료 ch-hiryo

tree 나무 namu; cherry tree 벗나무 pönnamu

tremendous (big) 커다란 k-hödaran

trendy 최신 유행의 ch-hweshin yuheng-e

trial (in court) 공판 kong-p-han

trim (verb) 다듬어요 tadmö-yo; please trim my mustache 코밑수염 좀 다듬어 주세요 k-homit-hsu-yöm chom tarmö juse-yo; just a trim please (hair) 대충 다듬어 주세요 tech-hung tadmö juse-yo

trip (voyage) 여행 yöheng; business trip 출장 ch-huljang; day trip 당일 여행 tang-il yöheng; I had a trouble-free trip 편안 한 여행였어요 p-hyönan han yöheng-yössö-yo; I want to go on a trip to ... ...까지 여행 하고 싶은데요 ...ggaji yöheng hago ship-hünde-yo

tripe 내장 nejang

tripod (photo) 삼각대 samgagde

Trojans (tm) (condom) 콘돔 k-hondom

tropical 열대(의) yölde(e)

trouble (noun) 문제 munje; engine trouble 엔진 의 고장 enjin e kojang; I'm in trouble 곤경에 빠져 있어요 kon-gyöng-e bbajyö issö-yo; have you found the trouble? 잘못된 데를 발견 했어요? chalmoddwen terl palgyön hessö-yo?

trousers 바지 paji

trout 송어 song-ö

truck 트럭 t-hürög

truck driver 트럭 운전수 t-hürög unjönsu

true 정말의 chöng-mare; it's not true 정말 아니에요 chöng-mal ani-e-yo

trunk (auto) 트렁크 t-hüröng-k-hü

trunks (swimming) 수영 복 su-yöng pog

truth 사실 sashil

try 해 봐요 he pwa-yo; let's try somewhere else 우리 다른 곳에 가 봐요

uri tarn kose ka pwa-yo; let me try it
내가 해 볼께요 nega he polg-ge-yo; I
haven't tried it 시험 한 일이 없어요
shihöm han iri öbsö-yo
tube (tire) 튜브 t-hyubü
Tuesday 화요일 hwa-yo-il; starting
Tuesday 화요일부터 hwa-yo-ilbut-hö;
no later than Tuesday 화요일까지 hwa-
yo-ilg-gaji
tulip 틀립 t-hyullib
tuna 참치 ch-hamch-hi
tuna fish 튜너 t-hyunö
tune (melody) 곡조 kogjo; a very
moving tune 매우 감동적인 선율 me-u
kamdong-jögin sönyul
tunnel 터널 t-hönöl
turkey 칠면조 ch-hilmyönjo
turn (rotate) 돌아요 tora-yo; (in road)
모퉁이 mot-hung-i; turn right 오른쪽
으로 돌아요 ornj-jogro tora-yo
turnips 순무 sunmu
turquoise 터키옥 t-hök-hi-og
TV 텔레비전 t-hellebijön
tweezers 쪽집게 jjogjibge
twice 두번 tubön
twin beds 트윈 베드 t-hüwin pedü
twin room 침대 둘 있는 방 ch-himde
tul innün pang
twins 쌍동이 ssang-dong-i
twist (sprain) 뼈요 bbyö-yo
type (kind) 타입 t-ha-ib; this type of
... 이 종류의 ... i jong-ryu-e ...;
her blood type is ... 그의 혈액형은 ...
이에요 k-e hyörek-hyöng-n ... i-e-yo
typewriter 타자기 t-hajagi
typhoon 태풍 t-hep-hung
typical (representative) 전형적인
chönyöng-jögin;
typical 전형적인 chönyöng-jögin

*

U

U-turn 유턴 yut-hön
ugly 미운 mi-un
Ukraine 우크라이나 uk-hüra-ina
ulcer 위궤양 wigwe-yang
umbrella 우산 usan; beach umbrella 비치
파라솔 pich-hi p-harasol
uncle 아저씨 ajösshi
uncomfortable 불편 한 pulp-hyön han
unconscious 기절 한 kijöl han
under ... (underneath) ... 밑에 ...
mit-he(less than) ... 이하 ... iha; (in
directory) ...의 항 ...e hang; under
age 미성년 misöng-nyön; LOTTE is
under "restaurants" 롯데는 식당 란에
있어요 roddenün shigdang rane issö-yo
undercooked: it's undercooked 덜
익었어요 töl igössö-yo
undergraduate 대학생 tehagseng
underpants 팬티 p-hent-hi
undershirt 런닝셔츠 rönning-shyöch-hü
undershorts (men's) 팬티 p-hent-hi
understand 알아요 ara-yo; I don't
understand Korean 한국말을 몰라요
han-gungmarl molla-yo; yes, I
understand 알았어요 arassö-yo; do you
understand? 아시겠어요? ashigessö-yo?
underwear 속옷 sogod; long underwear
내복 nebog
undo (untie) 풀어요 p-hurö-yo
uneatable 먹을 수 없는 mögl su ömnün
unemployed 실직 한 shiljig han
unfair 불공평 한 pulgong-p-hyöng han;
it's unfair 불공평 해요 pulgong-p-höng
he-yo
unforgettable: an unforgettable
experience 잊을 수 없는 경험 ijl su
ömnün kyöng-öm
unfortunately 유감스럽게도

yugamsröbgedo

unfriendly 불친절 한 pulch-hinjöl han

unhappy 슬픈 slp-hün

unhealthy (unhealthful) 좋지 않은 choch-hi anün; (person) 건강 하지 않은 kön-gang haji anün

union (labor) 노동 조합 nodong chohab

United Nations 국제 연합 kugje yönab

United States 미국 migug

university 대학 tehag

unleaded 보통 휘발유 pot-hong hwibaryu

unlimited milage (for car rental) 무제한 의 거리 mujehane köri

unlock 열어요 yörö-yo

unpack 짐을 풀어요 chiml p-hurö-yo

untie 풀러요 p-hullö-yo

until 까지 ggaji; not until after 7 o'clock 일곱시에 야 비로소 ilgobshi-e ya piroso; I will wait until my wife comes 안내 올 때까지 기다리겠어요 anne ol ddeg-gaji kidarigessö-yo

unusual 이상 한 isang han

up 위로 wiro; up in the mountains 산 위에 san wi-e; hang up (telephone) 끊어요 ggnö-yo; settle up 계산을 해요 kyesanl he-yo; is he up yet? 그는 일어났어요? knün irönassö-yo?; I'm fed up 진저리 나요 chinjöri na-yo; when I get up 내가 일어날 때에 nega irönal dde-e; we'll leave it up to you 당신의 판단에 맡기겠어요 tang-shine p-handane madk-higessö-yo; we're going to climb up 우리는 올라 가겠어요 urinün olla kagessö-yo; did the price go up? 값이 올랐어요? kabshi ollassö-yo?; you must go further up the hill 언덕 더 앞으로 올라가야 해요 öndög tö ap-hüro ollaga-ya he-yo; could you put me up for the night? 오늘 저녁 숙박 시켜 주시겠어요? onl chönyög sugbag shik-hyö jushigessö-yo?

upset stomach 배탈 pet-hal; have you got something for an upset stomach?

위통에 좋은 약 있어요? wit-hong-e chohün yag issö-yo?

upside down 거꾸로 kög-guro

upstairs 이층에 ich-hüng-e

urgent 긴급한 kin-gp-han

Uruguay 우루과이 urugwa-i

us 우리(들) uri(rl); both of us will come 두 사람 다 오겠어요 tu saram ta ogessö-yo; neither of us 어느 쪽 우리도 아니에요 önü jjog urido ani-e-yo; in front of us 우리 앞에(서) uri ap-he(sö); come and visit us 우리 한테 놀러 오세요 uri hant-he nollö ose-yo; one for each of us 우리에게 각각 한게씩 uri-ege kaggag han-gesshig

use (verb) 써요 ssö-yo; I used to swim a lot 수영을 자주 했었어요 su-yöng-l chaju hessössö-yo; may we use the bathroom? 화장실을 써도 좋아요? hwajang-shirl ssödo choha-yo?; can I use my sleeping bag? 내 침낭을 써도 돼요? ne ch-himnang-l ssödo dwe-yo?; it's for my personal use 그것은 내가 쓰는 것이에요 kgösn nega ssnün göshi-e-yo; would you let me use it? 그것을 사용 하게 해 주시겠어요? kgösl sa-yong hage he jushigessö-yo?

useful 편리 한 p-hyönri han; a useful phrase 편리 한 관용구 p-hyönri han kwanyong-gu

usual 보통의 pot-hong-e; at the usual table 평상의 테이블에서 p-hyöng-sang-e t-he-ibresö

usually 보통으로 pot-hong-ro; I usually get up late 나는 보통 늦게 일어나요 nanün pot-hong ndge iröna-yo

*

V

vacancy 빈방 pinbang
vacant 비었음 pi-össm
vacation 휴가 hyuga; winter vacation 겨울 휴가 kyö-ul hyuga; I'm on vacation 휴가 중이에요 hyuga chung-i-e-yo; a nice lazy vacation 한가한 휴가 han-gahan hyuga
vaccination 종두 chong-du
vacuum cleaner 진공 청소기 chin-gong ch-höng-sogi
valid (effective) 유효 한 yuhyo han
valley 골짜기 kolj-jagi
valuable (precious) 값비싼 kabbissan
valuables 귀중품 kwijung-p-hum
value (noun) 가치 kach-hi
van 밴 pen
vanilla 바닐라 panilla
variety show 버라이어티쇼 pöra-i-öt-hishyo
vase 화병 hwabyöng
VD (sexually transmitted disease) 성병 söng-byöng
veal 송아지 고기 song-aji kogi
vegetables 채소 ch-heso
vegetarian (person) 채식 주의자 ch-heshig chu-eja
vehicle 차 ch-ha
velvet 벨벳 pelbed
vending machine 자동 판매기 chadong p-hanmegi
venetian blind 차양 ch-ha-yang
Venezuela 베네수엘라 penesu-ella
venison 사슴 sasm
ventilator 환풍기 hwanp-hung-gi
very 대단히 tedani; very slowly 매우 천천히 me-u ch-hönch-höni; it's very confusing 대단히 복잡 해요 tedani pogjab he-yo; I'm very interested in

... ...는 매우 흥미가 있어요 ...nün me-u hüng-miga issö-yo; it's very spicy (hot) 매우 매워요 me-u mewö-yo; he was very helpful 그는 많이 도움이 됐어요 knün mani to-umi dwessö-yo; thank you very much 정말 감사 합니다 chöng-mal kamsa hamnida; I don't feel very well 몸이 불편 해요 momi pulp-hyön he-yo
via 경유 kyöng-yu; via Suwon 수원을 경유 suwönl kyöng-yu
video (recording) 비디오 pidi-o
Vietnam 베트남 pet-hünam
view 경치 kyöng-ch-hi; what a beautiful view! 참, 아름다운 경치에요! ch-ham, armda-un kyöng-ch-hi-e-yo!
viewfinder (of camera) 파인더 p-ha-indö
village 마을 ma-l; fishing village 어촌 öch-hon; folk village 민속촌 minsogch-hon; a mountain village 산촌 sanch-hon
vine (grape) 포도 나무 p-hodo namu
vinegar 식초 shigch-ho
vinyl 비닐 pinil
violet (flower) 제비꽃 chebig-goch
visa 비자 pija
visibility (vision) 시계 shigye
visit (verb) 방문 해요 pang-mun he-yo; New Year visit to a shrine 성묘 söng-myo; is this your first visit? 여기는 처음 오세요? yöginün ch-hö-m ose-yo?
vital 필요 한 p-hiryo han
vitamins 비타민 pit-hamin
vodka 보드카 podk-ha
voice 소리 sori
volcano 화산 hwasan
volleyball 배구 pegu
voltage 전압 chönab; what is the voltage? 전압은 몇 볼트에요? chönabn myöt polt-hü-e-yo?
vomit 토 해요 t-ho he-yo; I think I'm going to vomit 토 할 것 같아요 t-ho

hal göd kat-ha-yo

W

waist 허리 höri; the waist is too tight 허리가 좀 끼는데요 höriga chom gginünde-yo; I have to watch my waist 살찔까 봐 조심 해야 해요 saljjilg-ga pwa choshim he-ya he-yo
waistcoat 조끼 chog-gi
wait 기다려요 kidaryö-yo; wait just a moment 잠깐 기다려 주세요 chamg-gan kidaryö juse-yo; do I have to wait long? 오래 기다려야 돼요? ore kidaryö-ya dwe-yo?
waiter 웨이터 we-it-hö; waiter! 여보세요! yöbose-yo!; head waiter 헤드 웨이터 hedü we-it-hö; another waiter 다른 웨이터 tarn we-it-hö
waiting room 대합실 tehabshil
waitress 웨이추레스 we-ich-huresü
wake (up) 깨워요 ggewö-yo; will you wake me up at 8:30? 여덟시 반에 깨워 주시겠어요? yödölshi pane ggewö jushigessö-yo?
Wales 웨일스 we-ilsü
walk 걸어요 körö-yo; can I walk there? 거기에 걸어서 갈 수 있어요? kögi-e körösö kal su issö-yo?; it's a short walk 걸어서 금방이에요 körösö kmbang-i-e-yo; let's take a walk around the town 도시에 산책 나갈까요 toshi-e sanch-heg nagalg-ga-yo; I want to do some walking 산책 좀 하고 싶은데요 sanch-heg chom hago ship-hünde-yo
walking boots 등산화 tng-sanwa
walking stick 지팡이 chip-hang-i
walkman (tm) 워크맨 wök-hümen
wall 벽 pyög
wallet 지갑 chigab; I lost my wallet 지

갑을 잃어버렸어요 chigabl iröböryössö-yo
walnut 호두 hodu
wander 돌아다녀요 toradanyö-yo
want 싶어요 ship-hö-yo; want a lift? 태워 드릴까요? t-hewö trilg-ga-yo?; I want to make an appointment 약속 시간을 정하고 싶은데요 yagsog shiganl chöng-ago ship-hünde-yo; I want to go to ... ...에 가고 싶어요 ...e kago ship-hö-yo; I want to learn ... ...를 배우고 싶은데요 ...rl pe-ugo ship-hünde-yo; I want to go to the bathroom 화장실에 가고 싶은데요 hwajang-shire kago ship-hünde-yo; I want ... ...가 필요 해요 ...ga p-hiryo he-yo; we want to visit ... ...에 가 보고 싶은데요 ...e ka pogo ship-hünde-yo; I don't want to spend more than ... won ...원 이상은 쓰고 싶지 않아요 ...wön isang-n ssgo shibch-hi ana-yo; what do you want? 무엇을 원 하세요? mu-ösl wön hase-yo?
war 전쟁 chönjeng; Korean War 한국 전쟁 han-gug chönjeng
war movie 전쟁 영화 chönjeng yöng-wa
ward (hospital) 병실 pyöng-shil
warm 따뜻 한 ddad-düd han; foot warmer 발 보온기 pal po-on-gi; I feel very warm 나는 매우 따뜻 해요 nanün me-u ddad-düd he-yo
warmup suit 트레이닝 t-hüre-ining
warning (noun) 경고 kyöng-go; the warning light is on 위험 신호가 켜져요 wihöm shinoga k-hyöjyö-yo
was 었어요 yössö-yo
wash (verb) 씻어요 sshisö-yo; could you wash these clothes? 이것을 세탁 해 주시겠어요? igösl set-hag he jushigessö-yo?; I need to wash up 나는 씻어야 해요 nanün sshisö-ya he-yo
washcloth (for face) 세수 수건 sesu

sugön

washer (for screw) 워서 wöshyö

washing (laundry) 세탁 set-hag

washing machine 세탁기 set-haggi

wasp 말벌 malböl

wastepaper basket 휴지통 hyujit-hong

watch (wristwatch) 시계 shigye; **watch out!** 조심 해요! choshim he-yo!; **would you watch my bag(s) for me?** 이 가방을 좀 봐 주시겠어요? i gabang-l chom pwa jushigessö-yo?; **I have to watch my waist** 살찔까 봐 조심 해야 해요 salj-jilg-ga pwa choshim he-ya he-yo; **I want to watch television** 텔레비전을 보고 싶은데요 t-hellebijönl pogo ship-hünde-yo

watch band 손목 시계 줄 sonmog shigye chul

water 물 mul; **distilled water** 증류수 chüng-ryusu; **mineral water** 미네랄 워터 mineral wöt-hö; **potable water** 식수 shigsu; **soda water** 소다수 sodasu; **toilet water** 향수 hyang-su; **tonic water** 토닉 워터 t-honig wöt-hö; **is the water drinkable?** 이물 마셔도 되는 거예요? imul mashyödo dwenün köye-yo?; **please boil the water** 물을 끓여 주십시오 murl ggryö jushibshi-o; **a glass of water** 물 한잔 mul hanjan; **a jug of water** 한 항아리 가득의 물 han hang-ari kadge mul; **could we have some water?** 물을 좀 주시겠어요? murl chom chushigessö-yo?; **please give us more water** 물을 더 주세요 murl tö juse-yo; **there is no hot water** 뜨거운 물이 나오지 않아요 ddgö-un muri na-oji anö-yo

water polo 수구 sugu

water skis 수상 스키 susang sk-hi

water sports 수상 스포츠 susang sp-hoch-hü

watercolor 수채화 such-hehwa

watercress 양갓냉이 yang-ganneng-i

waterfall 폭포 p-hogp-ho

watermelon 수박 subag

waterproof (adjective) 방수 pang-su

waterski 수상 스키 susang sk-hi

wave (water) 파도 p-hado

wavy (hair) 웨이브진 we-ibjin

way (road) 길 kil; **go that way** 저쪽으로 가세요 chöj-jogro kase-yo; **right of way** (driving) 선행권 sönenggwön; **is it this way?** 이쪽으로 있어요? ij-jogro issö-yo?; **it's fine that way** 그래로 좋아요 krero choha-yo; **he's blocking the way** 방해가 돼요 pang-ega dwe-yo; **is it a long way?** 멀어요? mörö-yo?; **which is the fastest way?** 어느 쪽이 제일 빠른 방법이에요? önü jjogi che-il bbarn pang-böbi-e-yo?; **is it on the way to Namsan park?** 남산 공원 가는 길에 있어요? namsan kong-wön kanün kire issö-yo?

we 우리(들) uri(dl)

weak 약한 yak-han; **I have a weak back** 등이 약해요 tng-i yak-he-yo

wealthy 부유 한 pu-yu han

wear 입어요 ibö-yo; **must I wear a seat belt?** 좌석 벨트를 맬 필요가 있어요? chwasög pelt-hürl mel p-hiryoga issö-yo?

weather 날씨 nalshi; **because the weather is not good** 날씨가 나쁘기 때문에 nalshiga nab-bgi ddemune; **it's fine weather** 좋은 날씨에요 chohün nalshi-e-yo; **what awful weather!** 참 나쁜 날씨에요 ch-ham nab-bn nalshi-e-yo

weather forecast 일기 예보 ilgi yebo

wedding 결혼식 kyöronshig

wedding ring 결혼 반지 kyöron panji

Wednesday 수요일 su-yo-il; **last Wednesday** 지난 수요일 chinan su-yo-il; **not till Wednesday** 수요일에야 비로소 su-yo-ire-ya piroso; **can it be done by Wednesday?** 수요일까지 할 수 있어요? su-yo-ilg-gaji hal su issö-yo?

week 주 chu; **next week** 다음 주 ta-m

Pronounce: a father; e let; i machine; o note; ö löng; u rude; ü fürther

chu; a week from today 다음 주의
오늘 ta-m chu-e onl; until next week
다음주까지 ta-mjug-gaji; the whole
week 한 주일 han chu-il; within a
week 일주일 이내에 ilju-il ine-e;
Monday of next week 다음 주 월요일
ta-m chu wöryo-il; it's been rainy all
week 한주일 동안 비가 왔어요 hanju-il
tong-an piga wassö-yo; I want to
stay another week 일주일간 더 묵고
싶은데요 ilju-ilgan tö muggo ship-
hünde-yo
weekday 평일 p-hyöng-il
weekend 주말 chumal
weight (body) 몸무게 mommuge
weight lifting 역도 yögdo
weight limit 무게 제한 muge chehan
weird 이상 한 isang han
welcome (greeting) 어서 오세요 ösö
ose-yo; thank you -- you're welcome
고맙습니다 -- 천만에요 komabsmnida -
ch-hönmane-yo
well 잘 chal; well, I'm not sure 글쎄요,
잘 모르겠어요 klse-yo, chal
morgessö-yo; sleep well! 안녕히
주무세요 annyöng-i chumuse-yo; it's
well made 잘 만든 것이에요 chal
mandn göshi-e-yo; he's not well 그는
몸이 불편 해요 knün momi pulp-hyön
he-yo; did you sleep well? 잘
주무셨어요? chal chumushyössö-yo?;
I'm not feeling very well 몸이 불편
해요 momi pulp-hyön he-yo; these
three pictures didn't come out too
well 이 사진 세장은 잘 나오지 않았어요
i sajin sejang-n chal na-oji anassö-yo
well-done (cooked) 잘 익힌 chal ik-hin
well-run (hotel, organization) 서비스가
좋은 söbisga chohün
Welsh 웨일스의 we-ils-e
were ...였어요 ...yössö-yo; you were
right 당신이 옳았어요 tang-shini
orassö-yo
west 서쪽 söj-jog; the West 서양 sö-

yang
West Indian (adjective) 서인도 제도의
sö-indo chedo-e
West Indies 서인도 제도 sö-indo chedo
Western style food 양식 yang-shig
Western style room 침 대 방 ch-him te
pang
Westerner 서양 사람 sö-yang saram
Western style 서양식 sö-yang-shig; are
there Western or Korean meals? 음식은
양식이에요, 한식이에요? ümshign yang-
shigi-e-yo, hanshigi-e-yo?; I'd like
some Western food 양식을 먹고
싶은데요 yang-shigl möggo ship-
hünde-yo
wet 젖은 chöjn; it's gotten all wet 다
젖었어요 ta chöjössö-yo
whale 고래 kore
wharf 부두 pudu
what? 무엇? mu-öd?; what about a
drink? 술 한 잔 하는 게 어때 요? sul
han chan hanün ke öd-de yo?; what
do you advise? 어떻게 하면 좋을지
가르쳐 주십시오 öd-dök-he hamyön
chohülji karch-hyö jushibshi-o; what
does all that come to? 모두 얼마에요?
modu ölma-e-yo?; what did she
answer? 뭐라고 대답 했어요? mwörago
tedab hessö-yo?; what do you call
this? 이것을 뭐라고 불러요 igösl
mwörago pullö-yo; what nerve! 참
뻔뻔스럽기도 하군! ch-ham bbönb-
bönsröbgido hagun!; what does it
cost? 얼마에요? ölma-e-yo?; what
direction is it? 어느 쪽에 있어요? önü
jjoge issö-yo?; what should we do? 어
떻게 해야 할까요? öd-dök-he he-ya
halg-ga-yo?; what do you do? 지금 뭘
하세요? chigm mwöl hase-yo?; what
else? 그 밖에는 kü bag-genün; what is
this for? 뭣을 위한 것이에요? mwösl
wihan göshi-e-yo?; what is it like?
어때요? öd-de-yo?; what does this
word mean? 이 말은 무슨 뜻이에요? i

Pronounce: a father; e let; i machine; o note; ö löng; u rude; ü fürther

marn musn ddshi-e-yo?; what does she mean? 그의 말씀은 무슨 뜻이에요? k-e malsmn musn ddshi-e-yo?; what is your name? 이름이 무엇이에요? irmi mu-öshi-e-yo?; what did you say? 무 엇이라고 말씀 했어요? mu-öshirago malsm hessö-yo?; what did he say? 그 는 무엇이라고 말 했어요? knün mu-öshirago mal hessö-yo?; what a shame! 이게 무슨 창피냐! ige musn ch-hang-p-hinya!; what should I do? 어 떻게 할까요? öd-dök-he halg-ga-yo?; what sort of ...? 어떤 종류의 ...? öd-dön chong-ryu-e ...?; what do you suggest? 어떻게 하면 좋지요? öd-dök-he hamyön choch-hi-yo?; what do you think? 어떻게 생각 하세요? öd-dök-he seng-gag hase-yo?; what time is it? 지금 몇시에요? chigm myöt-hshi-e-yo?; what a beautiful view! 참, 아름다운 경치에요! ch-ham, armda-un kyöng-ch-hi-e-yo!; what do you want? 무엇을 원 하세요? mu-ösl wön hase-yo?; what beautiful weather! 참 좋은 날씨에요 ch-ham chohün nalshi-e-yo; what are you looking for? 뭘 찾으세요? mwöl ch-hajse-yo?; what credit cards do you take? 어떤 크레딧 카드를 받아요? öd-dön k-hüredid k-hadrl pada-yo?; what floor is the room on? 방이 몇 층에 있어요? pang-i myöt ch-hüng-e issö-yo?; what is the name of this wine? 이 포도주 이름이 무엇이에요? i p-hodoju irmi mu-öshi-e-yo?; what is the orchestra playing? 오케스트라가 무슨 곡을 연주 해요? ok-hest-hüraga musn kogl yönju he-yo?; what is this? 이것이 뭐에요? igöshi mwö-e-yo?; what kind of 무슨 musn; what teams are playing? 어느 팀이 나와요? önü t-himi nawa-yo?; what would you do? 당신은 어떻게 하시겠어요? tang-shinün öd-dök-he hashigessö-yo?; on what date? 며칠에?

myöt-hire?; at what time do you close? 몇시에 문을 닫으세요? myöt-hshi-e munl tadse-yo?; this is not what I asked for 이건 내가 주문한 것이 아니에요 igön nega chumunan göshi ani-e-yo; we don't know what to do 어찌 해야 좋을지 모르겠어요 öj-ji he-ya chohülji morgessö-yo

wheel 바퀴 pak-hwi; steering wheel 핸 들 hendl; the wheel wobbles 바퀴가 흔들려요 pak-hwiga hündllyö-yo

wheelchair 바퀴 달린 의자 pak-hwi tallin eja

when? 언제? önje?; when will he arrive? 언제 도착 해요? önje toch-hag he-yo?; when will it be available? 언 제 유효 할까요? önje yuhyo halg-ga-yo?; when can I see him? 언제 뵐 수 있을까요? önje pwel su isslg-ga-yo?; when does it begin? 언제 시작 해요? önje shijag he-yo?; when do you close? 몇시에 문을 닫으세요? myöt-hshi-e munl tadse-yo?; when does it finish? 언제 끝나요? önje ggt-hna-yo?; when do we arrive? 언제 도착 하겠어요? önje toch-hag hagessö-yo?; when I get up 내가 일어날 때에 nega iröronal dde-e; when does it open? 언제 문을 여세요? önje munl yöse-yo?; when will they be back? 언제 돌아오시지요? önje tora-oshiji-yo?; when shall we meet? 언제 만날까요? önje mannalg-ga-yo?; correct me when I make a mistake 실수 하면 고쳐 주세요 shilsu hamyön koch-hyö juse-yo

where? 어디? ödi?; where did you go? 어디에 갔다 오셨어요? ödi-e kadda oshyössö-yo?; where can you buy ...? 어디서 ...를 살 수 있어요? ödisö ...rl sal su issö-yo?; where do we catch the bus? 버스를 어디서 타요 pösrl ödisö t-ha-yo; where are you from? 어디서 오셨어요? ödisö oshyössö-yo?;

where do you get it from? 어디서 얻어요? ödisö ödö-yo?; where do I get off? 어디서 내려요? ödisö neryö-yo?; where are you going? 어디 가세요? ödi kase-yo?; where is he? 어디 있어요? ödi issö-yo?; where does this road lead to? 이건 어디 가는 길이지요 igön ödi kanün kiriji-yo; where do you live? 어디서 살고 있어요? ödisö salgo issö-yo?; where can we park? 어디에 주차 할 수 있어요? ödi-e chuch-ha hal su issö-yo?; where did you put the ...? ...를 어디다 두셨어요 ...rl ödida tushyössö-yo; where do we sign? 어디 에 서명 해요? ödi-e sömyöng he-yo?; where do I turn off? 어디서 길을 바꿔야 해요? ödisö kirl pag-gwö-ya he-yo?; where is the exit? 출구가 어디 있어요? ch-hulguga ödi issö-yo?; can you show me where we are on this map? 이 지도에서 우리가 있는 곳을 가리킬 수 있어요? i jido-esö uriga innün kosl karik-hil su issö-yo?

which 어느 önü; which platform is it? 어느 플랫폼이에요? önü p-hülledp-homi-e-yo?; which is the best route? 어느 쪽이 제일 좋은 길이에요? önü jjogi che-il chohün kiri-e-yo?; which street is it on? 어느 길에 있어요? önü kire issö-yo?; which way is it? 거기로 가는 길을 가르쳐 주세요 kögiro kanün kirl karch-hyö juse-yo

while 동안에 tong-ane; can you do it while I wait? 내가 기다릴 동안 해줄 수 있어요? nega kidaril tong-an hejul su issö-yo?; drop by once in a while 가 끔 들러 주세요 kag-gm tllö juse-yo; can she lie down a while? 그가 잠깐 누워도 좋아요? kga chamg-gan nuwödo choha-yo?

whipped cream 윕 크림 wib k-hürim

whisky 위스키 wisk-hi; a straight whisky 위스키 스트레이트 wisk-hi st-hüre-it-hü

whisper (verb) 속삭여요 sogsagyö-yo

white 흰색 henseg; do you have the same thing in white? 흰색으로 같은 것이 있어요? hensegro kat-hün göshi issö-yo?

white bread 빵 bbang

white collar worker 샐러리맨 sellörimen

white wine 흰 포도주 hen p-hodoju

whitebait 뱅어 peng-ö

who? 누구 nugu; who wrote it? 누가 썼어요? nuga ssössö-yo?; who is the person in charge here? 여기서 담임 사람은 누구에요? yögisö tamim saramn nugu-e-yo?; who did it? 누가 했어요? nuga hessö-yo?; who knows! 누가 알겠어요! nuga algessö-yo!; who? -- them. 누구에요? -- 그 사람들이에요 nugu-e-yo? - kü saramdri-e-yo; who is it? 누구세요? nuguse-yo?; who painted that picture? 저 그림은 누가 그렸어요? chö krimn nuga kryössö-yo?; who won? 누가 이겼어요? nuga igyössö-yo?; is there anyone who can help? 누구 도와줄 사람 있어요? nugu towajul saram issö-yo?; is there an operator who speaks English? 영어 하는 교환이 있어요? yöng-ö hanün kyohwani issö-yo?

whole 온 / 전부의 on / chönbu-e; a whole lot 많이 mani; the whole thing 전부 chönbu; I'll buy the whole lot 모 두 사겠어요 modu sagessö-yo

wholesale 도매 tome

whooping cough 백일해 pegire

whose 누구의 nugu-e; whose is this? 이 것은 누구 의 것이에요? igösn nugu e göshi-e-yo?

why? 왜? we?

wide 넓은 nölbn

wide-angle lens 광각 렌즈 kwang-gag renjü

widow 과부 kwabu

widower 홀아비 horabi

wife 아내 ane; his wife 부인 pu-in;

this is my wife 이 사람이 내 아내에요 i sarami ne ane-e-yo; I will wait until my wife comes 안내 올 때까지 기다리겠어요 anne ol ddeg-gaji kidarigessö-yo

wig 가발 kabal

will (do) 하겠어요 hagessö-yo; will you take care of it? (see to it) 준비를 해 주십시오 chunbirl he jushibshi-o; will you check? 조사해 주시겠어요? chosahe jushigessö-yo?; will you come too? 당신도 함께 오시겠어요? tang-shindo hamg-ge oshigessö-yo?; will you replace it? 바꿔 주시겠어요? pag-gwö jushigessö-yo?; will you give me these? 이것들을 주시겠어요? igöddrl chushigessö-yo?; will it stop raining soon? 비가 곧 그칠까요? piga kod kch-hilg-ga-yo?; when will he arrive? 언제 도착 해요? önje toch-hag he-yo?; we will bring it back 가져 오겠어요 kajyö ogessö-yo; that will do 괜찮아요 kwench-hana-yo; both of us will come 두 사람 다 오겠어요 tu saram ta ogessö-yo; I hope it will clear up 날씨가 맑으면 좋겠어요 nalshiga malgmyön chok-hessö-yo

willow 버드 나무 pödü namu

win (verb) 이겨요 igyö-yo

wind 바람 param; head wind 역풍 yögp-hung

wind chimes 범 종 pöm chong

window 창문 ch-hang-mun; shop window 점포의 진열장 chömp-ho-e chinyöljang; beside the window 창문 옆에 ch-hang-mun yöp-he; in the show window 진열장 안에 chinyöljang ane; a seat beside the window 창문 옆 자리 ch-hang-mun yöp chari

window seat 창가 옆자리 ch-hang-ga yöbch-hari

windshield 앞유리 ap-hyuri

windshield wipers 와이퍼 wa-ip-hö

windsurfing 윈드서핑 windsöp-hing; I like windsurfing 윈드서핑 하기를 좋아 해요 windsöp-hing hagirl choha he-yo

windy 바람 부는 param punün; a windy day 바람이 부는 날 parami punün nal; it's windy today 오늘은 바람이 잘 불어요 onrn parami chal purö-yo

wine 포도주 p-hodoju; red wine 붉은 포도주 pulgn p-hodoju; rice wine 막걸 리 maggölli; rice wine 정종 chöng-jong; white wine 흰 포도주 hen p-hodoju; a bottle of wine 포도주 한 병 p-hodoju han pyöng; could I have some more wine? 포도주 좀 더 주시겠어요? p-hodoju chom tö jushigessö-yo?

wine glass 포도주 잔 p-hodoju chan

wine list 포도주 리스트 p-hodoju rist-hü

wing 날개 nalge; left wing (political) 좌익 chwa-ig; right wing (politics) 우익 u-ig

winter 겨울 kyö-ul; in the winter 겨울 에 kyö-ure

winter vacation 겨울 휴가 kyö-ul hyuga

wipe 닦어요 tag-gö-yo

wire (a telegraph) 전보 chönbo; (electrical) 철사 ch-hölsa; fuse wire 퓨 즈선 p-hyujsön

wiring 배선 pesön

with ... 와 / 과 wa / gwa; with her 그 여자와 같이 kü yöjawa kat-hi; with him 그 사람과 같이 kü saramgwa kat-hi; with ice 얼음을 넣어 örml nöhö; with pleasure 기꺼이 kig-gö-i; with us 우리 같이 uri kat-hi; with you 당신과 함께 tang-shin-gwa hamg-ge; coffee with milk 프림을 탄 커피 p-hüriml t-han k-höp-hi; come with me 나와 함께 와요 nawa hamg-ge wa-yo; tea with milk 우유를 탄 홍차 u-yurl t-han hong-ch-ha; a room with a bath 욕실이 달린 방 yogshiri tallin pang; her behavior with me 나에 대한

그의 행동 na-e tehan k-e heng-dong; please come with me 나와 같이 가세요 nawa kat-hi kase-yo; the woman with the black skirt on 검은 스커트를 입는 사람 kömn sk-höt-hürl imnün saram; I write with a pen 펜으로 써요 p-henro ssö-yo; kimchee doesn't agree with me. 김치는 내 몸에 안 맞아요. kimch-hinün ne mome an maja-yo.; something is wrong with the brakes 브레이크가 잘못 됐어요 pre-ik-hüga chalmod dwessö-yo; can I pay with dollars? 달러로 내도 돼요? tallöro nedo dwe-yo?; we're not satisfied with the room 이 방으로 만족 하지 않아요 i bang-ro manjog haji anö-yo; may I sit with you? 함께 앉아도 좋아요? hamg-ge anjado choha-yo?; that's all right with me 그것은 괜찮어요 kgösn kwench-hanö-yo; may I speak with ...? (on phone) ...를 좀 바꿔 주세요? ...rl chom pag-gwö juse-yo?; I'm having trouble with ... ...에 문제가 생겼어요 ...e munjega seng-gyössö-yo; will you change places with me? 나와 자리를 바꾸겠어요? nawa charirl pag-gugessö-yo?; I don't have it with me 지금은 가지고 있지 않아요 chigmn kajigo idji anö-yo; I'm looking forward to working with you 함께 일 하게 되어서 기쁩니다 hamg-ge il hage dwe-ösö kib-bmnida; it's a pleasure to do business with you 당신과 일을 같이 하게되서 기뻐요 tang-shin-gwa irl kat-hi hagedwesö kib-bö-yo

within ... ... 이내에 ... ine-e; within easy reach 쉽게 갈 수 있는 거리에 swibge kal su innün köri-e; within a week 일주일 이내에 ilju-il ine-e

without 없이 öbshi; she pulled out without signalling 방향 지시 않고 튀어 나왔어요 pang-yang chishi ank-ho t-hwi-ö nawassö-yo

witness 증인 chüng-in; eye witness 목

격자 moggyögja; will you be my witness? 증인이 되어 주시지 않겠어요? chüng-ini dwe-ö jushiji ank-hessö-yo?

witty 재치 있는 chech-hi innün

wobble 흔들려요 hündllyö-yo

woman 여자 yöja; business woman 여류 사업가 yöryu sa-öbga; the woman with the black skirt on 검은 스커트를 입는 사람 kömn sk-höt-hürl imnün saram; that woman 그 여자 kü yöja women 여자들 yöjadl; many women 많은 여자 manün yöja

won (Korean money) 원 wön; 3500 won per bottle 한병에 삼천 오백원 hanbyöng-e samch-hön obegwön; 100 won coin 백원 짜리 동전 pegwön jjari tong-jön; 50,000 won fine 벌금 오만원 pölgm omanwön; almost 10,000 won 거의 만원 kö-e manwön; could you change this into won? 이것을 원화로 바꿔 주시겠어요? igösl wönwaro pag-gwö jushigessö-yo?; I don't want to spend more than ... won ...원 이상은 쓰고 싶지 않아요 ...wön isang-n ssgo shibch-hi ana-yo

wonderful 훌륭 한 hullyung han

wood (substance) 목재 mogje

woodblock prints 목판화 mogp-hanwa

wooden 나무의 namu-e

woods (forest) 숲 sup

wool 모 mo; cotton wool 탈지면 t-haljimyön

word 말 mal; what does this word mean? 이 말은 무슨 뜻이에요? i marn musn ddshi-e-yo?; please find the word in this book 이 책에서 그 말을 찾아 주세요 i ch-hegesö kü marl ch-haja juse-yo

word processor 워드 프로세서 wödü p-hürosesö

work (verb) 일 해요 il he-yo; (noun) 일 il; work hard 수고 해요 sugo he-yo; I work with him 그와 함께 일 하고 있어요 kwa hamg-ge il hago

Pronounce: a father; e let; i machine; o note; ö löng; u rude; ü further

issö-yo; it doesn't work 움직이지
않어요 umjigiji anö-yo; is there any
work for me to do? 내가 할 일이
있어요? nega hal iri issö-yo?
world 세계 segye
worn out (tired) 피곤 한 p-higon han
worry (be concerned) 걱정 해요
kögjöng he-yo; don't worry 걱정
마세요 kögjöng mase-yo
worse 더 나쁜 tö nab-bn
worst 가장 나쁜 kajang nab-bn
worth: worth seeing 볼 만한 pol
manan; it was worth waiting for 기다
린 보람이 있었어요 kidarin porami
issössö-yo
would (do) 하겠어요 hagessö-yo; would
you send it to my hotel? 내 호텔로
배달 해 주시겠어요? ne hot-hello pedal
he jushigessö-yo?
wound 상처 sang-ch-hö
wrap (verb) 포장 해요 p-hojang he-yo
wrapping (action) 포장 p-hojang
wrapping paper 포장지 p-hojang-ji
wrench (tool) 스패너 / 렌치 sp-henö /
rench-hi
wrestling (professional) 레슬링 reslling;
Korean wrestling 씨름 sshirm
wrist 손목 sonmog
write 써요 ssö-yo; please write your
name and phone number 성함과 전화
번호를 좀 써 주세요 söng-amgwa
chönwa pönorl chom ssö juse-yo; I
write with a pen 펜으로 써요 p-henro
ssö-yo; I'll write you a letter 편지
하겠어요 p-hyönji hagessö-yo
writer 작가 chagga
writing (letters) 글자 klja; Korean
writing 한글 han-gl
writing paper 편지지 p-hyönjiji
wrong 틀린 t-hüllin; something is
wrong with the brakes 브레이크가 잘못
됐어요 pre-ik-hüga chalmod dwessö-
yo; it's the wrong key 틀린 열쇠에요
t-hüllin yölswe-e-yo; the bill is

wrong 계산이 틀려요 kyesani t-hüllyö-
yo; we're on the wrong train 열차를
잘못 탔어요 yölch-harl chalmod t-
hassö-yo; is there something wrong
with it? 어디가 고장 났어요? ödiga
kojang nassö-yo?; I think I have the
wrong number 번호를 잘못 건 것
같군요 pönorl chalmod kön göd kadk-
hunyo

X

x ray 액스레이 egsre-i

Y

yacht 요트 yot-hü
yard (garden) 마당 madang
year 년 nyön; one year ago 일년 전에
ilnyön chöne; last year 작년
changnyön; New Year 새해 sehe; this
year 금년 kmnyön; last year 작년
changnyön; two years 이년 inyön;
three years ago 삼년 전 samnyön
chön; once per year 일년에 한 번씩
ilnyöne han pönshig; in a year 일년
지나면 ilnyön chinamyön; we will
come back next year 우리는 내년에
돌아 오겠어요 urinün nenyöne tora
ogessö-yo
yellow 노랑색 norang-seg
yellow pages 광고 안내 란 kwang-go
anne ran
yellowtail 방어 pang-ö
yen 엔 en
yes 에 / 네 ye / ne; yes, I see 네,
알았어요 ne, arassö-yo; yes, please 네,
좋아요 ne, choha-yo

Pronounce: a father; e let; i machine; o note; ö löng; u rude; ü fürther

yesterday 어제 öje; since yesterday 어제
부터 öjebut-hö; he went there
yesterday 어제 거기에 갔어요 öje kögi-
e kassö-yo; the day before yesterday
그저께 kjög-ge
yet 아직 ajig; not yet 아직도 ajigdo;
that's better yet 더욱 좋아요 tö-ug
choha-yo; is he up yet? 그는
일어났어요? knün irönassö-yo?; I don't
know yet 아직은 모르겠어요 ajign
morgessö-yo
yogurt 요구르트 yogurt-hü
you (singular) 당신 tang-shin; (plural)
당신들 tang-shindl; you promised it
for today 오늘짜지 해준다고 하셨는데요
onlj-jaji hejundago hashyönnünde-yo;
would you ...? (favor) ...어 주십시오
...ö jushibshi-o; it is for you 당신에
게 줄 것이에요 tang-shinege chul
göshi-e-yo
young 젊은 chölmn
young person 젊은이 chölmni
your 당신의 tang-shine; your colleague
당신의 동료 tang-shine tong-ryo; to
your health! 건배! könbe!; what is
your name? 이름이 무엇이에요? irmi
mu-öshi-e-yo?; is she your friend? 그
녀는 당신의 친구에요? knyönün tang-
shine ch-hin-gu-e-yo?; you don't
look your age 자기 나이로 보이지
않어요 chagi na-iro po-iji anö-yo;
would you put this in your safe? 이것
을 당신의 금고에 넣어 주시겠어요?
igösl tang-shine kmgo-e nöhö
jushigessö-yo?
yours 당신의 tang-shine; which one is
yours? 당신의 것은 어느 것이에요?
tang-shine gösn önü göshi-e-yo?
youth hostel 유스호스텔 yushost-hel;
I'm staying at the youth hostel 유스호
스텔에 묵어요 yushost-here mugö-yo

Z

zero 제로 chero
zipper 지퍼 chip-hö
zoo 동물원 tong-murwön
zoom lens 줌 렌즈 chum renjü
zucchini 서양호박 sö-yang-obag

Korean / English

This section of the dictionary is divided into two parts. The first part lists some frequently used Korean words. These words were selected from the definitions and sentence examples in the English / Korean section. They are listed in alphabetical order, according to our Romanized pronunciation system. You can use this list look up a word or expression you may have heard in Korean. Or you can look up some of the Korean words in the sentence examples from the English / Korean section in order to clarify your understanding of them.

The second part is subdivided into Traveller's Topics, subject sections where you can find the word you are looking for. The words listed here are for specific items needed by people travelling in Korea. They are arranged in the groups listed at the beginning. You are most likely to find these words written on signs, menus, etc. You need not learn the Korean writing system (Hangul) or its alphabetical order, however. Since the number of items in each group is limited, you can easily look through the whole group for the word which resembles the writing you see.

Pronounce: a father; e let; i machine; o note; ö löng; u rude; ü fürther

B

bbal¹i 빨리 quickly, fast, soon
bbang 빵 bread

A

C

ach-him 아침 morning
a-i 아이 kid (child)
a-illendü 아일랜드 Ireland
a-isk-hürim 아이스크림 ice cream
ajig 아직 still (yet); not yet
aju 아주 very, quite
allyö 알려 letting someone know
amudo 아무도 someone, anyone, nobody
amugöddo 아무것도 anything
an 안 inside, interior; not
anassö-yo 앉았어요 did not
ana-yo 앉아요 does not
andwe-yo 안돼요 no way, must not, will not do
ane 안에 inside
ani-e-yo 아니에요 is not, no
anjön 안전 safety, security
ank-hessö-yo 않겠어요 will not
anmyön 않으면 if not
anne 안내 information
anneso 안내소 information office
annewön 안내원 guide (person)
annyöng hase-yo? 안녕 하세요? how are you?
annyöng-i kyeshibshi-o 안녕히 계십시오 goodbye
anössö-yo 않었어요 did not
anö-yo 않어요 does not
anün 않은 which is not
ap-ha-yo 아파요 hurts, is painful
ap-he 앞에 ahead (forward, in front)
ap-hö-yo 아퍼요 ache (be painful)
arassö-yo 알았어요 yes, I understand
armda-un 아름다운 beautiful

cha 자 ruler (measure)
chabch-he 잡채 mixed vegetables with noodles
chadong 자동 automatic
chagn 작은 little
chajön-gö 자전거 bicycle
chak-hed 자켓 jacket
chal 잘 well
chalmod 잘못 error, mistake
chan 잔 cup
chang 장 boss; chest, cabinet; bowels
chari 자리 position, seat (location)
chebal 제발 please (please do)
chehan 제한 restriction, limitation
che-il 제일 most, number one, first
chemi 재미 fun (enjoyment)
ch-ha 차 car
ch-ham 참 really, truly, very
ch-hang-mun 창문 window
ch-hap-hyo 차표 rail ticket
ch-hijü 치즈 cheese
ch-himde 침대 bed (Western)
ch-hin-gu 친구 friend, companion
ch-hinjöl 친절 kindness, goodness
ch-hiryo 치료 cure (treatment)
ch-hode 초대 invitation
ch-hö-m 처음 beginning
ch-hönch-höni 천천히 material (cloth)
ch-höng-ö 청어 herring
ch-hönmane-yo 천만에요 you're welcome, don't mention it
ch-hulbal 출발 departure

ch-hulgu 출구 exit
ch-hung-bun 충분 full, satisfactory
ch-huwöl he-yo 추월 해요 pass, overtake
ch-hwiso 취소 cancellation
chi 지 (participle ending expressing doubt, negation)
chib 집 home
chibang 지방 fat (on meat)
chibe 집에 home, at home
chibul 지불 payment
chido 지도 map
chigm 지금 now
chigmn 지금은 now (as opposed to before)
chihach-höl 지하철 subway, metro (train)
chik-heng 직행 nonstop (direct)
chin 진 gin
chinan 지난 past, last
chinasö 지나서 beyond, past
chogag 조각 a carving
choging 조깅 jogging
chogm 조금 bit
chogmman 조금만 just a little
choha 좋아 well; likes, thinks well of
choha-yo 좋아요 good, okay, all right
chohün 좋은 good
chok-hessö-yo 좋겠어요 would be good; I wish
chöl 절 Buddhist temple
chom 좀 some (a little)
chön 전 whole, all; previous, before
chönbu 전부 all, the whole thing
chöne 전에 ago, before
chön-gi 전기 electricity
chöng-mal 정말 really
chöng-mallo 정말로 really, honestly
chön-gol 전골 casserole
chöng-ryujang 정류장 bus station
chön-gu 전구 bulb (light)
chönja 전자 electronic
chönjeng 전쟁 war
chönwa 전화 phone, telephone

chönyög 저녁 evening
chorim 조림 hard-boiled food
choshim 조심 caution; be careful!
chu 주 state (within country)
chuch-ha 주차 parking
chuch-hajang 주차장 car park
chu-e 주의 attention
chug 죽 porridge
chugessö-yo 주겠어요 I will give, will you give?
chul 줄 queue (noun)
chumun 주문 order, request
chunbi 준비 preparation, arrangements
chung-gug 중국 China
chung-i-e-yo 중이에요 is doing; is in the process of
chung-ryang 중량 weight
chuse-yo 주세요 please give, please do
chushibshi-o 주십시오 please do, please give
chushigessö-yo 주시겠어요 would you please do / give
chuso 주소 address
chusü 주스 juice, fruit juice
chu-yuso 주유소 filling station
chwö-yo 줘요 give
chyössö-yo 졌어요 became, got to be
chyusü 쥬스 juice

D

ddalgi 딸기 strawberry
ddara 따라 according to, following
dde 때 the time when
ddemune 때문에 the reason for, because
ddo 또 again; also; and, or
ddög 떡 rice cake
ddöna-yo 떠나요 leave, depart, go
dwen 된 -ized, having become
dwessö-yo 됐어요 became, was
dwe-yo 돼요 becomes

dwe-yo 되요 becomes, -izes

E

e 의 -'s; of
e 에 at, on, in
eja 의자 chair
ellibe-it-hö 엘리베이터 elevator
enjin 엔진 engine
esa 의사 doctor
esö 에서 at, in, on; from

G

ggaji 까지 until, up to; by (time); to
ggwe 꽤 fairly; considerably, quite
göd 것 thing, fact, the fact that, the one
göshi 것이 the thing (as subject); the fact
göshi-e-yo 것이에요 is a fact; is a thing; is so
gösl 것을 the thing, the fact (as object)
gösn 것은 the thing, the fact (as topic)

H

hage 하게 -ly (creates adverb); does so that
hagessö-yo 하겠어요 will do; will say
haggyo 학교 school
hago 하고 does and; with
haji 하지 (doesn't) do
hal 할 to be doing; which will do

halg-ga-yo 할까요 shall (we) do?
hamg-ge 함께 together, with
hamnida 합니다 does, says, -izes
hamnidaman 합니다만 does but; is but
hamyön 하면 would do; if one does then
han 한 one; which did, who did; -ish (turns noun into adjective)
hana 하나 one
hang-gong 항공 aviation, airline
han-gug 한국 Korea
han-gungmarl 한국말을 Korean language (as object)
hanjan 한잔 one cup, one glass
hanün 하는 doing, which does, who does
harin 할인 discount
harö 하러 (going to) do
hase-yo 하세요 you do
hashigessö-yo 하시겠어요 you will do
he 해 doing
he-an 해안 coast
hebyöne 해변에 at the seashore
hedo 해도 even though it is / does
hem 햄 ham
heng 행 destination, bound for
heng-dong 행동 behavior
he-ö 헤어 hair
hessö-yo 했어요 did, said
he-ya 해야 must do
he-yo 해요 do, does, says
hoju 호주 Australia
hong-ch-ha 홍차 black tea
honja 혼자 alone, by oneself
hot-hel 호텔 hotel
hu-e 후에 afterwards
hullyung han 훌륭 한 great, nice, fine
hura-i 후라이 frying, fried
hwagshil 확실 certainty, sureness
hwajang-shil 화장실 bathroom, toilet
hwanja 환자 patient
hweng-dan 횡단 intersection, crossing
hwesa 회사 company, corporation
hwibaryu 휘발유 gasoline

Pronounce: a father; e let; i machine; o note; ö löng; u rude; ü fürther

hwölshin 훨씬 by far, greatly
hyang 향 incense
hyönsang 현상 tongue
hyuga 휴가 vacation

J

jjari 짜리 bills (currency)
jjige 찌개 pot stew
jjim 찜 steamed dish

I

i 이 this; tooth
ibgu 입구 entrance
ich-hüng 이층 second story
i-e-yo 이에요 is, are
igöd 이것 this one
igöshi 이것이 this one (as subject)
igösl 이것을 this one (as object)
igösn 이것은 this one (as topic)
iha 이하 below, less than
i-inyong 이인용 two-person; for two people
ije 이제 now
il 일 work, business; fact
ilbon 일본 Japan
indo 인도 India
innün 있는 with; -full (changes noun into adjective)
insa 인사 greeting, bow
iri 일이 fact, business (as subject)
iri-e-yo 일이에요 is such a fact, is that kind of thing
irl 일을 fact, business (as object)
irm 이름 name
iröna-yo 일어나요 happen, happens
isang 이상 strangeness; above, more than
issm 있음 existence
issössö-yo 있었어요 there was; had
issö-yo 있어요 exists, there is; have, has

K

ka 가 going; (indicates the subject)
kabang 가방 bag, baggage
kabang-l 가방을 bag (as object)
kadda 갖다 carrying, bringing
kage 가게 shop, store
kagessö-yo 가겠어요 will go
kag-ga-un 가까운 near, close
kago 가고 going
kajang 가장 the most, -est
kaje 가재 crayfish
kaji 가지 eggplant; type, kind; branch; (doesn't) go
kajigo 가지고 taking, carrying
kajyö 가져 taking, carrying
kal 갈 being about to go
kalbi 갈비 ribs
kamgi 감기 a cold, flu
kamja 감자 potato
kamsa 감사 thanks, gratitude
kandan 간단 simplicity, brevity, lightness
kanün 가는 going
kara 갈아 changing, in exchange
karch-hyö 가르쳐 teaching, telling
kase-yo 가세요 you go
kassö-yo 갔어요 went
kat-ha-yo 같아요 is similar, is the same; is likely, seems
kat-hi 같이 along with; similarly

*

Pronounce: a father; e let; i machine; o note; ö löng; u rude; ü fürther

kat-hün 같은 similar, same
ka-ya 가야 must go
ka-yo 가요 goes
ke 게 crab
k-e 그의 his, her
k-ege 그에게 to him, to her, for him, etc.
kga 그가 he, she (as subject)
kgjang 극장 theater
kgöd 그것 this thing
kgöshi 그것이 this thing (as subject)
kgösl 그것을 this thing (as object)
kgösn 그것은 this thing (as topic)
k-hadü 카드 card
k-hagt-he-il 칵테일 cocktail
k-henada 캐나다 Canada
k-hendi 캔디 candy
k-holla 콜라 cola
k-honsent-hü 콘센트 electric outlet
k-höp-hi 커피 coffee
k-hot-hü 코트 coat
k-hüllöb 클럽 club
k-hün 큰 big
k-hürim 크림 cream
kijöl 기절 fainting
kil 길 road, way, street
kim 김 Kim (name); steam; laver
kimch-hi 김치 kimchee (hot pickled cabbage)
ki-ö 기어 gear
kirl 길을 the road (as object)
kjö 그저 still, without stopping
kmji 금지 prohibition, not allowed
knch-hö-e 근처에 in the area, nearby
knün 그는 he, she (as topic)
kod 곧 at once, immediately
kod 곳 place, the place where
kö-e 거의 almost, nearly; scarcely
kogi 고기 meat
kögi-e 거기에 there
kögjöng 걱정 worry, fear
kojang 고장 breakdown (auto, etc.)
köllyössö-yo 걸렸어요 took (time); hung; called (telephone)

köllyö-yo 걸려요 takes (time); hangs; calls (telephone)
komabsmnida 고맙습니다 thank you
komu 고무 rubber, eraser
könbe 건배 cheers, to your health
kön-gang 건강 health
kong-jung 공중 public
kong-p-ho 공포 fear, terror
kong-wön 공원 park, garden
körösö 걸어서 walking, on foot
kose 곳에 at the place where
krd 그릇 container; serving
kre-yo 그래요 yes, is so, does so; really?
krim 그림 picture, drawing, painting
kröch-hi 그렇지 (not) that way, (not) so
krök-he 그렇게 like that; so much
krön 그런 such a, like that
kü 그 this
kudu 구두 shoes
kug 국 soup
kugbch-ha 구급차 ambulance
kugje 국제 international, worldwide
kugsu 국수 noodles
kugyöng 구경 seeing, watching
ku-i 구이 Korean barbecue
kusög 구석 corner
kwa-il 과일 fruit
kwan-gwang 관광 sightseeing, tourism
kwench-hana-yo 괜찮아요 it's OK, not bad, will do
kwench-hanö-yo 괜찮어요 it's OK, not bad, will do
kyeran 계란 eggs
kyesansö 계산서 the bill, the check
kyese-yo 계세요 you are
kyesog 계속 continuation
kyohwan 교환 exchange
kyohwe 교회 church, chapel
kyöljöng 결정 decision, determination
kyöng-yu 경유 via; gasoline
kyöron 결혼 marriage
kyot-hong 교통 traffic, communication

Pronounce: a father; e let; i machine; o note; ö löng; u rude; ü fürther

M

mag 막 act (of play)
majimag 마지막 end, last
mal 말 language, speech; horse
malle-iji-a 말레이지아 Malaysia
malsm 말씀 words (honored), what you
  said
man 만 bay
mani 많이 a whole lot
manil 만일 if, supposing
manün 많은 many
mara-yo 말아요 don't, do not
marn 마른 thin, skinny
mase-yo 마세요 please do not
mashi 맛이 flavor (as subject)
megju 맥주 beer
menik-hyu-ö 매니큐어 manicure
me-u 매우 so (very)
me-un 매운 hot (spicy)
mi-an 미안 regret, I'm sorry
migug 미국 America
mist-hö 미스터 Mister
mod 못 not, cannot; bunion; pond
modn 모든 all (adjective)
modu 모두 all of them, all of it
molla-yo 몰라요 I don't know
momi 몸이 body (as subject)
morgessö-yo 모르겠어요 I wouldn't
  know, I don't understand
mörö-yo 멀어요 is far (away)
muggo 묵고 staying, residing
mul 물 water
mullon 물론 certainly (of course)
mune 무늬 pattern
munjega 문제가 door
munl 문을 door (as object)
mu-öd 무엇 what
mu-öshi-e-yo 무엇이에요 what is it?
mu-öshirago 무엇이라고 what is it

that...
murl 물을 the water (as object)
musn 무슨 which, what kind of
mu-u 무우 radish
myön 면 cotton (material)
myöndo 면도 razor, shaving
myönöjng 면허증 license
myöt 몇 how many
myöt-hshi-e 몇시에 what time?

N

nab-bn 나쁜 bad
nado 나도 me too
na-ege 나에게 to me, for me
najung-e 나중에 afterwards
nal 날 day
nalshi-e-yo 날씨에요 the weather is
nalshiga 날씨가 weather (as subject)
nam 남 male; south
namja 남자 man, fellow
namud-dalgi 나무딸기 raspberries
namul 나물 herbs, greens
nanün 나는 I (as topic)
narl 나를 me
nassö-yo 났어요 exited, went out
nawa 나와 with me
nawa-yo 나와요 come out
na-yo 나요 exits, goes out
ne 내 my
ne 네 yes, uh-huh, right
nega 내가 I (as subject)
ne-il 내일 tomorrow
neng-myön 냉면 cold soup
neryögan 내려간 having gone down
nöhün 넣은 inserted, included, put in
nok-ho 놓고 putting, placing
nömu 너무 too (much), very
nop-hün 높은 high
nuga 누가 who?
nugu 누구 someone (somebody)

Pronounce: a father; e let; i machine; o note; ö löng; u rude; ü fürther

nün 는 eye; snow

O

öbsössö-yo 없었어요 there wasn't any; I didn't have

öbsö-yo 없어요 there isn't any; I have none

öd-de-yo 어때요 what is it like? how is it?

öd-dök-he 어떻게 how

öd-dön 어떤 what kind of, some kind of, some

ödi 어디 where?

ödi-e 어디에 where

ödisö 어디서 where (does)

ogessö-yo 오겠어요 will come

ohu 오후 afternoon

o-i 오이 cucumber

o-il 오일 oil (lubrication)

öje 어제 yesterday

ölma-e-yo 얼마에요 how much is it?

ölmana 얼마나 how much

omlled 오믈렛 omelette

ömnün 없는 without; -less (creates negative adjective)

ön 언 language

on 온 having come out; all, whole

onch-hön 온천 hot springs

öndög 언덕 hill

önje 언제 when

onl 오늘 today

onlbam 오늘밤 tonight

onrn 오늘은 today

önü 어느 which

orenji 오렌지 orange

örisögn 어리석은 foolish

ose-yo 오세요 you come

oshigessö-yo 오시겠어요 you will come, will you come?

P

pa 바 way, means (bound noun)

pab 밥 boiled rice

pabo 바보 fool, idiot

pada 바다 sea, ocean

pada-yo 받아요 receive, get, accept

padse-yo 받으세요 you get, you accept

pag-ge 밖에 outside, besides, other than

pag-gwö 바꿔 in exchange

paji 바지 pants, trousers

pam 밤 evening, night

pan 반 half

panana 바나나 banana

pang 방 room, accommodations

pang-e 방에 in the room

parami 바람이 the wind (as subject)

paro 바로 exactly, just, immediately

pe 배 ship; stomach; pear

pedal 배달 delivery

p-ha-i 파이 pie

p-ha-inep-hül 파인애플 pineapple

p-hanme 판매 sale, selling

p-hanmegi 판매기 vending machine

p-hent-hi 팬티 undershorts, panties

p-hillip-hin 필리핀 Filipino

p-hillm 필름 film

p-himang 피망 pimento, green pepper

p-hiryo 필요 necessity, need

p-hiryoga 필요가 need (as subject)

p-hodo 포도 grape

p-hodoju 포도주 wine

p-hoham 포함 inclusion

p-huding 푸딩 pudding

p-hürang-sü 프랑스 France, French

p-hürogrem 프로그램 program

p-hyo 표 ticket

p-hyöndop-hyo 편도표 one-way ticket

p-hyönji 편지 letter

p-hyönri 편리 convenience, handiness

piga 비가 rain (as subject)

Pronounce: a father; e let; i machine; o note; ö löng; u rude; ü fürther

piheng-gi 비행기 airplane
pillyö 빌려 borrowing, renting
pip-hü 비프 beef
pöbön 버번 bourbon
poda 보다 than
podk-ha 보드카 vodka
pog-gm 볶음 roast, broiled food
pogjab 복잡 complexity, complication
pogo 보고 report; to (someone); sees / tries and...
pogyong 복용 dosage, dose
pohöm 보험 insurance
pölle 벌레 insect, bug
pölsö 벌써 already
pön 번 time, occasion, turn
pong-t-hu 봉투 envelope
pöno 번호 number
pönyög 번역 translation
pöryössö-yo 버렸어요 finished, completely
pösnün 버스는 the bus (as topic)
pösöd 버섯 mushroom
pösü 버스 bus
pot-hong 보통 ordinary, general
pot-hong-e 보통의 ordinary, general
pot-hü 보트 boat
po-yö 보여 showing, letting (someone) see
po-yö-yo 보여요 show, let (someone) see
pre-ik-hü 브레이크 brakes
puch-hyö 부쳐 sending, mailing
pu-in 부인 Mrs, madam, wife
pul 불 fire, light
pullö 불러 blowing; calling
pulp-hyön 불편 discomfort, inconvenience
pun 분 minute; honored person
purn 붙은 a light (as topic)
puröjin 부러진 broken
put-hag 부탁 request, favor
pwa 봐 trying, seeing
pwa-yo 봐요 see, try
pwebgessö-yo 뵙겠어요 will see, will meet

pyöllo 별로 especially, in particular
pyöng 병 bottle; illness
pyöng-wön 병원 hospital
pyöt-he 볕에 in the sun

R

remon 레몬 lemon
renjü 렌즈 lens
rl 를 (indicates object)
röshi-a 러시아 Russia
roshyön 로션 lotion

S

sagessö-yo 사겠어요 I'll buy it
sago 사고 accident
sagwa 사과 apple
sajin 사진 photograph (picture)
sajön 사전 dictionary
salgo 살고 living
salmn 삶은 person (as topic)
san 산 mountain
sang-ch-hö 상처 cut (wound)
saram 사람 person, people
saramdl 사람들 people
sarami 사람이 person (as subject)
sarami-e-yo 사람이에요 is that (kind of) person
se 새 bird
segwan 세관 Customs
sellödü 샐러드 salad
seng-gag 생각 idea, thought
seng-sön 생선 fish (food)
set-hagso 세탁소 dry cleaner
se-u 새우 shrimps
shibch-hi 싫지 (doesn't) want

Pronounce: a father; e let; i machine; o note; ö löng; u rude; ü fürther

shi-e 시에 at (that) hour
shigan 시간 hour
shigani 시간이 time (as subject)
shiganp-hyo 시간표 timetable (schedule)
shigdang 식당 dining room
shigmch-hi 시금치 spinach
shigsa 식사 meal
shigsarl 식사를 meal (as object)
shigye 시계 clock, watch
shihöm 시험 exam
shijag 시작 start (beginning)
shijang 시장 market (marketplace)
shine 시내 downtown
shinmun 신문 god
ship-hö-yo 싶어요 want, wants
ship-hünde-yo 싶은데요 wants, want
shyöbid 서빗 sherbet
shyop-hing 쇼핑 shopping
sk-hach-hi 스카치 scotch (whisky)
sk-hi 스키 ski (noun)
soge 소개 introduction
sogm 소금 salt
sogogi 소고기 beef
sömyöng 서명 signature
sön 선 line
son 손 hand
söng 성 gender, sex; castle
song-aji 송아지 calf
sönmul 선물 gift
sönt-heg 선택 choice
sont-hob 손톱 fingernail
sori 소리 sound, voice
söryu 서류 document
ssan 싼 cheap
ssö 써 using, writing
ssödo 써도 (may) use; (may) write
ssö-yo 써요 use (verb)
st-he-ik-hü 스테이크 steak
su 수 ability, possibility
suga 수가 ability, possibility
sugbag 숙박 watermelon
su-ib 수입 earnings
sul 술 alcoholic drink
sup-hü 수프 soup

sup-hülle 수플레 souffle
sup-hyo 수표 check (financial)
sup-hyorl 수표를 check (as object)
suri 수리 repair, fixing
susang 수상 prime minister
su-yöng 수영 swimming
swi-un 쉬운 easy

T

ta 다 all, completely
ta-i-öt-hü 다이어트 diet
tal 달 moon, month
talg 닭 chicken
talla-yo 달라요 is different, differs
tallin 달린 hanging
ta-m 다음 next, following
tambe 담배 tobacco, cigarette
tamberl 담배를 cigaret (as object)
tang-shine 당신의 your
tang-shini 당신이 you (as subject)
tang-shinl 당신을 you (as object)
tarn 다른 different, another, other
tashi 다시 again
tedani 대단히 very; seriously
tehab 대합 waiting
tehabshil 대합실 waiting room, lounge
tesagwan 대사관 embassy
teshine 대신에 instead, in place
t-hang 탕 soup
t-hassö-yo 탔어요 rode, took; burned
t-ha-yo 타요 ride, take; burn
t-hegshi 택시 taxi
t-he-ibl 테이블 table
t-he-ip-hü 테이프 tape
t-hellebijön 텔레비전 television
t-henisü 테니스 tennis
t-hewö 태워 riding, carrying; burning
t-homat-ho 토마토 tomato
t-hong-eng 통행 traffic
t-hong-wa 통화 currency; telephone

Pronounce: a father; e let; i machine; o note; ö löng; u rude; ü fürther

call

t-honig 토닉 tonic

t-hüllin 틀린 wrong, mistaken

t-hwigim 튀김 batter-fried food; tempura

tisk-ho 디스코 disco

tisk-hü 디스크 disk

tng-rog 등록 registration

tö 더 more, farther

to 도 also, too

toch-hag 도착 arrival

togil 독일 Germany

tojagi 도자기 pottery, ceramics

töl 덜 less, little

tollyö 돌려 spinning, around

ton 돈 money

tong-an 동안 period (of time), while

tong-ryo 동료 associate, colleague

toni 돈이 money (as subject)

tonl 돈을 money (as object)

tora 돌아 turning, in return, back

toro 도로 road, highway

tö-un 더운 warm, hot

towa 도와 helping

töwö-yo 더워요 is hot, is warm

tra-i 드라이 dry (cleaning)

trö 들어 into, putting in, entering

trö-yo 들어요 enters, goes in

tu 두 two

tubu 두부 tofu, bean curd

tut-hong 두통 headache

tweji 돼지 pig

U

uch-hegug 우체국 post office

ül 을 (indicates object)

ümryo 음료 drink, beverage

ümshig 음식 food

ün 은 (indicates topic); silver (substance)

undong 운동 luck

üneng 은행 bank

unjön 운전 driving

unjönsu 운전수 driver

up-hyön 우편 mail, postal

uri 우리 we, us; our

uri-e 우리의 our

urinün 우리는 we (as topic)

üro 으로 by, through, with; (sometimes indicates object)

W

wassö-yo 왔어요 came

wa-yo 와요 come

we 왜 why?

wech-hul 외출 going out

wi-e 위에 above

wihöm 위험 danger

wön 원 won (Korean money)

wöryo-il 월요일 Monday

wöt-hö 워터 water

Y

yag 약 about

yagsog 약속 appointment

yang 양 sheep

ye-yag 예약 example

yo 요 mattress (Korean style)

yöbose-yo 여보세요 hello (on phone); excuse me (to get attention)

yöbsö 엽서 postcard

yög 역 station

yögi 여기 here

yögi-e 여기에 here

yögisö 여기서 here; from here

yogm 요금 fare

Pronounce: a father; e let; i machine; o note; ö löng; u rude; ü fürther

yögwan 여관 guesthouse, Korean inn
yögwön 여권 passport
yöheng 여행 travel, journey
yöheng-ja 여행자 traveller
yöja 여자 woman
yöl 열 fever
yölch-ha 열차 train
yön 연 kite
yöng-gug 영국 Britain
yöng-ö 영어 English language
yöng-öro 영어로 in English
yöng-wa 영화 film, movie
yönrag 연락 connection
yöp-he 옆에 beside, at the side of
yori 요리 cooking, cuisine
yössö-yo 였어요 was
yuhyo 유효 validity

Pronounce: a father; e let; i machine; o note; ö löng; u rude; ü fürther

Traveller's Topics

Abbreviations
Air Travel
Banks
Buses, Bus Stations
Calendar
Cars (Rental / Repair)
Countries of the World
Customs
Department Store Sections
Doctors
Drinks (Alcoholic)
Drinks (Non-Alcoholic)
Eating and Drinking Places
Emergencies
Expressions, Greetings
Food
Forms and Documents
Geographical

Hairdressers and Barbers
National Holidays
Hotels and Hostels
Labels (on Products)
Night Life
Place Names
Post Offices
Public Buildings
Rest Rooms
Road Signs
Schedules
Store / Shop Names
Signs
Taxis
Telephones
Theaters (Movies, Plays)
Tourism
Trains and Subways (Metro)

세관 [segwan] customs
출발 [ch-hulbal] departure
출발 하는 곳 [ch-hulbal hanün kod] departure gate
출발 [ch-hulbal] departure(s)
목적지 [mogjögji] destination
국내항공 [kungnehang-gong] domestic airlines
면세점 [myönsejöm] duty-free shop
출구 [ch-hulgu] exit
출입국 관리소 [ch-huribgug kwanriso] immigration
안내 [anne] information
대한 항공 [tehan hang-gong] Korean Air Lines
여권 [yögwön] passports
예약 [ye-yag] reservations
택시 [t-hegshi] taxis
경유 [kyöng-yu] via

ABBREVIATIONS
(생략 / seng-ryag)

AAR Asiana Airlines
AFKN American Forces Korean Network
DDD Direct Distance Dialling
DMZ Demilitarized Zone
DPRK Democratic People's Republic of Korea
ISD International Subscriber Dialling
KAL Korean Air Lines
KASA Korean Amateur Sports Assoc
KBS Korean Broadcasting Service
KIST Korean Institute of Science and Technology
KNR Korean National Railroad
KNTC Korean National Tourism Corp
KTA Korea Telecommunication Authority
MBC Munhwa Broadcasting Company
RAS Royal Asiatic Society
ROK Republic of Korea
USO United States Service Organization
W Won (Korean money)

BANKS
(은행 / üneng)

은행 구좌 번호 [üneng kujwa pöno] account number
금액 [kmeg] amount
달러 [tallö] dollar(s)
환율 [hwanyul] exchange rate
외국환 [weguk-hwan] foreign exchange
이율 [i-yul] interest rate
송금환 [song-gmwan] money order
파운드 [p-ha-undü] pound(s)
서명 [sömyöng] signature
여행자 수표 [yöheng-ja sup-hyo] traveler's check
원 [wön] won (Korean currency)
엔 [en] yen

AIR TRAVEL
(항공 / hang-gong)

항공 [hang-gong] airline
항공권 [hang-gong-gwön] airline ticket
공항 [kong-ang] airport
도착 하는 데 [toch-hag hanün te] arrival gate
도착 [toch-hag] arrival(s)
게이트 [ke-it-hü] boarding gate
보딩 패스 [poding p-hesü] boarding pass
...행 [...eng] bound for...
버스 [pösü] buses

BUSES, BUS STATIONS
(버스 / pösü)

회수권 [hwesugwön] book of tickets
버스 정류장 [pösü chöng-ryujang] bus

Pronounce: a father; e let; i machine; o note; ö löng; u rude; ü fürther

stop
버스표 판매소 [pösp-hyo p-hanmeso]
  bus ticket kiosk
고속 [kosog] express
요금 [yogm] fare
직행 [chik-heng] limited express
완행 [waneng] local
버스 터미널 [pösü t-höminöl] terminal

CALENDAR
(달력 / tallyög)

일월 [irwöl] January
이월 [iwöl] February
삼월 [samwöl] March
사월 [sawöl] April
오월 [owöl] May
유월 [yuwöl] June
칠월 [ch-hirwöl] July
팔월 [p-harwöl] August
구월 [kuwöl] September
시월 [shiwöl] October
십일월 [shibirwöl] November
십이월 [shibiwöl] December
일요일 [iryo-il] Sunday
월요일 [wöryo-il] Monday
화요일 [hwa-yo-il] Tuesday
수요일 [su-yo-il] Wednesday
목요일 [mogyo-il] Thursday
금요일 [kmyo-il] Friday
토요일 [t-ho-yo-il] Saturday
일주일 [ilju-il] one week
이주일 [iju-il] two weeks

CARS (RENTAL / REPAIR)
(자동차 / chadong-ch-ha)

보증금 [pojng-gm] deposit
디젤 [tijel] diesel
운전 면허증 [unjön myönöjng] driver's
  license
빵꾸 [bbang-ggu] flat tire
연료 [yönryo] gas / petrol
주유소 [chu-yuso] gas station

보험료 [pohömryo] insurance
점퍼 케이블 [chömp-hö k-he-ibul]
  jumper cable
마일수 [ma-ilsu] milage
엔진 오일 [enjin o-il] oil
레귤러 [regyullö] regular (gas)
수퍼 [sup-hö] super
타이어 [t-ha-i-ö] tires
물 [mul] water

COUNTRIES OF THE WORLD
(국민 / kungmin)

아르헨티나 [arhent-hina] Argentina
오스트레일리아 [ost-hüre-illi-a]
  Australia
벨기에 [pelgi-e] Belgium
브라질 [prajil] Brazil
캐나다 [k-henada] Canada
중국 [chung-gug] China
크로아티아 [k-hüro-at-hi-a] Croatia
체코 [ch-hek-ho] Czechoslovakia
에쿠아도르 [ek-hu-adorü] Ecuador
이집트 [ijibt-hü] Egypt
영국 [yöng-gug] England
프랑스 [p-hürang-sü] France
독일 [togil] Germany
그리스 [krisü] Greece
네덜란드 [nedöllandü] Holland
인디아 [indi-a] India
인도네시아 [indoneshi-a] Indonesia
이란 [iran] Iran
아일랜드 [a-illendü] Ireland
이스라엘 [isra-el] Israel
이태리 [it-heri] Italy
요르단 [yordan] Jordan
한국 [han-gug] Korea
쿠웨이트 [k-huwe-it-hü] Kuwait
레바논 [rebanon] Lebanon
말레이지아 [malle-iji-a] Malaysia
멕시코 [megshik-ho] Mexico
뉴질랜드 [nyujillendü] New Zealand
노르웨이 [norwe-i] Norway
파키스탄 [p-hak-hist-han] Pakistan

Pronounce: a father; e let; i machine; o note; ö löng; u rude; ü fürther

폐루 [p-heru] Peru
필리핀 [p-hillip-hin] Philippines
폴란드 [p-hollandü] Poland
포르투갈 [p-hort-hugal] Portugal
러시아 [röshi-a] Russia
사우디아라비아 [sa-udi-arabi-a]   Saudi
  Arabia
세르비아 [serbi-a] Serbia
싱가폴 [shing-gap-hol] Singapore
남아프리카 [namap-hürik-ha]   South
  Africa
스페인 [sp-he-in] Spain
스웨덴 [sweden] Sweden
스위스 [swisü] Switzerland
태국 [t-hegug] Thailand
우크라이나 [uk-hüra-ina] Ukraine
미국 [migug] United States
우루과이 [urugwa-i] Uruguay
베네수엘라 [penesu-ella] Venezuela

CUSTOMS
(세관 / segwan)

관세 [kwanse] customs
세관 서류 [segwan söryu]   customs
  declaration form
관세 [kwanse] customs duties
출발 [ch-hulbal] departure
출입국 기록 [ch-huribgug   kirog]
  embarkation / disembarkation card
입국 [ibgug] entry into a country,
  immigration
외국인 [wegugin] foreign nationals
한국인 [han-gugin] Korean nationals
여권 [yögwön] passport
소지품 [sojip-hum] personal effects
검역 [kömyög] quarantine

DEPARTMENT STORE SECTIONS
(백화점 / pek-hwajöm)

도자기 [tojagi] china
커피 숍 [k-höp-hi shyob] coffee shop
엘리베이터 [ellibe-it-hö] elevator

에스컬레이터   [esk-hölle-it-hö]
  escalator
수공예품 [sugong-yep-hum] handicrafts
가정용품   [kajöng-yong-p-hum]
  housewares
안내소 [anneso] information desk
보석 [posög] jewelry
여자 화장실 [yöja hwajang-shil]   ladies'
  room
여행 가방 [yöheng kabang] luggage
신사복 [shinsabog] men's clothing
남자 화장실 [namja   hwajang-shil]
  men's room
잡화 [chap-hwa] notions
식당 [shigdang] restaurant
구두 [kudu] shoes
스낵 바 [sneg pa] snack bar
전화 [chönwa] telephone
물 마시는 곳 [mul mashinün   kod]
  water fountain
부인복 [pu-inbog] women's clothing

DOCTORS
(의사 / esa)

구급차 [kugbch-ha] ambulance
화상 [hwasang] burn
진료소 [chinryoso] clinic
감기 [kamgi] cold
변비 [pyönbi] constipation
치과 의사 [ch-higwa esa] dentist
진단 [chindan] diagnosis
설사 [sölsa] diarrhea
병 [pyöng] disease
의사 [esa] doctor
안과 의사 [an-gwa esa] eye doctor
유행성 감기 [yuheng-söng kamgi]   flu
  / influenza
두통 [tut-hong] headache
병원 [pyöng-wön] hospital
불면증 [pulmyönjng] insomnia
진찰 [chinch-hal] medical examination
약 [yag] medicine
이비인후과 [ibi-inugwa] nose, ear and

throat hospital
수술실 [susulshil] operating room
외래 환자 [were hwanja] out patient
환자 [hwanja] patient
알약 [aryag] pill
적십자 [chögshibja] Red Cross
외과 [wegwa] surgery
체온 [ch-he-on] temperature
치통 [ch-hit-hong] toothache
상처 [sang-ch-hö] wound
엑스 선실 [egsü sönshil] X-ray room

DRINKS (ALCOHOLIC)
(주류 / churyu)

맥주 [megju] beer
한 병 [han pyöng] a bottle
반병 [panbyöng] half a bottle
버번 [pöbön] bourbon
버번 하이볼 [pöbön ha-ibol] bourbon
  and soda
버번 워터 [pöbön wöt-hö] bourbon
  and water
버번 언 더 락 [pöbön ön tö rag]
  bourbon on the rocks
브랜디 [prendi] brandy
칵테일 [k-hagt-he-il] cocktail
생맥주 [seng-megju] draught beer
진 토닉 [chin t-honig] gin and tonic
진 피즈 [chin p-hijü] gin fizz
진 언 더 락 [chin ön tö rag] gin on
  the rocks
라이트 비어 [ra-it-hü pi-ö] light beer
마이 타이 [ma-i t-ha-i] Mai Tai
맨하탄 [menat-han] Manhattan
마티니 [mat-hini] martini
포트 와인 [p-hot-hü wa-in] port
레드 와인 [redü wa-in] red wine
로제 [roje] rose
럼 [röm] rum
스카치 [sk-hach-hi] scotch
스카치 하이볼 [sk-hach-hi ha-ibol]
  scotch and soda
스카치 워터 [sk-hach-hi wöt-hö]

scotch and water
스카치 언 더 락 [sk-hach-hi ön tö rag]
  scotch on the rocks
스크루드라이버 [sk-hürudra-ibö]
  screwdriver
셰리 [shyeri] sherry
버번 스트레이트 [pöbön st-hüre-it-hü]
  straight bourbon
스카치 스트레이트 [sk-hach-hi st-hüre-it-hü] straight scotch
딸기 화채 [ddalgi hwach-he] strawberry
  punch
밀감 화채 [milgam hwach-he]
  tangerine punch
보드카 [podk-ha] vodka
보드카 토닉 [podk-ha t-honig] vodka
  and tonic
보드카 언 더 락 [podk-ha ön tö rag]
  vodka on the rocks
위스키 [wisk-hi] whisky
백포도주 [pegp-hodoju] white wine
포도주 [p-hodoju] wine

DRINKS (NON-ALCOHOLIC)
(음료수 / ümryosu)

사과 주스 [sagwa jusü] apple juice
칡차 [ch-hilch-ha] arrowroot tea
코카 콜라 [k-hok-ha k-holla] Coca
  Cola
콜라 [k-holla] cola
다이어트 음료 [ta-i-öt-hü ümryo] diet
  soda
과일 주스 [kwa-il chusü] fruit juice
진저 엘 [chinjö el] ginger ale
생강차 [seng-gang-ch-ha] ginger tea
인삼차 [insamch-ha] ginseng tea
포도 주스 [p-hodo chusü] grape juice
쌍화차 [ssang-wach-ha] herb tea
냉커피 [neng-k-höp-hi] iced coffee
냉홍차 [neng-ong-ch-ha] iced tea
율무차 [yulmuch-ha] job's tears tea
사이다 [sa-ida] lemon lime soda
밀크 쉐이크 [milk-hü swe-ik-hü] milk

shake
미네랄 워터 [mineral wöt-hö] mineral water
오렌지 주스 [orenji chusü] orange juice
복숭아 쥬스 [pogsung-a chyusü] peach juice
펩시 콜라 [p-hebshi k-holla] Pepsi Cola
파인애플 주스 [p-ha-inep-hül chusü] pineapple juice
들깨차 [tlg-gech-ha] sesame tea
홍차 [hong-ch-ha] tea
레몬차 [remonch-ha] tea with lemon
토마토 주스 [t-homat-ho chusü] tomato juice
토닉 워터 [t-honig wöt-hö] tonic water
호두차 [hoduch-ha] walnut tea

EATING AND DRINKING PLACES
(음식점 / ümshigjöm)

바 [pa] bar
불고기집 [pulgogijib] barbecue meat restaurant
비어 홀 [pi-ö hol] beer hall
다방 [tabang] coffee shop
만두집 [mandujib] dumpling restaurant
스낵집 [snegjib] fast food place
삼계탕집 [samgyet-hang-jib] ginseng chicken restaurant
한식집 [hanshigjib] restaurant (Korean style)
레스토랑 [rest-horang] restaurant (western style)
분식집 [punshigjib] snack shop
백반집 [pegbanjib] steamed rice restaurant
생선회집 [seng-sönwejib] sushi (raw fish) restaurant

*

EMERGENCIES
(긴급 / kin-gb)

구급차 [kugbch-ha] ambulance
비상구 [pisang-gu] emergency exit
불 [pul] fire
화재 경보기 [hwaje kyöng-bogi] fire alarm
소화기 [sohwagi] fire extinguisher
소화전 [sohwajön] fire hydrant, fireplug
응급처치 [üng-gbch-höch-hi] first aid
구급상자 [kugbsang-ja] first aid kit / box
의사를 불러 주세요 [esarl pullö juse-yo] get a doctor
가세요! [kase-yo!] go away!
사람 살려! [saram sallyö!] help!
구명정 [kumyöng-jöng] lifeboat
들으세요 [trse-yo] listen
보세요 [pose-yo] look
경찰 [kyöng-ch-hal] police
빨리! [bballi!] quickly!
도둑놈 잡아요! [todungnom chaba-yo!] stop thief!

EXPRESSIONS, GREETINGS
(대화 / tehwa)

미안 합니다 / 실례 합니다 [mi-an hamnida / shille hamnida] excuse me
네, 안녕 하세요? [ne, annyöng hase-yo?] fine thanks, and you?
안녕 하세요? [annyöng hase-yo?] hello, how are you?
못 알아 듣겠어요 [mod ara tdgessö-yo] I don't understand
알겠어요 [algessö-yo] I see
괜찮아요 [kwench-hanö-yo] it doesn't matter / it's okay
잠깐만 기다리세요 [chamg-ganman kidarise-yo] just a moment, please

Pronounce: a father; e let; i machine; o note; ö löng; u rude; ü fürther

아니오 [ani-o] no
아직 [ajig] not yet
제발 ... [chebal ...] please ...
부탁 합니다 [put-hag hamnida] please
...를 주세요 [...rl chuse-yo] please
 give me ...
만나서 반갑습니다 [mannasö pan-
 gabsmnida] pleased to meet you
정말이에요? [chöng-mari-e-yo?]
 really?
감사 합니다 / 고맙습니다 [kamsa
 hamnida / komabsmnida] thank you
...가 있어요 [...ga issö-yo] there is /
 are ...
예 / 네 [ye / ne] yes
천만에요 [ch-hönmane-yo] you're
 welcome

FOOD
(음식 / ümshig)

Appetizers
(마른 안주 / marn anju)

모듬전채 [modmjönch-he] assorted
 appetizers
캐비아 [k-hebi-a] caviar
셀러리 올리브 [sellöri ollibü] celery
 and olives
치즈 [ch-hijü] cheese
대합 [tehab] clams on the half-shell
게살 [kesal] crab meat
생선전 [seng-sönjön] fillet of fish
고추전 [koch-hujön] fried hot green
 pepper stuffed w ground beef
햄 [hem] ham
청어 [ch-höng-ö] herring
마른 안주 [marn anju] Korean
 appetizers (in general)
바닷 가재 [padad kaje] lobster
멜런 [mellön] melon
빈대떡 [pinded-dög] mung bean

pancakes
버섯 [pösöd] mushrooms
굴 [kul] oysters on the half-shell
중 새우 [chung se-u] prawns
무우 [mu-u] radishes
샐러드 [sellödü] salad
살라미 [sallami] salami
정어리 [chöng-öri] sardines
소시지 [soshiji] sausage
잡채 [chabch-he] shredded beef,
 vegetables, vermicelli in spicy sauce
작은 새우 [chagn se-u] shrimp

Soups
(탕, 국 / t-hang, kug)

전복 죽 [chönbog chug] abalone
 porridge
콩나물국 [k-hong-namulgug] bean
 sprout soup
설렁 탕 [söllöng t-hang] beef soup
 with noodles and ginger
치킨 수프 [ch-hik-hin sup-hü] chicken
 soup
조개국 [chogegug] clam soup
냉면 [neng-myön] cold noodles
콩소메 [k-hong-some] consomme
콘 수프 [k-hon sup-hü] corn soup
크림 수프 [k-hürim sup-hü] cream
 soup
당파국 [tang-p-hagug] green onion
 soup
김치국 [kimch-higug] kimchee soup
만두국 [mandugug] meat dumpling
 soup
어니언 수프 [öni-ön sup-hü] onion
 soup
잣 죽 [chad chug] pine nut porridge
떡 국 [ddög kug] rice cake soup
미역국 [mi-yöggug] seaweed soup
갈비 탕 [kalbi t-hang] short rib soup
된장국 [dwenjang-gug] soybean paste
 soup
매운 탕 [me-un t-hang] spicy fish

soup

육계 장 [yuggye chang] spicy hot beef soup with been sprouts

시금치 국 [shigmch-hi kug] spinach soup

토마토 수프 [t-homat-ho sup-hü] tomato soup

야채 스프 [yach-he sp-hü] vegetable soup

Egg Dishes
(계란 / kyeran)

베이컨 에그 [pe-ik-hön egü] bacon and eggs

삶은 계란 [salmn kyeran] boiled eggs

치즈 오믈렛 [ch-hijü omlled] cheese omelet

계란 [kyeran] eggs

계란 후라이 [kyeran hura-i] fried eggs

햄 에그 [hem egü] ham and eggs

햄 오믈렛 [hem omlled] ham omelet

계란 완숙 [kyeran wansug] hard-boiled eggs

오믈렛 [omlled] omelet

풀어서 한 계란 후라이 [p-hurösö han kyeran hura-i] scrambled eggs

계란 반숙 [kyeran pansug] soft-boiled eggs

알찜 [alj-jim] steamed egg (Korean style)

Fish and Seafood Dishes
(생선 / seng-sön)

앤초우비 [ench-ho-ubi] anchovy

생선 구이 [seng-sön ku-i] basted broiled fish

낙지 볶음 [nagji pog-gm] braised small octopus with spicy sauce

생선 구이 [seng-sön ku-i] broiled fish

조기 구이 [chogi ku-i] broiled porgy

모캐 [mok-he] burbot

잉어 [ing-ö] carp

대합 [tehab] clam

대합 구이 [tehab ku-i] clam meat in shell

대구 [tegu] cod / haddock

게 [ke] crab

가재 [kaje] crayfish

갈치 조림 [kalch-hi chorim] cutlass fish hard-boiled

홍합 [hong-ab] dried mussels

뱀장어 [pemjang-ö] eel

굴전 [kuljön] egg-rolled oysters

멸치 볶음 [myölch-hi pog-gm] fried dried anchovies

생선전 [seng-sönjön] fried fillets

생선과 야채볶음 [seng-sön-gwa yach-hebog-gm] fried fish and vegetables

넙치 [nöbch-hi] halibut

청어 [ch-höng-ö] herring

다랑어 [tarang-ö] horse mackerel

훈제한 청어 [hunjehan ch-höng-ö] kipper

바닷 가재 [padad kaje] lobster

고등어 [kodng-ö] mackerel

숭어 [sung-ö] mullet

굴 [kul] oyster

굴무침 [kulmuch-him] oyster with vegetable salad

농어 [nong-ö] perch

곤들매기 [kondlmegi] pike

도미 [tomi] porgy

죽 새우 [chug se-u] prawn

생선 초밥 [seng-sön ch-hobab] raw fish rolls (sushi)

생선회 [seng-sönwe] raw fish sliced (sashimi)

연어 [yönö] salmon

정어리 [chöng-öri] sardine

전갱이 [chön-geng-i] scad

가리비 [karibi] scallop

해물 전골 [hemul chön-gol] seafood, octopus, vegetables in spicy sauce

잔 새우 [chan se-u] shrimp

모듬냄비 [modmnembi] shrimp, fish, chicken, vegetables

Pronounce: a father; e let; i machine; o note; ö löng; u rude; ü fürther

홍어 [hong-ö] skate
혀가자미 [hyögajami] sole
(생선) 매운 탕 [(seng-sön) me-un t-hang] spicy fish soup
게 찜 [ke jjim] stuffed crab
새우 찜 [se-u jjim] stuffed shrimp
송어 [song-ö] trout
참치 [ch-hamch-hi] tuna / tunny
가자미 [kajami] turbot
뱅어 [peng-ö] whitebait
방어 [pang-ö] yellowtail

Meat and Meat Dishes
(고기 / kogi)

베이컨 [pe-ik-hön] bacon
닭 구이 [talg ku-i] barbecued chicken
쇠고기 [swegogi] beef
완자전 [wanjajön] beef and bean curd patties
쇠고기 버섯 무침 [swegogi pösöd much-him] beef and mushrooms
장조림 [chang-jorim] beef boiled in soy sauce
곱창 전골 [kobch-hang chön-gol] beef intestines, tripe, noodles, vegetables
갈비 찜 [kalbi jjim] beef rib stew
불갈비 [pulgalbi] beef ribs
비프 스테이크 [pip-hü st-he-ik-hü] beefsteak
가슴 고기 [kasm kogi] breast
불고기 [pulgogi] broiled beef
닭 찜 [talg jjim] broiled chicken
송아지 골 [song-aji kol] calf's brains
샤토브리앙 [shyat-hobri-ang] chateaubriand
닭 [talg] chicken
갈비 고기 [kalbi kogi] chops
모듬 냉육 [modm neng-yug] cold cuts
커틀렛 [k-höt-hülled] cutlets
오리 [ori] duck
고기전 [kogijön] egg-rolled meatballs
필레 고기 [p-hille kogi] fillet
삼계탕 [samgyet-hang] ginseng chicken

거위 [köwi] goose
햄 [hem] ham
고추전 [koch-hujön] hot green pepper stuffed with beef
콩팥 [k-hong-p-hat] kidney
새끼양 고기 [seg-gi-yang kogi] lamb
새끼양 갈비 [seg-gi-yang kalbi] lamb chops
도가니 [togani] leg
간 [kan] liver
양 고기 [yang kogi] mutton
목덜미 고기 [mogdölmi kogi] neck
잡채 [chabch-he] noodles with meat and vegetables
쇠꼬리 [sweg-gori] oxtail
꿩 [ggwöng] pheasant
비둘기 [pidulgi] pigeon
송이 전골 [song-i chön-gol] pine mushroom and beef pot
돼지 고기 [dweji kogi] pork
돼지 갈비 [dweji kalbi] pork chops
돼지 갈비 [dweji kalbi] pork ribs
메추리 [mech-huri] quail
육회 [yuk-hwe] raw beef shredded & marinated
갈비탕 [kalbit-hang] rib soup
갈비찜 [kalbij-jim] rib stew
고기만두 [kogimandu] rissoles
로스트 비프 [rost-hü pip-hü] roast beef
소고기 편채 [sogogi p-hyönch-he] roast beef thinly sliced
로스트 포크 [rost-hü p-hok-hü] roast pork
등심 고기 [tng-shim kogi] saddle
소시지 [soshiji] sausage
어깻살 [ög-gessal] shoulder
소의 허릿고기 [so-e höridgogi] sirloin
산적 [sanjög] skewered beef and vegetables
즉석 전골 [chügsög chön-gol] sliced beef and vegetables (sukiyaki)
징기스칸 [ching-gisk-han] sliced beef, noodles and vegetables

Pronounce: a father; e let; i machine; o note; ö löng; u rude; ü fürther

참새 [ch-hamse] sparrow
육회 [yuk-hwe] spiced raw beef
스테이크 [st-he-ik-hü] steak
스튜 고기 [st-hyu kogi] stew
혀 [hyö] tongue
투르느도 [t-hurndo] tournedos
내장 [nejang] tripe
칠면조 [ch-hilmyönjo] turkey
송아지 고기 [song-aji kogi] veal
송아리 로스 고기 [song-ari rosü   kogi]
  veal cutlets
송아지 지라 [song-aji chira] veal
  sweetbreads
사슴 [sasm] venison
멧돼지 [meddweji] wild boar

Korean-style Barbecue
(구이 / ku-i)

불 고기 [pul kogi] beef slices barbecue
갈비 [kalbi] boneless short rib
닭 구이 [talg ku-i] boneless   sliced
  chicken
소금 구이 [sogm ku-i] frozen   beef
  barbecue
표고 버섯 구이 [p-hyogo pösöd   ku-i]
  marinated shiitake mushrooms
조기 구이 [chogi ku-i] porgy /   sea
  bream
산적 구이 [sanjög ku-i] shish kebab
염통 구이 [yömt-hong ku-i]   sliced
  beef heart
혀밑 구이 [hyömit ku-i] sliced   beef
  tongue
혀밑 소금 구이 [hyömit sogm   ku-i]
  sliced beef tongue without marinade
양 구이 [yang ku-i] sliced beef tripe
돼지 구이 [dweji ku-i] sliced pork
방자 구이 [pang-ja ku-i] thick-sliced
  beef without marinade

*

Rice Dishes
(밥 / pab)

만두국밥 [mandugugbab]   dumpling
  soup with rice
오곡밥 [ogogbab] five-grain rice
비빔 밥 [pibim pab] fried meat or
  vegetables over rice
육회 비빔밥 [yuk-hwe pibimbab] raw
  beef over rice
회덮밥 [hwedöbp-hab] raw fish over
  rice
떡 볶음 [ddög pog-gm] rice   cakes
  with vegetables
콩나물 밥 [k-hong-naml pab]   rice
  with soybean sprouts
떡국 [ddöggug] ricecake soup
장국밥 [chang-gugbab] sliced beef and
  rice in broth

Vegetables
(채소 / ch-heso)

아스파라거스 [asp-haragösü] asparagus
사탕무우 [sat-hang-mu-u] beet (root)
도라지 [toraji] bellflower root
잠두 [chamdu] broad beans
브라컬리 [prak-hölli] broccoli
싹는 양배추 [ssangnun   yang-bech-hu]
  brussels sprouts
양배추 [yang-bech-hu] cabbage
당근 [tang-gn] carrots
꽃양배추   [ggoch-hyang-bech-hu]
  cauliflower
셀러리 [sellöri] celery
이집트콩 [ijibt-hük-hong] chick peas
옥수수 [ogsusu] corn on the cob
오이 [o-i] cucumber
가지 [kaji] eggplant
꽃상치 [ggoch-hsang-ch-hi] endive
강남콩   [kang-namk-hong]   French
  beans

Pronounce: a father; e let; i machine; o note; ö löng; u rude; ü fürther

마늘 [manl] garlic
작은 오이 [chagn o-i] gherkins
파강회 [p-hagang-we] green onion bundles
피망 [p-himang] green pepper
서양고추냉이 [sö-yang-goch-huneng-i] horseradish
뚱딴지 [ddung-ddanji] Jerusalem artichokes
강남콩 [kang-namk-hong] kidney beans
파전 [p-hajön] korean scallion pancake
부추 [puch-hu] leeks
렌즈콩 [renjk-hong] lentils
상치 [sang-ch-hi] lettuce
비빔밥 [pibimbab] mixed rice and vegetables
모듬 야채 [modm yach-he] mixed vegetables
잡채 [chabch-he] mixed vegetables with noodles
빈대떡 [pinded-dög] mung-bean pancake
버섯 [pösöd] mushroom
양파 [yang-p-ha] onions
파슬리 [p-haslli] parsley
완두 [wandu] peas
피망 [p-himang] pimento
감자 [kamja] potatoes
무우 [mu-u] radishes
붉은 양배추 [pulgn yang-bech-hu] red cabbage
고추 [koch-hu] red pepper
쌀 [ssal] rice (uncooked)
샐러드 [sellödü] salad
감자 조림 [kamja chorim] salted potatoes
실파 [shilp-ha] scallions / green onions
콩나물 [k-hong-namul] seasoned bean sprouts
시금치 나물 [shigmch-hi namul] seasoned spinach

시금치 [shigmch-hi] spinach
호박전 [hobagjön] stuffed zucchini
사탕옥수수 [sat-hang-ogsusu] sweet corn
김 [kim] toasted seaweed
도마도 [tomado] tomatoes
순무 [sunmu] turnips
양갓냉이 [yang-ganneng-i] watercress
서양호박 [sö-yang-obag] zucchini

Salads
(샐러드 / sellödü)

오이 생채 [o-i seng-ch-he] cucumber salad
가지 나물 [kaji namul] eggplant salad
그린 샐러드 [krin sellödü] green salad
겨자채 [kyöjach-he] mustard sauce salad
무우 생채 [mu-u seng-ch-he] radish salad
삼색 나물 [samseg namul] three vegetable salad
토마토 샐러드 [t-homat-ho sellödü] tomato salad

Noodles
(국수 / kugsu)

우동 [udong] big noodles with onions, bean curd and egg (udon)
온면 [onmyön] buckwheat noodles with beef in broth
모밀 국수 [momil kugsu] buckwheat noodles with sweet radish sauce
냉면 [neng-myön] cold noodles
라면 [ramyön] instant noodles in broth (ramen)
잡채 [chabch-he] mixed vegetables with noodles
냉면 사리 [neng-myön sari] plain buckwheat noodles
콩 국수 [k-hong kugsu] wheat noodles in soymilk soup

Pronounce: a father; e let; i machine; o note; ö löng; u rude; ü fürther

오뎅 국수 [odeng kugsu] wheat noodles with fishcakes

Bean Curd
(두부 / tubu)

두부 조림 [tubu chorim] bean curd with beef
완자전 [wanjajön] beef and bean curd patties
양념 두부 [yang-nyöm tubu] boiled bean curds in sauce
두부 부침 [tubu puch-him] fried bean curd
된장 찌개 [dwenjang jjige] soy bean paste stew

Fruits and Nuts
(과일과 견과 / kwa-ilgwa kyön-gwa)

아몬드 [amondü] almonds
사과 [sagwa] apple
살구 [salgu] apricots
바나나 [panana] banana
버찌 [pöj-ji] cherries
밤 [pam] chestnuts
야자 열매 [yaja yölme] coconut
대추야자 열매 [tech-hu-yaja yölme] dates
무화과 [muhwagwa] figs
구즈베리 [kujberi] gooseberries
그레이프프루트 [kre-ip-hüp-hürut-hü] grapefruit
포도 [p-hodo] grapes
개암 [ke-am] hazelnuts
키위 [k-hiwi] kiwi
레몬 [remon] lemon
멜론 [mellon] melon
올리브 [ollibü] olives
오렌지 [orenji] oranges
파파야 [p-hap-ha-ya] papaya
복숭아 [pogsung-a] peach
땅콩 [ddang-k-hong] peanuts
배 [pe] pear

감 [kam] persimmon
파인애플 [p-ha-inep-hül] pineapple
서양오얏 [sö-yang-o-yad] plums
말린 오얏 [mallin o-yad] prunes
나무딸기 [namud-dalgi] raspberries
딸기 [ddalgi] strawberries
귤 [kyul] tangerine
호도 [hodo] walnuts
수박 [subag] watermelon

Desserts
(디저트 / tijöt-hü)

아몬드 수플레 [amondü sup-hülle] almond souffle
애플 파이 [ep-hül p-ha-i] apple pie
바나나 플람베 [panana p-hüllambe] banana flambe
바나나 튀김 [panana t-hwigim] banana fritters
케이크 [k-he-ik-hü] cake
밤 단자 [pam tanja] chestnut balls
체스넛 타트 [ch-hesnöd t-hat-hü] chestnut tart
초콜렛 푸딩 [ch-hok-holled p-huding] chocolate pudding
커피 케이크 [k-höp-hi k-he-ik-hü] coffee cake
아이스크림 커피 [a-isk-hürim k-höp-hi] coffee ice cream
쿠키 [k-huk-hi] cookies
슈크림 [shyuk-hürim] cream puff
카스데라 [k-hasdera] custard
나무딸기 수플레 [namud-dalgi sup-hülle] frozen raspberry souffle
프루트 칵테일 [p-hürut-hü k-hagt-he-il] fruit cocktail
프루트 타트 [p-hürut-hü t-hat-hü] fruit tart
약과 [yaggwa] honey cookies
아이스크림 [a-isk-hürim] ice cream
레몬 아이스크림 [remon a-isk-hürim] lemon ice cream
레몬 수플레 [remon sup-hülle] lemon

souffle

멜런 서빗 [mellön shyöbid] melon sherbet

오렌지 서빗 [orenji shyöbid] orange sherbet

페이스트리 [p-he-ist-hüri] pastry

피치 멜바 [p-hich-hi melba] peach melba

붉은 포도주에 조린 배 [pulgn p-hodoju-e chorin pe] pears baked in red wine

크림을 넣고 조린 배 [k-hüriml nök-ho chorin pe] pears cooked with cream

파인애플 서빗 [p-ha-inep-hül shyöbid] pineapple sherbet

버찌 브랜디에 담근 파인애플 [pöj-ji prendi-e tamgn p-ha-inep-hül] pineapples with kirsch

푸딩 [p-huding] pudding

나무딸기 아이스크림 [namud-dalgi a-isk-hürim] raspberry ice cream

럼을 넣은 오믈렛 [röml nöhün omlled] rum omelet

서빗 [shyöbid] sherbet

수플레 [sup-hülle] souffle

딸기 아이스크림 [ddalgi a-isk-hürim] strawberry sundae

단 오믈렛 [tan omlled] sweet omelet

약식 [yagshig] sweet spiced rice

바닐라 아이스크림 [panilla a-isk-hürim] vanilla ice cream

윕 크림 [wib k-hürim] whipped cream

Kimchee
(김치 / kimch-hi)

김치 [kimch-hi] chinese cabbage kimchee

오이소박이 [o-isobagi] cucumber kimchee

깍두기 [ggagdugi] hot radish kimchee

김치 찌개 [kimch-hi jjige] kimchee stew

나박 김치 [nabag kimch-hi] radish and

cabbage kimchee

총각김치 [ch-hong-gaggimch-hi] small radish kimchee

백김치 [peggimch-hi] white cabbage kimchee

Snacks
(가벼운 식사 / kabyö-un shigsa)

맥주 [megju] beer

비스켓 [pisk-hed] biscuits

도시락 [toshirag] box lunch

빵 [bbang] bread

케이크 [k-he-ik-hü] cake

캔디 [k-hendi] candy

담배 [tambe] cigarettes

코코아 [k-hok-ho-a] cocoa

커피 [k-höp-hi] coffee

콜라 [k-holla] cola

과자 [kwaja] cookies

크래커 [k-hürek-hö] crackers

프렌치 토스트 [p-hürench-hi t-host-hü] French toast

햄 [hem] ham

햄버거 [hembögö] hamburger

아이스크림 [a-isk-hürim] ice cream

쥬스 [chyusü] juice

땅콩 [ddang-k-hong] peanuts

푸딩 [p-huding] pudding

청주 [ch-höng-ju] rice wine

샌드위치 [sendwich-hi] sandwich

새우깡 [se-ug-gang] shrimp chips

토스트 [t-host-hü] toast

Chinese Food
(중국 음식 / chung-gug ümshig)

마파두부 [map-hadubu] bean curd Szechuan style (hot)

난자완스 [nanjawansü] beef patties

닭 고기 로메인 [talg kogi rome-in] chicken lo mein

라조기 [rajogi] chicken with red pepper sauce

Pronounce: a father; e let; i machine; o note; ö löng; u rude; ü fürther

만두 [mandu] dumplings

계란탕 [kyerant-hang] egg drop soup

볶음밥 [pog-gmbab] fried rice

짜장밥 [jjajang-bab] fried rice with brown sauce

사라탕 [sarat-hang] hot and sour soup

파소고기 볶음 [p-hasogogi pog-gm] mongolian beef

양장피 [yang-jang-p-hi] mustard sauce salad

짜장면 [jjajang-myön] noodles with black bean sauce

돼지 고기 로메인 [dweji kogi rome-in] pork lo mein

짬뽕밥 [jjamb-bong-bab] rice with chop suey soup

짬뽕 [jjamb-bong] spicy seafood noodle soup

소고기 탕수육 [sogogi t-hang-su-yug] sweet and sour beef

탕수육 [t-hang-su-yug] sweet and sour pork

원탕 [wönt-hang] wonton

Japanese Food
(일식 / ilshig)

회덮밥 [hwedöbp-hab] chirashi (asstd raw fish on rice)

후도마끼 [hudomag-gi] futo maki

까스 [ggasü] katsu (cutlet)

소고기 구이 [sogogi ku-i] negimaki (scallions rolled in beef)

생선회 [seng-sönwe] sashimi

스끼야끼 [sg-gi-yag-gi] sukiyaki

생선초밥 [seng-sönch-hobab] sushi

튀김 [t-hwigim] tempura

데리야끼 [teri-yag-gi] teriyaki

우동 [udong] udon (noodles)

Side Dishes
(반찬 / panch-han)

완자전 [wanjajön] beef and bean curd patties

도라지 [toraji] bellflower root

두부 부침 [tubu puch-him] fried bean curd

멸치 볶음 [myölch-hi pog-gm] fried dried anchovies

풋고추전 [p-hudgoch-hujön] fried stuffed peppers

콩 나물 [k-hong namul] seasoned bean sprouts

시금치 나물 [shigmch-hi namul] seasoned spinach

두부 조림 [tubu chorim] steamed bean curd

호박전 [hobagjön] stuffed zucchini

김 [kim] toasted seaweed

Basics, Condiments
(조미료 / chomiryo)

후춧가루 [huch-hudgaru] black pepper

빵 [bbang] bread

버터 [pöt-hö] butter

크림 [k-hürim] cream

꿀 [ggul] honey

잼 [chem] jam

케첩 [k-hech-höb] ketchup

김치 [kimch-hi] kimchee (picked vegetable)

레먼 [remön] lemon

마가린 [magarin] margarine

마멀레이드 [mamölle-idü] marmalade

마요네즈 [ma-yonejü] mayonnaise

겨자 [kyöja] mustard

기름 [kirm] oil

올리브유 [ollib-yu] olive oil

감자 [kamja] potatoes

고추장 [koch-hujang] red pepper paste

고춧가루 [koch-hudgaru] red pepper powder

밥 [pab] rice (steamed, white)

소금 [sogm] salt

조미료 [chomiryo] seasoning

간장 [kanjang] soy sauce

Pronounce: a father; e let; i machine; o note; ö löng; u rude; ü fürther

설탕 [sölt-hang] sugar
시럽 [shiröb] syrup
식초 [shigch-ho] vinegar
포도주 [p-hodoju] wine

Methods of Preparation
(요리법 / yoriböb)

구운 [ku-un] baked
불 [pul] barbecued
백반 [pegban] basic Korean meal of steamed rice and side dishes
튀김 [t-hwigim] batter-fried (tempura)
삶은 [salmn] boiled
볶음 [pog-gm] braised
전골 [chön-gol] casserole
채 [ch-he] chopped
만두 [mandu] dumpling
전 [chön] grilled
조림 [chorim] hard-boiled
요리 [yori] main dishes
떡 [ddög] pancake
김치 [kimch-hi] pickled vegetable
죽 [chug] porridge
찌개 [jjige] pot stew
화채 [hwach-he] punch (honeyed fruit juices)
구이 [ku-i] roasted and seasoned meat
나물 [namul] seasoned with herbs
반찬 [panch-han] side dishes
국 [kug] soup
무침 [much-him] spiced, seasoned
찜 [jjim] stewed, steamed
속을 넣은 [sogl nöhün] stuffed

Miscellaneous
(기타 / kit-ha)

각색전 [kagsegjön] fried fillet, pepper and squash
모듬전 [modmjön] fried meatballs, fish, peppers, pancakes
신선로 [shinsönro] Korean celebration firepot

구절판 [kujölp-han] nine kinds of Korean hors d'oeuvre
해장국 [hejang-gug] pork-blood & vegetable soup
번데기 [pöndegi] steamed silkworm larvae

FORMS AND DOCUMENTS
(용지 / yong-ji)

날짜 [nalj-ja] date
생일 [seng-il] date of birth
성 [söng] family name
여 [yö] female
이름 [irm] given name
주소 [chuso] home address
숙박 기간 [sugbag kigan] length of stay
남 [nam] male
이름 [irm] name
국적 [kugjög] nationality
직업 [chigöb] occupation
여권 번호 [yögwön pöno] passport number
서명 [sömyöng] signature

GEOGRAPHICAL
(지리 / chiri)

만 [man] bay
대도시 [tedoshi] big city
수도 [sudo] capital
도시 [toshi] city
해안 [he-an] coast
시골 [shigol] countryside
언덕 [öndög] hill
온천 [onch-hön] hot springs
섬 [söm] island
호수 [hosu] lake
지방 [chibang] land area
지도 [chido] map
산 [san] mountain
산맥 [sanmeg] mountain range
국립공원 [kugribgong-wön] national

Pronounce: a father; e let; i machine; o note; ö löng; u rude; ü fürther

park
바다 [pada] ocean
인구 [in-gu] population
도 [to] province
도청 소재지 [toch-höng sojeji] provincial capital
강 [kang] river
소도시 [sodoshi] town
마을 [ma-l] village
폭포 [p-hogp-ho] waterfall

HAIRDRESSERS AND BARBERS
(이발 / ibal)

갈색 [kalseg] auburn
단발 [tanbal] bangs
이발소 [ibalso] barber shop
턱수염 [t-högsu-yöm] beard
미장원 [mijang-wön] beauty parlor
금발 [kmbal] blond
흑색 [hügseg] brunette
염색 [yömseg] color tint
마사지 [masaji] facial massage
헤어 스프레이 [he-ö sp-hüre-i] hair spray
헤어 커트 [he-ö k-höt-hü] haircut
매니큐어 [menik-hyu-ö] manicure
안마 [anma] massage
콧수염 [k-hossu-yöm] mustache
파마 [p-hama] permanent
샴푸 [shyamp-hu] shampoo
샴푸와 드라이 [shyamp-huwa tra-i] shampoo and blow dry
면도 [myöndo] shave
구렛나루 [kurennaru] sideburns
샴푸와 세트 [shyamp-huwa set-hü] wash and set

NATIONAL HOLIDAYS
(국경일 / kuggyöng-il)

신정 [shinjöng] Jan 1, New Year's Day
구정 [kujöng] Lunar New Year
삼일절 [samiljöl] Mar 1, Independence Day
식목일 [shingmogil] Apr 5, Arbor Day
석가 탄신일 [sögga t-hanshinil] Buddha's Birthday (Lunar)
어린이날 [örininal] May 5, Children's Day
현충일 [hyönch-hung-il] Jun 6, Memorial Day
제헌절 [chehönjöl] Jul 17, Constitution Day
광복절 [kwang-bogjöl] Aug 15, Liberation Day
추석 [ch-husög] Korean Thanksgiving (Lunar)
국군의 날 [kuggune nal] Oct 1, Armed Forces Day
개천절 [kech-hönjöl] Oct 3, Foundation Day
한글날 [han-glnal] Oct 9, Hangul Day
크리스마스 [k-hürismasü] Dec 25, Christmas

HOTELS AND HOSTELS
(호텔 / hot-hel)

에어콘 [e-ök-hon] air conditioning
빠 [bba] bar
목욕탕 [mogyogt-hang] public bathhouse
화장실 [hwajang-shil] bathroom
침대 [ch-himde] bed
벨보이 [pelbo-i] bellhop
카테일 라운지 [k-hagt-he-il ra-unji] cocktail lounge
식당 [shigdang] dining room
엘리베이터 [ellibe-it-hö] elevator / lift
체육관 [ch-he-yuggwan] gym
헬스 클럽 [helsü k-hüllöb] health club
호텔 [hot-hel] hotel (western)
여관 [yögwan] Korean inn
소등 시간 [sodng shigan] lights out time

Pronounce: a father; e let; i machine; o note; ö löng; u rude; ü fürther

청소부 [ch-höng-sobu] maid
지배인 [chibe-in] manager
식사 시간 [shigsa shigan] meal time
회원증 [hwewönjng] membership card
화장실 [hwajang-shil] rest room (toilet)
방 [pang] room
민박 [minbag] room in private house
룸써비스 [rumsöbisü] room service
사우나 [sa-una] sauna
샤워실 [shyawöshil] shower
슬리핑 백 [sllip-hing peg] sleeping bag
수영장 [su-yöng-jang] swimming pool
전화 [chönwa] telephone
텔레비전 [t-hellebijön] television
테니스 코트 [t-henisü k-hot-hü] tennis court
온돌 [ondol] underfloor heating
기상 [kisang] wakeup time

LABELS (ON PRODUCTS)
(설명서 / sölmyöng-sö)

식후 [shik-hu] after meals
취침전 [ch-hwich-himjön] before going to bed
식전 [shigjön] before meals
조리 (방)법 [chori (bang)böb] cooking directions
무명 [mumyöng] cotton
복용량 [pogyong-ryang] dosage
그램 [krem] grams
성분 [söng-bun] ingredients
가죽 [kajug] leather
중량 [chung-ryang] net weight
나일론 [na-illon] nylon
폴리에스터 [p-holli-est-hö] polyester
한국산 [han-gugsan] product of Korea
공단 [kong-dan] satin
조리예 [chori-ye] serving suggestion
실크 [shilk-hü] silk
일일 ...회 복용 [iril ...we pogyong] take ... times a day

복용 [pogyong] to be taken internally
비닐 [pinil] vinyl
원 [wön] Won (price)
울 [ul] wool

NIGHT LIFE
(밤의 유흥 / pame yuhüng)

바 [pa] bar
연주회 [yönjuhwe] concert
디스코 [tisk-ho] disco
플로어 쇼 [p-hüllo-ö shyo] floor show
기생집 [kiseng-jib] Korean geisha restaurant
막걸리 집 [maggölli chib] Korean-style bar
영화 [yöng-wa] movie / cinema
나이트 클럽 [na-it-hü k-hüllöb] nightclub
오페라 [op-hera] opera
예약 [ye-yag] reservation

PLACE NAMES
(지명 / chimyöng)

춘천 [ch-hunch-hön] Ch'unch'on
충청북도 [ch-hung-ch-höng-bugdo] Ch'ungch'ongbuk-do
충청남도 [ch-hung-ch-höng-namdo] Ch'ungch'ongnam-do
제주도 [chejudo] Chejudo
전라북도 [chönrabugdo] Chollabuk-do
전라남도 [chönranamdo] Chollanam-do
인천 [inch-hön] Inch'on
강원도 [kang-wöndo] Kangwon-do
한국 [han-gug] Korea
광주 [kwang-ju] Kwangju
경기도 [kyöng-gido] Kyonggi-do
경주 [kyöng-ju] Kyongju
경상북도 [kyöng-sang-bugdo] Kyongsangbuk-do
경상남도 [kyöng-sang-namdo] Kyongsangnam-do
포항 [p-hohang] P'ohang

Pronounce: a father; e let; i machine; o note; ö löng; u rude; ü fürther

부산 [pusan] Pusan
동해 [tong-e] Sea of Japan (East Sea)
서울 [sö-ul] Seoul
대구 [tegu] Taegu
대전 [tejön] Taejon
황해 [hwang-e] Yellow Sea

POST OFFICES
(우체국 / uch-hegug)

주소 [chuso] address
항공 엽서 [hang-gong yöbsö] aerograms
항공 우편 [hang-gong up-hyön] airmail letter
중앙 우체국 [chung-ang uch-hegug] Central Post Office
세관 신고용지 [segwan shin-go-yong-ji] customs declaration form
봉투 [pong-t-hu] envelope
유치 우편 [yuch-hi up-hyön] general delivery / poste restante
편지 [p-hyönji] letter
우체통 [uch-het-hong] mailbox
우체부 [uch-hebu] mailman
우편환 [up-hyönwan] money order
사서함 [sasöham] P.O. Box
소포 [sop-ho] parcel
우체국 [uch-hegug] post office
우편 요금 [up-hyön yogm] postage
엽서 [yöbsö] postcard
인쇄물 [inswemul] printed matter
등기 우편 [tng-gi up-hyön] registered letter
발신인 주소 [palshinin chuso] return address
속달 우편 [sogdal up-hyön] special delivery letter
우표 [up-hyo] stamp(s)
세금 [segm] tax

*

PUBLIC BUILDINGS
(공공 건물 / kong-gong könmul)

수족관 [sujoggwan] aquarium
화랑 [hwarang] art gallery
교회 [kyohwe] church
시청 [shich-höng] city hall
영사관 [yöng-sagwan] consulate
회의장 [hwe-ejang] convention hall
대사관 [tesagwan] embassy
체육관 [ch-he-yuggwan] gymnasium / gym
병원 [pyöng-wön] hospital
중학교 [chung-aggyo] junior high school
법정 [pöbjöng] law court
도서관 [tosögwan] library
박물관 [pangmulgwan] museum
궁전 [kung-jön] palace
우체국 [uch-hegug] post office
국민 학교 [kungmin haggyo] primary school
고등학교 [kodng-aggyo] senior high school
경기장 [kyöng-gijang] stadium
증권거래소 [chüng-gwön-göreso] stock exchange
절 [chöl] temple
중심가 [chung-shimga] town center
대학교 [tehaggyo] university

REST ROOMS
(화장실 / hwajang-shil)

남자용 / 신사용 [namja-yong / shinsa-yong] gentlemen
여자용 / 숙녀용 [yöja-yong / sungnyö-yong] ladies
사용중 [sa-yong-jung] occupied
당기시오 [tang-gishi-o] pull
미시오 [mishi-o] push
비었음 [pi-össm] vacant

Pronounce: a father; e let; i machine; o note; ö löng; u rude; ü fürther

ROAD SIGNS
(도로 표지 / toro p-hyoji)

노면불량 [nomyönbullyang] bad road surface

자전거 전용 [chajön-gö chönyong] bicycles only

버스 정류장 [pösü chöng-ryujang] bus stop

주의 [chu-e] caution

보행자 주의 [poheng-ja chu-e] caution: pedestrians

위험 [wihöm] danger

위험 커브 [wihöm k-höbü] dangerous curve / bend

막혔음 [mak-hyössm] dead end / cul-de-sac

우회로 [uhwero] detour / diversion

안전운행 [anjönuneng] drive safely

비상 전화 [pisang chönwa] emergency telephone

입구 [ibgu] entrance

출구 [ch-hulgu] exit

높이 제한 [nop-hi chehan] height limit

좌회전 가능 [chwahwejön kanüng] left turn anytime

건널목 있음 [könnölmog issm] level (railroad) crossing

자갈길 [chagalgil] loose gravel

주차 금지 [chuch-ha kmji] no parking

주정차 금지 [chujöng-ch-ha kmji] no parking or stopping

추월 금지 [ch-huwöl kmji] no passing / overtaking

횡단 금지 [hweng-dan kmji] no pedestrian crossing

회전 금지 [hwejön kmji] no U turn

차량 통행 금지 [ch-haryang t-hong-eng kmji] no vehicles

일방 통행 [ilbang t-hong-eng] one-way traffic

주차 [chuch-ha] parking

횡단 보도 [hweng-dan podo] pedestrian crossing

보행자 전용 [poheng-ja chönyong] pedestrians only

감속운행 [kamsoguneng] reduce speed

우선 [usön] right of way / priority

통행 금지 [t-hong-eng kmji] road closed

도로 공사중 [toro kong-sajung] roadworks in progress

서행 [söheng] slow

천천히 [ch-hönch-höni] slow down

비포장 도로 [pip-hojang toro] soft shoulder

정지 [chöng-ji] stop

전방에 간선도로 있음 [chönbang-e kansöndoro issm] thoroughfare ahead

본선 [ponsön] through traffic

톨게이트 [t-holge-it-hü] tollgate

전방에 신호등 있음 [chönbang-e shinodng issm] traffic light ahead

중량 제한 [chung-ryang chehan] weight limit

SCHEDULES
(시간표 / shiganp-hyo)

도착 [toch-hag] arrival

출발 [ch-hulbal] departure

시간표 [shiganp-hyo] schedule / timetable

...행 [...eng] to ...

경유 [kyöng-yu] via

STORE / SHOP NAMES
(상점 이름 / sang-jöm irm)

골동품점 [koldong-p-humjöm] antique shop

화랑 [hwarang] art gallery

빵집 [bbang-jib] bakery

서점 [söjöm] bookstore

카메라점 [k-hamerajöm] camera shop

도자기점 [tojagijöm] ceramics store

Pronounce: a father; e let; i machine; o note; ö löng; u rude; ü fürther

백화점 [pek-hwajöm] department store
양장점 [yang-jang-jöm] dressmaker (modern)
한복집 [hanbogjib] dressmaker (traditional)
약국 [yaggug] drugstore
장어가죽 제품점 [chang-ögajug chep-humjöm] eel skin shop
전자제품점 [chönjajep-humjöm] electrical appliance store
주유소 [chu-yuso] filling station
수산물 시장 [susanmul shijang] fish market
꽃집 [ggojch-hib] florist
표구사 [p-hyogusa] frame shop
모피상 [mop-hisang] furrier
인삼가게 [insamgage] ginseng shop
식료품점 [shigryop-humjöm] grocery store
철물점 [ch-hölmuljöm] hardware store
건재약국 [könje-yaggug] herbal medicine shop
보석상 [posögsang] jewelry store
피혁상 [p-hihyögsang] leather goods store
시장 [shijang] market (open air)
신문 판매대 [shinmun p-hanmede] newsstand
안경점 [an-gyöng-jöm] optician
사진관 [sajin-gwan] photography studio
우체국 [uch-hegug] post office
레코드 가게 [rek-hodü kage] record store
구둣방 [kudüdbang] shoe repair shop
양화점 [yang-wajöm] shoe store
주단가게 [chudan-gage] silk shop
선물가게 [sönmulgage] souvenir shop
운동구점 [undong-gujöm] sporting goods store
문방구점 [munbang-gujöm] stationary store
수퍼마켓 [sup-hömak-hed] supermarket
양복점 [yang-bugjöm] tailor

담배가게 [tambegage] tobacco shop
완구점 [wan-gujöm] toy store
여행사 [yöheng-sa] travel agency
시계방 [shigyebang] watch and clock store

SIGNS
(간판 / kanp-han)

개조심 [kejoshim] beware of dog
버스 정류장 [pösü chöng-ryujang] bus stop
캐셔 [k-hyeshyö] cashier
주의 [chu-e] caution
닫혔음 [tat-hyössm] closed
커피숍 [k-höp-hishyop] coffee shop
위험 [wihöm] danger
치명적 위험 [ch-himyöng-jög wihöm] danger of death
손대지 마시오 [sondeji mashi-o] do not touch
엘리베이터 [ellibe-it-hö] elevator
비상구 [pisang-gu] emergency exit
사용중 [sa-yong-jung] engaged
입구 [ibgu] entrance
에스컬레이터 [esk-hölle-it-hö] escalator
출구 [ch-hulgu] exit
소화기 [sohwagi] fire extinguisher
세 놓습니다 [se nohsmnida] for rent / hire
판매 [p-hanme] for sale
... 금지 [... kmji] forbidden to ...
서행 [söheng] go slow
병원 [pyöng-wön] hospital
안내 [anne] information
잔디에 들어가지 마시오 [chandi-e trögaji mashi-o] keep off the grass
출입금지 [ch-huribgmji] keep out
남자용 [namja-yong] men
입장사절 [ibjang-sajöl] no admittance
사진 촬영 금지 [sajin ch-hwaryöng kmji] no cameras allowed
입장금지 [ibjang-gmji] no entrance

Pronounce: a father; e let; i machine; o note; ö löng; u rude; ü fürther

낚시 금지 [nag-gshi kmji] no fishing
좌회전 금지 [chwahwejön kmji] no
left turn
주차 금지 [chuch-ha kmji] no parking
주정차 금지 [chujöng-ch-ha kmji] no
parking or stopping
추월 금지 [ch-huwöl kmji] no passing
금연 [kmyön] no smoking
수영금지 [su-yöng-gmji] no swimming
회전 금지 [hwejön kmji] no U turn
차량 통행금지 [ch-haryang t-hong-eng-
gmji] no vehicles
열렸음 [yöllyössm] open
주차 [chuch-ha] parking
벨을 눌러 주세요 [perl nullö juse-yo]
please ring bell
신발을 닦으시오 [shinbarl tag-gshi-o]
please wipe your feet
사유지 [sa-yuji] private property
당기시오 [tang-gishi-o] pull
미시오 [mishi-o] push
예약 [ye-yag] reserved
화장실 [hwajang-shil] rest room
(toilet)
세일 [se-il] sale
스넥 코너 [sneg k-honö] snack shop
품절 [p-humjöl] sold out
정지 [chöng-ji] stop
전화 [chönwa] telephone
수리중 [surijung] under repair
비었음 [pi-össm] vacant
경고 [kyöng-go] warning
환영 [hwanyöng] welcome
칠 주의 [ch-hil chu-e] wet paint
여자용 [yöja-yong] women

TAXIS
(택시 / t-hegshi)

택시 미터기 [t-hegshi mit-högi] fare
meter
빈차 [pinch-ha] for hire, free
택시 [t-hegshi] taxi
택시 승차장 [t-hegshi sng-ch-hajang]

taxi stand

TELEPHONES
(전화 / chönwa)

구역 번호 [ku-yög pöno] area code
통화중 [t-hong-wajung] busy
수화인 지불 통화 [suhwa-in chibul t-
hong-wa] collect call
혼선 [honsön] crossed wire
비상 전화 [pisang chönwa] emergency
call
교환 번호 [kyohwan pöno] extension
시내 전화 [shine chönwa] local call
시외 전화 [shiwe chönwa] long
distance call
국제 전화 [kugje chönwa] overseas
service
지명 통화 [chimyöng t-hong-wa]
person to person call
공중 전화 [kong-jung chönwa] public
telephone
전화 박스 [chönwa pagsü] telephone
booth
전화 요금 [chönwa yogm] telephone
charges
전화 번호부 [chönwa pönobu]
telephone directory
전화 교환국 [chönwa kyohwan-gug]
telephone exchange
통화 [t-hong-wa] telephone message
전화 번호 [chönwa pöno] telephone
number
전화 교환수 [chönwa kyohwansu]
telephone operator
틀린 번호 [t-hüllin pöno] wrong
number

THEATERS (MOVIES, PLAYS)
(극장 / kgjang)

입장료 [ibjang-ryo] admission
만화 영화 [manwa yöng-wa] animated
cartoon

Pronounce: a father; e let; i machine; o note; ö löng; u rude; ü fürther

관객 [kwan-geg] audience
이층 [ich-hüng] balcony
매표소 [mep-hyoso] box office
희극 [hegüg] comedy
감독 [kamdog] director
영어 자막 [yöng-ö chamag] English subtitles
입구 [ibgu] entrance
출구 [ch-hulgu] exit
영화 [yöng-wa] film
만 원 [man wön] full house
사극 [sagüg] historical drama
휴게 시간 [hyuge shigan] intermission
낮 흥행 [nad hüng-eng] matinee
이층 앞쪽 [ich-hüng ap-hj-jog] mezzanine
영화관 [yöng-wagwan] movie theater
뮤지칼 [myujik-hal] musical
미스테리 [mist-heri] mystery
연극 [yön-güg] play
극작가 [kgjagga] playwright
영화 제작자 [yöng-wa chejagja] producer
프로그램 [p-hürogrem] program
애정물 [ejöng-mul] romance
공상 과학 영화 [kong-sang kwahag yöng-wa] science fiction film
무대 [mude] stage
극장 [kgjang] theater
공포 영화 [kong-p-ho yöng-wa] thriller / horror film
매표소 [mep-hyoso] ticket office
표 [p-hyo] ticket(s)
자막 [chamag] title
비극 [pigüg] tragedy
전쟁 영화 [chönjeng yöng-wa] war film

TOURISM
(관광 / kwan-gwang)

(국립) 공원 [(gugrib) kong-wön] (national) park
청와대 [ch-höng-wade] Blue (President's) House
절 [chöl] Buddhist temples
안내원 [annewön] guide (person)
민속촌 [minsogch-hon] Korean Folk Village
한국 역사 [han-gug yögsa] Korean history
대한 여행사 [tehan yöheng-sa] Korean Travel Bureau
박물관 [pangmulgwan] museum
궁전 [kung-jön] palace
...사 [...sa] ...temple

TRAINS AND SUBWAYS (METRO)
(기차와 전철 / kich-hawa chönch-höl)

도착 [toch-hag] arrival
...행 [...eng] bound for...
출발 [ch-hulbal] departure
식당칸 [shigdang-k-han] dining car
보통칸 [pot-hong-k-han] economy class
입구 [ibgu] entrance
출구 [ch-hulgu] exit
특급 열차 [t-hüggb yölch-ha] express train
요금 [yogm] fare
일등칸 [ildng-k-han] first class
반액 요금 [paneg yogm] half fare
안내소 [anneso] information office
막차 [magch-ha] last train
우등 열차 [udng yölch-ha] limited express train
완행 열차 [waneng yölch-ha] local train
편도표 [p-hyöndop-hyo] one-way ticket
예약 접수처 [ye-yag chöbsuch-hö] reservation office
지정석 차표 [chijöng-sög ch-hap-hyo] reserved seat ticket
화장실 [hwajang-shil] rest room (toilet)
왕복표 [wang-bogp-hyo] round-trip /

return ticket

시간표 [shiganp-hyo] schedule / timetable

침대칸 [ch-himdek-han] sleeping car

표 [p-hyo] standing ticket

역 [yög] station

지하철 지도 [chihach-höl chido] subway map

지하철 역 [chihach-höl yög] subway station

고속 열차 [kosog yölch-ha] super express train

직행 열차 [chik-heng yölch-ha] through train

차표 자동 판매기 [ch-hap-hyo chadong p-hanmegi] ticket machine

매표구 [mep-hyogu] ticket window

승강장 [sng-gang-jang] to the platforms

...번선 [...bönsön] track

보통석 차표 [pot-hong-sög ch-hap-hyo] unreserved seat ticket

대합실 [tehabshil] waiting room

Hangul

(Korean Writing)

Koreans are proud of their writing system, which is more accurate than most alphabets, and simpler as well. The following are some elementary rules for reading Hangul:

1. Each Korean symbol represents a whole syllable, not just a sound. Like English, Korean is read from left to right and from top to bottom.

2. Each syllable is composed of letters, also read from left to right and then top to bottom.

3. The vowels are linear, and the consonants have square or rounded designs (see table below).

4. Each syllable starts with a consonant, followed by a vowel, optionally followed by up to two more consonants.

5. If a syllable begins with a vowel, then a filler consonant (the circle) is substituted.

6. All the entries in this dictionary have been supplied with Hangul plus pronunciation. This could provide practice examples for the reader who wishes to learn Hangul.

CONSONANTS

ㄱ	g	ㄲ	gg	ㅋ	k-h	ㅇ	ng	ㅎ	h
ㄷ	d	ㄸ	dd	ㅌ	t-h	ㄴ	n	ㅅ	s
ㅂ	b	ㅃ	bb	ㅍ	p-h	ㅁ	m		
ㅈ	j	ㅉ	jj	ㅊ	ch-h	ㄹ	r		

VOWELS

ㅏ	a	ㅐ	e	ㅒ	e	ㅓ	ö
ㅣ	i	ㅗ	o	ㅜ	u	ㅡ	ü
ㅑ	ya	ㅒ	ye	ㅖ	ye	ㅕ	yö
		ㅛ	yo	ㅠ	yu		

Pronounce: a father; e let; i machine; o note; ö löng; u rude; ü fürther